SWEET MYSTERY

A BOOK OF REMEMBERING

A Deep South Book

SWEET

MYSTERY

A BOOK OF

REMEMBERING

Judith Hillman Paterson

THE UNIVERSITY OF ALABAMA PRESS
Tuscaloosa and London

Published by arrangement with Farrar, Straus and Giroux, LLC
First published in 1996 by Farrar, Straus and Giroux
First paperback edition published by Farrar, Straus and Giroux, 1997
Reprinted paperback edition published by
The University of Alabama Press, 2001
The University of Alabama Press
Tuscaloosa, Alabama 35487-0380
Manufactured in the United States of America

9 8 7 6 5 4 3 2 1
08 07 06 05 04 03 02 01 00

Cover Design by Michele Myatt Quinn

Typeface: Granjon

∞

The paper on which this book is printed meets the minimum requirements of
American National Standard for Information Science-Permanence of Paper for
Printed Library Materials, ANSI Z39.48-1984.

Library of Congress Cataloging-in-Publication Data

Paterson, Judith Hillman, 1936–
Sweet mystery : a book of remembering / Judith Hillman Paterson.
p. cm. — (Deep South books)
Originally published: New York: Farrar, Straus, and Giroux, 1996.
ISBN 0-8173-1090-8 (pbk.)
1. Paterson, Judith Hillman, 1936—Childhood and youth. 2. Montgomery
(Ala.)—Biography. 3. Hillman, Emily, 1914–1946. 4. Adult children of
alcoholics—Alabama—Montgomery—Biography. 5. Adult children of
dysfunctional families—Alabama—Montgomery—Biography. 6. Children of
the mentally ill—Alabama—Montgomery—Biography. I. Title. II. Series.

F334.M753 P39 2001
976.1'47063'092—dc21
[B]   00-050935
British Library Cataloguing-in-Publication Data available

In memory of

Emily Hillman and Julius Porter Paterson

and in honor of

their six grandchildren

Preface: Setting Out

People talk to you a great deal about your education, but some good,
sacred memory, preserved from childhood, is perhaps the best education. [If one] carries many such memories with him into life, he
is safe to the end of his days, and if one has only one good memory
left in one's heart, even that may sometime be the means of saving
us.

—Dostoevsky, *The Brothers Karamazov*
Translated by Constance Garnett Black

 My mother died when I was nine and she was thirty-
one, so of course I remembered her. Her fear of being
alone, the insomnia, the terrible fights with my father,
the uncontrollable drinking, the vacant stare and slack
mouth. The tart yeasty smell of beer on her breath,
powder and tobacco loose in her purse, a favorite plaid dress gone
rank with sweat. No matter how hard I tried to forget, I remembered.

After she died, the whole family—my father most of all—
wanted nothing so much as to forget her suffering, forget the short
life she had lived, forget the failed mother everyone assumed she
had been. My three siblings and I seemed to have no choice but
to go along with the mandate, especially me because of my deep
love and emotional bondage (no lesser word will do) to my father.
And so I developed enough defenses to fortify a psychological
Maginot Line—workaholism, perfectionism, obsessive fears, re-
sentments, denial—and still the memories returned willy-nilly in

Technicolor images, frozen in time and totally unwilling to be banished.

The weight of those memories increased a thousandfold when two children were born to me and instantly—as if by some symbiotic magic—reactivated my own childhood. I would start to say something to my small son or daughter and there my own exiled mother would be—in a tone of voice and words so long suppressed that I thought they were gone. Another day the words and voice might be those of my grandmother when I was small or the housekeeper who had lived with us for as long as my mother lived and then vanished with a finality as total as my mother's death had been. Sometimes the memories surfaced suddenly and in complete narrative episodes akin to the flashbacks associated with traumatic losses and fears. Sometimes they appeared in response to some reminiscent beauty in nature, linked more to a longing for a time that was lost than to any remembered anguish. Occasionally they came out of unexplained periods of depression, like the one that came on an afternoon late in the winter of 1964 when my children were still quite young. This is the way I recall it:

Not knowing what is wrong with me, I sit in despair in a dark-paneled room in a suburban house outside Montgomery, Alabama. Finally, I pull myself up and go outside to fetch my small daughter home from the yard next door where she is playing. Air that I expect to be cold wraps around me like a warm cloud, promising spring, the way it sometimes does in Alabama long before anyone has thought to look for it. The hum of insects blocks all other sound. A moon-like sun paints the woods in front of me red. The present vanishes and suddenly I am back to a time before my mother died, in a moment so pleasurable and so lost that in order to bear that it existed at all I have had to forget it.

In memory I am the same age as the daughter who stands before me; my sister Jane and I are tumbling down the hill in front of our house in the glorious pink light of dusk in the country. Bats swoop lower and lower out of the pine marsh beyond the framed house where an old black couple named Idabell and Jim Thomas live with their children and grandchildren.

We toss rocks into the sky and someone says, "You can't hit a bat with a rock. Bats hang in trees by their toes. They are blind and see at night with something inside them that won't let them bump into things or get hit." They stream in long black ribbons across the sky, darting lower and lower. We throw and throw and sling our arms out wide, spinning in circles until we hit the ground too dizzy and queasy to stand any longer.

The others circle around me calling, "Sister, sister," as if the name were both a joke and a title of distinction. "Y'all mind Sister, now," my father yells. Jane is my only sister for a long time, so the other spinners must be cousins or the children of Momma's friends.

Their parents sit with ours on the long side yard that slopes down the hill toward the Thomas house. They drink beer or whiskey and talk about the Japs and the Germans. Daddy sits militarily tall and talks of going to war to fight for freedom. Tonight it doesn't matter that my father, Duke, and my mother, Emily, disagree violently about this.

Emily's friends and her Aunt Bessie say my mother is beautiful, but she isn't really. Her eyes and nose are fashionably bold, but her chin is weak and her mouth small, making the two halves of her face look like they belong to different people. Only her dark eyes and the tawny lushness of her skin recall an Italian ancestor and the stunning combination of darkness and light that once marked her mother's fabled beauty.

Although her small-boned frame is topped by large round breasts, her femininity is soft and malleable, more like that of a child than of a woman who has borne two children and is carrying another. Against the purpling sky, she wears a white blouse and a big, flowered skirt. Her short, permed hair falls loose around

5

her face. She is teasing my father and clowning for her friends in a slew-footed parody of Charlie Chaplin that is also a parody of the comical way she walks herself. Her ballooning belly makes her look even funnier—like a cartoon character about to topple under its own weight. The barbs are aimed at herself, and everyone laughs.

Emily has a big belly. She is laughing. The sky darkens. The moment sticks in a twinkling of time that may have come near the end of her seven months' pregnancy with my brother James Porter, who will be born July 16, 1941, live two days, die, and in dying start an endless hemorrhage of sorrow in the heart of our family. Or, by then—since early-childhood memory knows neither time nor chronology—she may have been carrying my second sister, Joan Elizabeth, bred to replace the dead brother and keep my father home from war.

Such moments were not rare, but since they were rarely so compelling, I usually just looked away, slammed the door on a heart full of childhood anguish, and hurled my energies in some other direction. A few years after that, I started commuting the fifty miles from Montgomery to Auburn University to get a Ph.D. in English and begin a career as a teacher and writer. I did that in part, I believe, because the work was relentless enough and compelling enough to keep my memories at bay. I did it, too, because it gave me great pleasure and satisfaction and was a very good thing for me to do. After all, able young women in the sixties and seventies were not supposed to sit in the dark-paneled rooms of suburban tract houses and nurse their depressions.

And still the memories and themes of my childhood returned unbeckoned—triggered by reminiscent fears, associations, certain kinds of weather, the cast of light on the side of a building, a fragment of a song or an odor remembered—and hurtled me into episodes of anger and sadness that, because they often seemed

6

unrelated to present circumstances, baffled and disturbed my husband and children as well as myself. February 9, 1973, brought back another set of memories that I would never forget:

I take my children to school and head for the university library, as I usually do on the days when I have no classes to teach. By the time I get there, a light snow—a rare thing indeed in our part of the state—has started to fall.

As soon as I get out of the car, the feel of cold air and wet flakes on my face sinks me in sadness so absolute that it seems to come from the heart of existence itself. I chat with the librarian, pick up some books, and sit down in front of a window that becomes a canvas for a set of memories linked by snow, cold air, and sorrow—not repressed memories but memories that have presented themselves a thousand times before and a thousand times been driven back into their cave. Today they refuse to go, and I sit still as a monk in a cell and watch them play themselves out against a colorless sky.

In the first of them, I am very small. It is snowing and I want to go outside. My mother acts strange and says it is too cold. I am indignant at first and then realize, with a heartbreak I never forget, that something is wrong with my mother.

All the other snow memories took place on Long Island, New York, where we lived for a year when I was seven and where my mother was sick and nearly insane with her addictions. The themes and associations are the same: the snow is lovely, the air is cold on my face, something is wrong with my mother, and I am alone with a loneliness as bottomless as the sea.

Finally, someone comes and tells me the campus is closing and I have to go. I drive slowly in the few inches of snow that collect on the ground, remembering and remembering, until I hear on the car radio that schools have been closed for hours and parents should have picked up their children. What I remember next is

7

the look on the face of my ten-year-old son, Charles, when I arrived to find him the last child left at his school, with the lone teacher who had waited with him.

"I thought you weren't coming," he says, and suddenly I see in his face an image of myself as a child much younger than he is and already terrified that my mother is going to leave me, die, go away, and never come back. All I remember after that was my feeble attempt to explain where I had been and the fact that there was something in the moment that neither my son nor I ever forgot—as if all the fear of abandonment that had been in me had somehow leaped out of my body and into his. And still, despite that day and others bearing the same message, I held the line for many more years against that place inside me that wanted to remember the truths of my own childhood.

By 1980, my children were approaching adulthood, my marriage had ended in divorce, my father had undergone surgery for lung cancer, and the family I grew up in had started to collapse under a great weight of addictions, emotional problems, and griefs never faced. By the time my father died in 1985, the flower-growing complex that had been the hub of the extended family of my childhood had come close to bankruptcy and been sold, the first marriages of all my father's children had failed, and my two sisters were suffering the effects of the same virulent combination of mental illness and alcoholism that had killed my mother. On the first anniversary of my father's death, my brother died at forty-one of an aneurysm triggered, I always thought, by heavy drinking and smoking combined with family pressures and the stress of financial failure.

My stepmother died the next year and I spent the summer of 1987 cleaning out and preparing to sell the house that held the memories I didn't want to face. I can still see myself standing amid the debris, the inheritor of a head full of memories and several trunks full of newspaper clippings and memorabilia—the only person in my family still standing, lonelier than I had ever thought it possible to be, and still reluctant to admit that the family psychology that had destroyed the others had also damaged me.

The next spring, following an instinct I didn't know I had and could not possibly have put into words, I drove to Kentucky to see what I could learn about the family of my mother's seldom-mentioned father, and without knowing it began a journey of family and personal discovery that would occupy every spare moment for almost seven years and produce a book I never intended to write. For two years, I haunted courthouses, libraries, archives, and the attics and kitchens of newly found relatives—in Ohio, Kentucky, Maryland, Virginia, and all across the Deep South. When I was not on the road I was holed up in the National Archives or the Library of Congress, where I followed one thread after another until I knew more about my extended family on both sides than I had ever thought it possible to know. I followed the tracks of the long history of mental illness and addiction in my mother's family. I also unearthed some secrets in my father's family, including the never-told story of my Irish-immigrant great-great-grandfather, who had been so moved by the plight of the enslaved Africans in the South that he had joined the Union Army at thirty-six and died fighting for his idea of America, thus inspiring his daughter to get the education she needed and go South to teach the freed slaves. Together she and the Scottish missionary-educator she married established the Patersons in Alabama in a way that was much more unusual and controversial than I had ever been led to believe.

But as soon as I started to write the "objective" family story that my experience as a student of literature, history, and journalism had prepared me to write, I began suffering episodes of writer's block, insomnia, and migraine headaches like nothing I had ever experienced before. And when the attacks were over, I would find on the page, not social history and analysis, but vivid

—sometimes strange, almost surrealistic—accounts of those troublesome, long-ignored memories of my childhood.

First I wrote my memory of the day my mother died, and, while I wrote, endured a degree of physical and emotional pain that I would not have thought possible to endure—as if all the backed-up, unexpressed anguish of that day and the losses, abandonments, and fears of the days that led up to it and the days that followed it were literally blasting themselves out of the places in my body where they had been stored all those years. And when the writing was finally done, the relief was as intense as the suffering had been.

Next I wrote my recollection of twirling on the hill at dusk that the image of my young daughter standing in front of a late-winter sunset had called back with such force some twenty years earlier. By the time the snow memories emerged and became a sort of outline for the story of sadness and stress that I associated with my mother's illness and death, I knew I was writing something entirely different from what I had planned. And so I kept going, writing history one day and memoir the next, until finally the two approaches started to become one.

As I wrote, I noticed that the spontaneous memories had an unusual quality to them. The remembrance of color and light seemed unusually vivid. The moment of recollection often hurled me back in time, causing the remembered feelings to act themselves out in my mind and body as if the event were ongoing and no time had passed. I also noticed that the child I was in memory seemed to understand what was going on in a way far beyond her years; sometimes I seemed to be standing outside myself watching, the way we do in dreams. A long time passed before I began reading about the effects that loss, stress, and trauma have on both children and adults and learned that such peculiarities often characterize traumatic or very stressfully experienced memory. What I also found in my own experience, however, was that the intensely pleasurable memories often shared those same qualities in a way that tempered the pain of remembering and kept me writing.

My family was no exception to the rule that troubled families teach their children to keep their problems to themselves. And though it was a message I learned so well that until my father died I never questioned it, I gradually realized I would have to unlearn it if the book I was trying to write was ever to be written. Eventually I began calling, writing, and finally seeing in person many of the people I had known when I was small who, for various reasons, had gone out of my life either before or shortly after my mother died. The singular highlight of this part of my quest came when I discovered my first cousin James Hoggatt Hillman III living in Salisbury, Maryland, only a few hours away from where I lived in Washington.

Jimmy (which is what I will always call him, though no one else does) had lived with my maternal grandmother, been partially raised by my parents, and been as much a part of my family as I was myself until I was six and he was thirteen—when he was sent to live with the mother he hadn't seen since she left for New York when he was three to make a career for herself singing and teaching music. Though his going took something from us as real and grievous as the amputation of a limb might have done, the loss was barely acknowledged at the time and seldom mentioned afterwards, reflecting an attitude that ran deep in our family and revealed the kind of damage that had already been done.

And when Jimmy Hillman opened the door I finally knocked on, I saw not the towheaded trickster I remembered but a sixty-year-old businessman with children and grandchildren, a man so marked by the history of my mother's family and so imprinted with the mannerisms and habits of my father that it was like seeing several ghosts at once and having things I thought I had made up turn out to be true. Slowly . . . slowly . . . for remembering came no easier to him than it did to me, we pieced together our own histories and our own childhoods and I learned how he fared after we put him on a train for New York with nothing but a photograph of his mother to know her by and nothing to comfort him but his belief in my father's promise that his Cushman motorcycle would arrive on a later train.

I learned how the Cushman finally came and how Jimmy lived at the Algonquin Hotel for a year and drove the motorcycle all over Manhattan before going with his mother and her third husband to live on the Eastern Shore of the Chesapeake Bay in Maryland and driving it there until he finally sold it. And how he saw it in the hands of an antique automotive dealer shortly before he got the letter from me saying I was about to show up, too, and ask him to remember things that he had tried as hard to forget as I had—and for many of the same reasons.

One day, in the midst of trying to make sense of both the family history and my own memories, I heard the child psychologist Bruno Bettelheim tell a television interviewer that his idea of a healthy childhood boiled down to one thing: "Somebody has got to be crazy about that kid."

Indeed, amid all the troubles we had, I was blessed to have a number of people who were crazy about me—my parents, my Grandmother Ila, my Great-aunt Bessie, our housekeeper Mary Willie, my father's brother, Sonny. I was also blessed, I now see, to have been born at the center of a vast extended family that nurtured both my imagination and my talents. Nevertheless, it has taken me a long journey through all the sorrow that came with those blessings to get back a sense of my own childhood and how it made me who I am.

Cardiology Associates of Montgomery, P.C.

1758 Park Place, Suite 101 • Montgomery, Alabama 36106

(334) 264-9191

John A. Williams, M.D.	Howard L. Brazil, M.D.	Charles E. Hastey, M.D.

For:

Rx   Disp.   Date:

Sig   Refill

1. Martha - I'm sorry we can't

2. come to the murktin. Jennifer

3.

4.

5. is in a parade in Troy. See you so—

Product selection permitted

_____ M.D.

DEA# AW9443158
State # 9622

DEA# BB2792489
State # 20966

Dispense as written

_____ M.D.

DEA# BH3396733
State # 08667

Emily and Duke

 Emily and Duke came from families about as different from one another as two families that had been in Montgomery for several generations could possibly be. My mother's forebears had gambled all on the Civil War and been staunchly post-Confederate ever since. My father's, on the other hand, had come to Alabama as abolitionist missionaries and founders of schools for the freed slaves during Reconstruction. The conflicts were deep and everlasting and, I believe, had something to do with what went wrong between my parents. Nevertheless, the two families had some things in common: they did not grieve, and they did not admit failure: the Ware–Walker–Hillmans out of shame for having failed so utterly and lost so much; the Patersons out of fear that if outsiders like themselves showed weakness, they would be destroyed or driven out of the place where they had come and wanted to stay.

Montgomery, Alabama. On the banks of a big river where there had never been anything but Creek Indians until the French came in 1715 and built a fort impossible to hold against the wilderness and the Alibamu tribe of Creeks, for whom they named the place. After that, nothing but a few trappers and traders mixing white blood with red blood for a hundred years until Tennessee militia General Andrew Jackson plucked 22 million acres out of the heart of the Creek Nation and turned it over to people like my ancestors,

Robert and Judith Anthony Ware, who brought African slaves, money, and the idea of aristocracy from North Georgia, where they had fought the Revolution, given up their Quaker–Baptist opposition to slavery, and fallen in love with what the cotton gin might do for their fortunes.

"The Wares were here before there was a place," my maternal Great-aunt Bessie Ware Walker liked to say, meaning nobody in Montgomery had a longer local pedigree and more right to pride of place than we did. Be that as it may, the Wares arrived in 1822, bringing forty slaves and a tribe of kinsmen.

Robert was sixty-two. Judith was fifty. I can't imagine what they were thinking. They certainly found no aristocracy there, just a frontier village with some sixty (mostly log) houses and a population of 239 white people, 156 slaves, and six free men of color, set down near the banks of a river along a line of the most cantankerous soil anybody ever tried to plow, with air so close you could hardly breathe in it and fevers worse than Georgia's.

Still, some of the settlers survived, and by 1850 black bodies and short-staple cotton had turned black dirt into black gold and made Robert and Judith's children "rich as God," some people said. Rich enough for their son James Anthony and his wife, Jane, to swap the log plantation house for an Italian villa in town and then trade it for a Greek Revival mansion furnished with china and silver from England and a rosewood bed said to have been ordered by Queen Victoria but rejected because it was too short for Prince Albert. Rich enough to turn frontiersmen into aristocrats and Revolutionary patriots into rebels gambling all on a civil war that hadn't a prayer. And still they prayed to a God they thought still listened, until, in the end, they had fought their own country and lost almost everything, including, I believe, their moral moorings.

And when the war was over, most of the plantations lay fallow. Black people and white flocked to town and camped out in shacks all around it. Rich and poor alike ate whatever they could get their hands on. The carcasses of starved horses and mules piled up in the streets. What could anybody do?

The first thing they did was refuse to repent and resist all efforts to make them act like a conquered people. And by the time the Congressional Reconstruction began two years later, the demoralized James Anthony had died, and the once prideful, now chastened Jane Ware had moved her family upstairs and rented the ground floor of her columned mansion to the officers of the Occupying Army for $125 a month. Never mind that their neighbors thought it shameful to profit off the horrors of the Reconstruction (carpetbaggers, scalawags, and niggers running everything), Aunt Bessie's Grandmother Jane saved the family plantation when all around her were losing theirs. And before her husband was cold in the ground, she abandoned what was left of the Wares' hardshelled, Georgia–Baptist religion and took herself back to the sweet-smelling Episcopal Church of her own forebears to be comforted in the dark certainty that God's ways were unknowable to man—as if the whole thing had been the fault of a Baptist god, and the Wares, the cotton gin, and slavery had nothing to do with it.

I don't know at what point it began to be so, but the Wares as I knew them were a bitter, resentful people, convinced that the Civil War had unjustly and tragically divested them of wealth and a way of life that had been rightfully theirs—never mind that both were built on human enslavement. The two great myths of their lives—that they had been wrongly bereft of their wealth and that they were better than their circumstances—left them diminished in mind and spirit and shackled to a set of values that freed them to break the small rules of ordinary life while binding them to the complicated social and racial dance they called the Southern Way of Life.

Though Emily behaved in every way to deny it, the words "We have been deprived of what was ours; we are entitled to more;

we are better than other people" burned like a live coal in a dark corner of her own heart. And that darkness married itself to something in Duke that was similar—though the circumstances that had put it there could hardly have been more different.

Just as the prematurely white-haired Grandmother Jane was turning her mansion in town over to the Yankees to save a 2,000-acre plantation in the country, the seventeen-year-old William Burns Paterson, who would be Duke's grandfather, was leaving a dirt-floored cottage in the rural village of Tullibody, Scotland, and going down to the docks at Glasgow to hop a freighter for New York. As the brightest and most ambitious of the nine children of landless farmers and brewery workers, Will had gone to school just long enough to fall in love with learning and dream of doing something worthwhile with his life.

But first he wanted to see America, which is what he did for three years, seeing all but three states of it, traveling sometimes with just "a dog, a gun, and a fishing line," working at anything that paid, and discovering a country vast and free beyond his dreams. Until, sometime in 1870, still seeing America, still working at anything that paid, he had followed the Reconstruction railroad boom north from New Orleans to Hale County, Alabama, and there found himself standing at the heart of that band of dark soil that had once made a few white people very, very rich, where impoverished freedmen now made up over half the population, and blacks and whites alike now labored night and day just to feed their children.

It was there, in the rural Black Belt, eighty miles west of Montgomery, that he started to teach black railroad workers to read and write and do figures. And it was there that he began to dance the fine line (which it would be his destiny to dance for the rest of his life) between his belief in education and human betterment and the traditions of a place built on class and caste, where learning was often ridiculed, where before the Civil War there had been little public education, and where now there was none.

By 1871 he had built the one-room schoolhouse he called Tullibody Academy in the county seat at Greensboro and by 1878 had gone to head the American Missionary Association's Lincoln School at Marion, Alabama, which, in the last days of its strength, the Reconstruction legislature had made the first state normal college for Negroes. There he and Margaret (Maggie) Flack, the Ohioborn, Oberlin-educated missionary teacher he married, created a model school and had a daughter and four sons. My grandfather was born there in 1883 and named James Porter Paterson for Maggie's father, a private in the Union Army killed marching toward Georgia to free the slaves.

Soon, Lincoln School and Normal University graduates were in demand to teach all over the South. Maggie and Will had the school of their dreams, and it looked as if Alabama was going to nurture one of the most useful institutions ever to take hold in American soil. And then, in a flicker of time on a dark night in the winter of its ninth year, the campus went up in flames set by vigilantes hostile to higher education for Negroes and outraged by the racial integration at the Lincoln School.

In the wake of the fire, the legislature ordered the Normal School moved to the state capital at Montgomery, and as soon as it got there withdrew all funding, leaving the school to be supported by black churches, Northern contributions, and the free labor of the teachers. And when funding was finally restored two years later, it was restored mainly for industrial training. And still the school prospered and trained teachers, and the Patersons built a long shotgun house near the campus and put a tiny greenhouse in the back yard and gardened the acres around the house and started a nursery business they called Rosemont Gardens.

That is where they were living the night they awoke to find a cross-shaped straw scarecrow burning in the yard and a note left at the door giving the "nigger teacher" twenty-four hours to get out of town or have his house burned to the ground with his family in it. My father remembered his father telling the story: how he lay on the floor with his mother and siblings and some teachers from the school and smelled the straw burning and saw the cross silhouetted on the wall and waited all night for the sound of boots on the porch that never came.

Creeping through the brush the next night to make good their promise to set fire to the house and the school if the teacher was still there when they returned, the Klansmen found Will sitting on the porch of his house rocking in a rocking chair, back and forth, back and forth, with a book in his lap. Coming closer, they saw what they had missed in the dark, five Confederate veterans, the best shots in the county, sitting in chairs behind the teacher, their guns on their knees. So the cowardly vigilantes retreated much faster than they had come; and every year after that, for as long as the school's defenders lived, the family sent roses to them on their birthdays, doing it, my father said, long after Maggie and Will were dead and some of their descendants had forgotten why we honored this particular set of old men in this way.

Though he wasn't among them, I think Emily's grandfather, Henry (Hal) Tabb Walker, was the sort of man who might have done such a thing. Hal had come to Montgomery to read law the year the Civil War ended and had married Eliza Ware, the short, plain daughter of the short, plain Grandmother Jane who had saved the plantation. Captain Hal was stocky like the Wares and not much taller than his 5'3" wife, but he was a personable, well-spoken young man who had spent four of the first five years of his life in a suite at the White House, where his father served as personal secretary to his uncle and former law partner, President James Knox Polk.

Though the Knox–Polk–Walkers of Tennessee were business

people, lawyers, and natural-born Jacksonian Democrats with little to gain from cotton and slaves, when their state seceded, so did they. Hal's urbane father, knowing nothing of war, had raised a Confederate infantry regiment from among the Irishmen of Memphis and taken the Irishmen and the seventeen-year-old Hal to fight at Belmont and then at Shiloh Church—where North and South would learn, along with the Walkers, that the war was going to be about death and destruction and disillusionment beyond anything anybody had imagined or bargained for. Twenty-three thousand men fell at Shiloh and thousands more (including Hal's father) came down with typhoid and dysentery. Within a month, the forty-four-year-old Colonel Walker had gone home to die, broken in body by exposure, exhaustion, and dysentery and in spirit by the sight of carnage nothing in his life had prepared him to look on.

With that, Hal joined the cavalry as aide-de-camp to his brother-in-law, Confederate General Frank Crawford Armstrong, and with him served at Chickamauga, Missionary Ridge, Knoxville, Atlanta, Franklin, Nashville, and Selma. But the gregarious, Union-reconciled Hal Walker did not do well in Montgomery, married to the war-embittered, antebellum-minded Eliza Ware.

For a while during the Reconstruction, he tried journalism. But when the planters criticized his paper for opposing the Ku Klux Klan and promoting organized labor, land reform, the education of Negroes, and cooperation with the Reconstructionists, Hal gave it up and afterwards became a general in the United Confederate Veterans, dabbled in politics, brokered cotton, backed an electric amusement park that made a little money and lost a little, and never did much of anything with his life. He had wanted to be more than he was, I am sure, but the resistance of the Wares combined with some weakness in his own character held him back.

The Yankee officers were still occupying the ground floor of the Greek Revival mansion when my grandmother, Augusta Knox

Walker, was born there on January 14, 1871. The second child and first daughter of a family needing something to hope for, Knoxie, as she was always called, was gorgeous, with golden hair, dark eyes, and tawny skin. She was high-strung from birth, hard to keep occupied, and as willful as her older brother, Croom, whom Grandmother Jane favored and spoiled. A son named James but called Boise was born on Christmas Day three years after Knoxie. But it was my Aunt Bessie, born ten years after that, who became her father's favorite. The two certainly looked alike, with their short, broad shapes, wiry black hair, and long Walker jaws. Both loved good talk, good food, and the old ways that were passing and would never come back.

As soon as Bessie was born, the family sold the Greek Revival mansion and moved to the Victorian townhouse where my mother grew up, which they always called "410" because of its address, 410 South Court Street. They moved, they said, because the new house was modern and had both a kitchen and a bathroom in the main building. They moved, too, I suspect, to get the money to educate and launch the Walker children in society. Both Croom and Boise attended the preparatory academy at Sewanee, and Boise completed a year of law school at the University of the South, but both young men went to work early in the insurance business. It was Knoxie on whom the family lavished the luxuries of expensive trips, jewelry, and clothes, expecting their beautiful daughter to marry a man rich enough and prominent enough to restore the family to its rightful place in the scheme of things.

Though the campus of the "colored college" where Maggie and Will were raising and educating their own children was only a few miles from the antebellum part of town where the Ware–Walkers lived, the families were separated by a social divide so vast that no one would have believed it possible to breach it at all, much less as swiftly and fully as the gifted, ambitious, and personable children of Maggie and Will were going to breach it. All four of their sons graduated from Alabama Polytechnic Institute (now Auburn University) and made names for themselves as students and athletes and came home to take over a nursery business that by then included a shop downtown and a complex of greenhouses and gardens on a stretch of suburban land bought with money inherited from Maggie's mother—the same war-widowed, Irish-born mother who had sold part of her tiny farm in Canfield, Ohio, to send her daughter to study with the abolitionists at Oberlin.

Will and Maggie believed in hard work and self-reliance and the American dream, but they held their children close and taught them to trust only one another and to put the needs of the family above all personal desires and to live above reproach. Failure to thrive and failure to understand the intricacies of black-and-white mores when they came there could have meant death, exile, or the end of their work—until, finally, failure and doubt and the need for help from outside the family had become a shameful, unacceptable thing among them. There was a streak of sadness and defensiveness in the Patersons as I knew them that came, I believe, from the realization that it was not going to be possible for them to be who they were and still be as admired and loved as they wanted to be.

In truth, the need to stick together and defend themselves against attack seemed never to end, and when Maggie died of Bright's disease in 1904 and was buried across the line in the black section of the segregated cemetery (making a statement even in death), the main building of the school burned to the ground. "I cannot think it was set fire," the ever-sanguine Will told a reporter. "Rather, the fire has revealed to me the great interest there is in our work and how many friends we do have."

My grandfather Jim Paterson was twenty years old when his mother died—a good student in his junior year at college, a star football player, captain of the baseball team, and already a skilled horticulturist. He was, I believe, something of a poet in his feelings and more interested in making friends and pursuing his own interests than in fighting to raise the family in the eyes of the world, a role that fell to his brothers—Will Jr. and Haygood—who did it extremely well.

Jimmy, the gentle one, the one closest to his mother, was a fair-skinned, energetic fellow with a wiry build and stark, plain features—"so homely somebody had to love him," my Grandmother Ila said to explain her love for a man who was not only plain-looking but self-conscious about his looks and vain enough to want to make up for them with perfect grooming and a dapper style of dress. He had something to be self-conscious about, I suppose, since he had been born with a large upper lip with a ridge in the middle of it, as if two lips had been intended rather than one—"nigger lip" being something he and his brothers believed they had to fight about (though his parents told them not to) every time his schoolmates said it.

The double lip seems also to have been a blessing, since his going into the hospital to have it "cut down and stitched up" was the occasion of his meeting the dark-eyed nurse he would marry. But Jim was bashful as well as vain and all the stories the down-to-earth Ila Watson told about their courtship and early marriage emphasized those two qualities.

First there was the unnecessary surgery on his upper lip, which looked all right the way it was, she said, and didn't look much better afterwards. Then there was the time he borrowed a fine horse and buggy to take her for a ride. Trouble was, the horse had diarrhea and slung "liquid manure" all over them and the buggy every time it swished its tail. The point of the tale was twofold: the difficulty my grandmother had not further embarrassing the mortified Jim by howling with laughter (which she always did when she told it), and Jim's vanity in wanting to come courting a country girl like herself in a finer style than he (plain and poor as he was) had a right to.

While plain Jim Paterson courted the country girl Ila, Knoxie played the Southern belle to the point of parody and continued a debut that lasted thirteen years. Only a woman as independent and beautiful as Knoxie could get away with it for so long, everybody said, without being pitied as an old maid—though I think some people must have seen the loneliness and confusion beneath the flamboyance and pitied her anyway.

At some point during those years, Knoxie began a strange, lifelong romance with a reserved and soft-spoken man named Charles Poellnitz Gunter, born in the last days of the Civil War to a family that had backed the Confederacy with such fervor that when the hostilities ended some of them took their slaves and migrated to Brazil. Nobody knows why Charlie Gunter and Knoxie courted so long and never married. Aunt Bessie said Knoxie never loved anybody else. Some people said Charlie was too much in love with the ease of living at home with his mother and sisters to think seriously of marrying anybody. Some said they both knew he would never make enough money to afford the spoiled and extravagant Knoxie.

Eliza said her daughter was so flighty *nobody* would have her, and it was in response to that gibe, some people said, that Knoxie married Jim Hillman, who had first come calling on the much younger, much less beautiful Bessie. The family put it out that Jim Hillman was very rich and that Knoxie had finally found someone good enough for her. In truth, the rather mysterious Mr. Hillman from Birmingham and Kentucky was far from rich and, even if all his prospects of inheritance had come true, would still not have been rich enough to match the rumors the family spread.

And so it was that on January 5, 1905, two weeks before her thirty-fourth birthday, Knoxie (who by then had changed her name from Augusta Knox to Knoxie Polk) married James Hoggatt Hillman in the Victorian parlor of the house at 410. Family lore has it that on the morning of the wedding Knoxie sent Charlie Gunter a note saying, "Come get me." Instead, he came to the wedding and shook the hand of the groom like the good friend of the family he had always been.

The thirty-five-year-old groom was a pleasant-looking man with bright blue eyes and regular features. He was intelligent, mild-mannered, and a lover of books and literature, but so passive in his approach to life that I have never heard of anyone who had a strong sense of who or what he was. What I do know is that he was a binge drinker, with a record of personal and business failure that left him largely dependent on his half brother Thomas Tennessee (Tenny) Hillman. A brilliant, hunchbacked little man who had pioneered the steel industry in Birmingham, Tenny was one of a long line of Hillmans who had fallen in love with the idea of turning mineral ore into tools made of iron, and followed that yearning south from New Jersey to Kentucky to Birmingham. The Hillmans brought with them a heritage that combined monumental ambition with a depressive gene (sometimes manic, sometimes not) that runs in that side of my family as deep as any mineral runs in the earth.

As heir to that heritage, Tenny and Jim's father, Daniel Hillman, had built an iron-making empire on the land between the Cumberland and Tennessee rivers in Kentucky and then sacrificed half of what he had made to the Confederacy, and afterwards, when he was fifty-eight years old, taken a young Nashville heiress named Mary Ann Gentry to be his second wife. Though broken in mind and spirit by then, he was still healthy enough to add three sons (my grandfather being the last of them) to the four legitimate (for there seem to have been quite a few others) children he already had. And still sagacious enough to buy large mineral properties in Alabama for Tenny, who—to complicate matters—had by then married his stepmother's younger sister, Emily Gentry.

And so it was that the man Knoxie married had grown up almost fatherless in the isolation of a defunct Kentucky iron compound that had once worked thousands of slaves and made millions of dollars. My grandfather was eleven years old when his father was admitted to the Western State Asylum for melancholia and fifteen when he died of what the hospital called exhaustion. When he was seventeen, Jim was enrolled in Phillips Exeter Academy in New Hampshire but stayed only a few months. Afterwards he worked off and on for Tenny in Birmingham and then went into the Army for a while. He was married briefly to a Birmingham woman who, with the help of a servant, "escaped" the family home in Kentucky on the train and refused to go back. By 1905, when Knoxie married him, Jim was living in Birmingham again and running an ornamental-brick-manufacturing business financed by Tenny and the Aunt Emily who was also his half-sister-in-law.

Unlike Knoxie, who was (as F. Scott Fitzgerald said of the Montgomery woman he married) "reared to be idle," my Grandmother Ila believed that the only approach to life that made any sense at all was working and scrimping and saving, which is what she was doing at the Laura Hill Infirmary in Montgomery when Jim Paterson showed up to have his double lip reduced. Though I doubt Ila ever knew true privation, the history of it in a family descended, as hers was, from the slaveless, hard-laboring farmers of plantation-dominated Wilcox County, Alabama, was so real and so recent that she never lost her fear of it.

And then came love and sweetness with a man she didn't marry for four years because she feared they couldn't afford it. And when they did finally marry, they moved into Will Paterson's crowded cottage on the edge of campus, where in March 1910 their first child was born. He was named William Burns Paterson III, for one of the heroes of education in Alabama who happened also to be the sweet-faced, frumpily dressed old man who was the baby's grandfather. Though named for his grandfather, Ila and Jim's firstborn was called Sonny, and the name stuck with him for life—an earnest, lovable child who looked and acted just like his father and was so adored by his mother (and was so adoring of her) that Ila said she wouldn't mind his being an only child. But Sonny was not to be an only child, and by the time Ila found herself pregnant again, the cottage they were building behind the Greenhouse (as the growing complex of Rosemont Gardens greenhouses was always called; in honor, I suppose, of its tiny back-yard beginnings) was almost done. And so she hoped for a daughter, but the daughter she hoped for turned out to be my father, born on March 10, 1913, and named Julius Porter for his father and his two grandfathers, but eventually called Duke, a nickname derived from Ila's baby-talk endearment "Dookie."

Will Paterson died two years later at sixty-six, still doing the work he believed the Almighty had put him on earth to do, still going before the legislature every year to call for a level of education for Negroes considered almost as radical in Alabama in 1915 as it had been in 1870. After their father's death, Will's four sons (though not his daughter) grew increasingly cautious in their identification with the beliefs that had brought their parents to Alabama. If my father knew that he and his father had been named for an abolition-minded Union soldier killed marching through Georgia with Sherman's Army, he never told it and neither did anyone else in the family. His generation seldom spoke of the remarkable community at Marion into which their parents had been born and the terrible blow the loss of the school had been to their grandparents. They seldom spoke of the insecurities, insults, and privations the family endured in Montgomery for the sake of the unpopular work they had brought there. Though they maintained a loyalty to Alabama State Teachers' College (now Alabama State University) and supported it in numerous practical ways, philosophically they drifted steadily in the direction of the mainstream in which they now lived and made their living.

By the time Duke was born, two sons—Dan and James Hoggatt Jr.—had also been born to Knoxie and Jim Hillman in Birmingham. By then my grandfather's mother had died and left him enough money to form a real-estate partnership with a Mr. William Watts. Tenny was dead by then, having left his two half-brothers one dollar each, believing he had done too much for them already and knowing that their Aunt Emily would give them whatever they needed. As it turned out, Jim Hillman and his family were going to need a great deal.

Whatever the pressures were (his mother's death, his half-brother's death and disinheritance, one full brother dead of tongue cancer at twenty-one, the other gone West without a trace, his and Knoxie's incompatibility, the challenges of fatherhood to a man who had himself been practically fatherless), soon Jim Hillman was going for days without sleep, hearing voices and imagining terrible things happening to his sons. Some say he lost his mind like his father, some say he had a brain tumor, others say it was syphilis. In any case, his paranoia turned (who knows why) toward his partner Watts—until, one day in the winter of 1914, my Grandfather Hillman, a master marksman, took his gun to work and shot and seriously wounded Mr. Watts, who, fortunately for all concerned, did not die.

Perhaps because he was, by then, truly insane, perhaps to save him from being tried for attempted murder, Jim was declared *non compos mentis* and hospitalized in private quarters on the wooded grounds of a private sanatorium in Louisville, Kentucky, where he stayed for nearly two years at the expense of his aging, childless, and wealthy Aunt Emily. And there in a cottage where my mad or nearly mad grandfather lived (with "a servant and all the amenities," Aunt Bessie always said), my mother, Emily Gentry Hillman, was conceived, an unwanted child if ever there was one.

She was born on November 6, 1914, in a hospital in Birmingham, and handed almost immediately into the care of her unmarried thirty-one-year-old Aunt Bessie. Her seventy-year-old Great-aunt Emily added her namesake to her will and died two years later. Her father, whom she never saw, died a year after that in the state asylum at Anchorage, Kentucky, of what funeral records called apoplexy. He was forty-eight. Knoxie was forty-six, and Charlie Gunter was waiting in the wings to be her lover again and cause a minor scandal by spending unchaperoned weekends in the house on Mountain Avenue in Birmingham.

For self-indulgence and flamboyance, Knoxie's widowhood almost rivaled her debut. She traveled, partied, drank, smoked, dressed to the nines, went about with Charlie, and paid so little attention to her children that soon they were spending almost as much time in Montgomery with Bessie as they did in Birmingham with their mother. Finally Knoxie ran out of money and moved the whole family back to 410 South Court Street in Montgomery.

Duke's life was as different from that as could be, and would on the surface seem to have been made for happiness, and I believe there was great happiness in it. And yet my father seemed almost from birth to have felt himself an outsider in a family of insiders—an outsider simply by temperament and by his own definition rather than theirs, for, in truth, I don't think any of the Patersons ever lost the sense of themselves as a people barricaded together and out to prove they were "as good as anybody."

Duke was a wistful, temperamental child whose initial lack of interest in school and competition (and long hours spent walking wordlessly through the Greenhouse at his father's side or curled up in the crawl space under the house, building toy cars from spools and scraps of metal) filled everyone except his father with consternation. My father had trouble in school from the beginning, and because school was one of the ways in which the Patersons proved themselves and because his brother was so good at it, the trouble seemed worse than it was.

By the 1920s, Ila and Jim had started to prosper both from the family business and from a poultry-breeding enterprise they ran on their own. Jim bought a camera before most people had one and owned one of the first radios in town. When Duke was nine, his father and a friend took a boat from Miami to Cuba and bootlegged enough Prohibition rum back into the country for Jim to buy a Roamer touring car. He taught the whole family, including his small son, to drive, and on the weekends took carloads of friends over fifty miles of country road to see Auburn play football.

Then suddenly Jim, the father, the playmate, the one who had loved his mother most, the one who could work circles around all his brothers and had two paying jobs and more friends than all the rest of them put together, began to lose his strength from a heart-muscle infection that, in those days, could not be cured. And so he was dying, but dying slowly, until around Easter 1927, near the time of Duke's fourteenth birthday, when the terrible, painful death from a ruptured appendix began.

And Ila said, "Let him die at home then, where he belongs and where I can look after him to the end," and Duke alternated between pacing the rows of sweet-scented lilies in the Greenhouse and watching his father twist and stiffen and suppress the pain and go white and then gray and finally die in the black leather chair where he had sat listening to the radio and reading the papers for as long as his son could remember. And Ila, not ordinarily inclined to sentiment, got a wooden gift box her husband had given her and took a little bottle of perfume he had given her and put a drop of sweetness on a lace handkerchief he had given her and sat down to shed the only tears anybody ever saw her shed over him, and afterwards declared to everyone that there would be no more tears and no more sorrow and that her sons would go back to school on Monday and they would get by somehow and life would go on as it always had.

Duke remembered his father's writhing with pain, his mother's grief, the smell of the lilies, and his father's regret that he was going to die without seeing what the Model A Ford would look like. Neither Duke nor Sonny ever cried over anything in Ila's presence after their father died that I ever heard of, though I heard often how she would say, "Straighten up your face, boy," to Duke to stop him from crying even when he was very small.

At bottom, my Grandmother Ila seems to have thought suffering and sorrow were either too useless or too threatening to be countenanced, and I never saw any evidence that anything that befell her changed her mind.

She was a woman soaked in reality, with almost no interest at all in anything imaginary—and there was a small, hard knot of judgment and fear inside her that brooked "no foolishness" from anyone who saw life less matter-of-factly than she did.

Within days of her husband's death, she had agreed to let the family support her and her sons rather than go back to nursing and running the poultry business on her own. Whatever reservations she had about financial dependency (and I think they must have been substantial) were overcome. And after the decision was made, she seemed never to have questioned her right to the tiny pension she received from her husband's family for the rest of her life.

Unfortunately for Duke, the sting of "charity case" (and submitting to the authority and high standards of his father's oldest brother, Will) added its opprobrium to the death of his father in a family in which the father-son bond was practically sacred and in which sorrow, failure, and the need to be comforted were not allowed. And the wound ached and ached and my father matured slowly and haltingly and resented all efforts to make him do otherwise. And it must have been at that time that he started to develop the haughty, intolerant, sometimes violent side of the Jekyll-and-Hyde nature that I knew in him—a usually witty, sensitive man, painfully vulnerable to the suffering of others, whom a drink of whiskey or the stab of some feeling too painful to bear could turn, without warning, into a tornado of rudeness and fury.

Emily was thirteen in 1928 when the now debt-ridden, now heavily drinking Knoxie sold her house in Birmingham and moved her family in with Bessie. Emily, who couldn't have been happier, showed up for the eighth grade at the Lawrence Street public school wearing knickers and a ruffled blouse, looking like no other girl there, and began at that point to make friends of her own and to dress in the tailored, conventional style she had always liked— no matter what Knoxie said, no matter what Bessie wanted her to do. It was also there, I believe, that she began to take a heavy load of the hardest courses and to panic whenever her schoolwork wasn't perfect and to turn from everybody's pal and the best sandlot athlete in town into a soft-featured beauty with breasts bigger than she ever wanted them to be and boys pressing her for attention and her trying to be equally nice to everybody.

What she wanted most was to enjoy her friends and do the things they did without displeasing Knoxie and Bessie any more than she had to. Most of all, she wanted to be different from Knoxie—to be kind to people, to marry for love and belong to a big, happy family of people who loved one another.

And then, who knows why (the unstable family life? an inherited fragility? adolescence gone wrong?), something inside her started to slip. She attended Sidney Lanier High School for a year and dropped out the next fall because the crowds in the halls frightened her and too many people were smarter than she was—and spent the rest of the year keeping Bessie and Knoxie company at home and enjoying the baby Jimmy, recently born to her brother James H. and his wife.

Though he had no idea who she was, Emily remembered Duke in high school as a handsome, well-built young man, somber and tense in a way that translated (to her) as pure sex appeal. He was making a name for himself playing football but doing so poorly in school that the family sent him to Georgia Military College, where for two years he quarterbacked the football team to victory and had more success in school than he had ever had before and glimpsed (and, I believe, understood) what a highly disciplined life might have made of him. He wanted to join the Navy and see the world, but the family was of one mind: he should go to Auburn, join a fraternity (now that fraternities would have them), play football, get a degree, and come back to work in the family business like all the others.

But Auburn was too big for my father, he missed his friends in Georgia, he couldn't adjust, he skipped classes and got in fights, and—though he captained the freshman swimming team and played football—he wasn't disciplined enough for either college sports or college academics. It was there that he began to drink in a troubling way and to fight a brooding disappointment in himself and his failure to live up to the expectations of the people who loved him.

Fourteen million Americans were out of work in the spring of 1933 when Duke dropped out of college and set out to make a living on his own, saying the last thing in the world he wanted was to join his cousin Bill running the Greenhouse under his Uncle Will's thumb. Instead, he borrowed enough money to open a gas station with a friend and supplemented his income selling life insurance.

Emily, meanwhile, had fallen in love with a brilliant University of Virginia law student named Sam and gone off to a finishing school in Manhattan run by Charlie Gunter's sister, Mrs. Rosa Gunter Semple. She would go to Mrs. Semple's for a year, she thought, and then she would marry Sam, whom Knoxie admired for his Virginia roots and his reputation for brilliance and his plans to practice law in Montgomery. In love with the image and reflected glory of a man she thought far above herself, Emily went to New York expecting to get engaged to Sam over the summer. A few weeks after she left, Sam's younger brother was killed in an automobile accident. The family was in chaos, and Sam was devastated.

Emily sympathized from afar, perhaps not knowing she ought to come home, perhaps unable to face the kind of suffering she was sure to see if she did, perhaps thinking it was kinder and more polite to let the family grieve alone. Another young woman saw it differently and made it her business to go to the house every day and to do what she could for the family and Sam. Emily was so happy in New York (rooming with one of Mrs. Semple's nieces, going to the museums, the opera, a different historic church every Sunday, the Bronx Zoo, Coney Island, all the best shops and big department stores, celebrating her nineteenth birthday in a tea room on Fifth Avenue, learning a little French and some Spanish, going to dances with West Point cadets) that she "fairly glowed" when she got off the train at Christmas, and had more admirers than ever before, though she only had eyes for Sam. In February, her roommate's sister and the woman who had comforted Sam came on the train to New York to see the sights and visit their friends at school.

Sam's new friend had an invitation to take them to tea at the apartment of that famous Alabamian, Tallulah Bankhead. Only they didn't drink tea; they drank whiskey. Everybody except Emily, that is, who never drank anything with alcohol in it and ordered hot tea even in bars, telling her friends she feared the tendency to abuse alcohol was in her genes. After tea, they walked around Manhattan and then went to dinner in a restaurant. They were all having so much fun, smoking cigarettes in public and laughing about Emily's short haircut and all the strange doings at home and who was "going with" whom—until Emily started noticing looks being passed across the table, as if the others knew something she didn't know, until finally Sam's friend took her left hand out of her lap and flashed a diamond engagement ring, blindingly bright in the light from the lamp on the table.

She was going to marry Sam in June, she said. She and her friend came to New York to tell Emily. Sam wouldn't tell her, so she came herself. Somebody had to do it.

Emily didn't believe them. It must be a joke. How could he have pretended at Christmas? How could he have written the letters he wrote? Impossible for anybody to be so cruel.

Something locked inside the woman who was to be my mother and for two days she acted as if nothing had happened and woke up on the morning of the third day in a blast of light too bright to be borne. The sound of her roommate splashing cold water on her face went off in her head like the shot of a gun. The sun was too bright, the air too cold, tiny noises were magnified a thousandfold. Her pulse pounded in her head and she felt like someone was cutting her heart out of her chest with a knife.

By afternoon, her bags were packed and she was stepping on the train in a state of bliss—so happy to be going home (to sleep forever in her own bed and forget everything that had happened since she left there) that she thought she would never be sad again. But the sadness had only begun.

For months she confined herself to the third floor at 410—not eating, not sleeping, not talking, not crying, not howling, not banging her head on the wall—comforted only by the sweetness of her three-year-old nephew, Jimmy, as recently and totally abandoned by his parents as she had been by her sweetheart. She pulled the shades and stared into blackness. When she ate at all, she ate sitting on the bed, feeding and being fed by a three-year-old child.

Bessie paced the wide halls downstairs, railing at Sam, his fiancée, and all their relations, wringing her fat little hands and sobbing into them the way Emily should have been doing but wasn't. They were all so young and stupid, and Sam was such a fool.

Emily was just too good for Sam, Knoxie said, and would soon forget all about him. She herself had loved and lost scores of beaux and spent her whole life apart from the only one she really wanted. "All things pass for the young," she said.

As it turned out, things did not pass quickly for Emily. Sam married. She postponed the debut she was expected to make in September. The only thing that gave her pleasure was the party she arranged for Jimmy's fourth birthday and the company of a few friends. She stopped caring about her looks and grew as thin and pale as Knoxie.

By fall, she had gotten her spirits up enough to talk the trustees of her Aunt Emily's estate into letting her buy the maroon Chevrolet she wanted. Soon she was taking everybody she knew for drives and picnics in the country. Her brother Dan and his wife, Helen, had a daughter now, Emily's goddaughter and first niece. Hope grew in her that her family might be coming alive again, with the little boy Jimmy at 4 and the baby Helen out at the house Dan had built not far from the old plantation house to which her Uncle Boise had returned from Texas with a family of cousins her age and younger.

I don't know what else my mother did that year besides master golf with a speed that amazed her friends, but by Christmas 1934 her small, athletic body was as lithe and voluptuous as ever; her skin was soft and rosy. Her fine brown eyes glowed and the gold shone again in her chestnut hair.

Narrow Lane Road

I associate two images with my parents' coming together in the spring of 1935. In the first, Emily stands
alone on the golf course at the Montgomery Country
Club. Duke drives by and thinks she is the most
beautiful girl he has ever seen. He doesn't know who
she is, but he honks. She waves, not because she recognizes him
(though she would have if he had been closer), but because she
waves at everybody.

In the second, they are in a crowded bar with friends. Duke
always drinks when they go out (everybody does). He wants her
to join him and so she drinks too, just a little, telling her friends
she is being careful because she still believes, as she always has,
that the weakness for alcohol is in her blood. Maybe she believed
it because of the way Knoxie drank and the way she remembered
her Grandfather Hal drinking and because of what she knew or
suspected about her father. Maybe she believed it because the little
drinking she had already done had shown her that once she started
she didn't want to stop. And so she starts drinking with Duke,
just a little, because he wants it so much and she is so in love with
him and things go so much better between them when they both
drink a little. Just a little.

Though their emotional instability and potential for alcoholism
seemed to have given their love a troubled, almost violent edge

from the start, nobody noticed at first, certainly not Bessie and Knoxie, who were too disconcerted by Duke's lack of social standing to think about anything else. How *could* Emily be serious about Duke? There were so many *suitable* young men in Montgomery. That the Patersons had come from the North and Scotland during Reconstruction to start schools for colored people didn't bother them all that much, since (now almost everybody agreed) what they did had been a good thing; but they were *trades*men, and (though people said they were fine people and accomplished and some of them lived well enough) they didn't *have* anything and their lives were so *plain*.

Nevertheless, by fall, the romance was serious enough for Bessie and Knoxie to plan a party at 410 to introduce Duke to their friends in a proper way. Emily objected. Duke didn't like parties. Her friends already knew him. He didn't like many people outside his own family. But, they insisted, he was a young businessman. Some of the best people in town would be there; he should know them. Finally Emily acquiesced and talked Duke into agreeing to come, though he thought it a terrible, snooty idea—having a party like that for no reason, for people you don't care about and hardly knew.

The famous claw-footed table where Jefferson Davis dined was laid out with a starched white tablecloth for the first time in years. Special cooks were hired to prepare a meal in the old style. The best bartenders and waiters in town came to serve. All the right people were gathered in the regal old house, which looked, for the first time in a long time, the way it looked when Bessie and Knoxie had beaux of their own. Everybody was there except Duke.

They waited and waited, until Emily was in tears, and finally started dinner without him. And when he arrived, he arrived drunk, wearing a dinner jacket (as they had said he must), and with a smirk on his face that mocked them all. He was as good as they were. He had something better to do.

Somehow he and Emily made it up. Emily's debut party at the Montgomery Country Club two weeks before Christmas became famous for two things: the skimpiness of refreshments (just fruit-cake, and not enough champagne to go around), for which Knoxie was famous, and the yards and yards of red-and-white-twined smilax garlands with which Duke had draped the upper balcony overlooking the ballroom. The floral decorations were so elegant that half the article in the next day's newspaper was devoted to them.

"Miss Emily Hillman made her bow in a Milgrim debutante period model of imported ivory chiffon velvet," the unsigned article read. "The smart ultra bodice had a halter neckline, and left the shoulders bare. The circular skirt, closely fitted, ended in a long train. Miss Hillman wore magnificent heirloom pearls. Her flowers were a long, loose arrangement of Templar roses and white calla lilies tied with silver ribbons which reached to the floor."

Emily's brother Dan and his dark-eyed wife, Helen (without doubt, everybody agreed, the most beautiful woman of their generation), along with other members of the extended family, were there. Sam's wife and the woman who came with her to New York to tell Emily that Sam had decided to marry someone else presided over a "great silver punch bowl massed around with asparagus plumosa fern, the whole being garlanded with lilies of the valley, white sweet peas and white Killarney roses." The idea of honoring those two in that way rather than choosing two of my mother's less well-married, less well-connected friends could only have originated with Knoxie and Bessie.

"That way," I can hear Bessie saying, "no one will think you are still pining over Sam, and everybody will see how happy and beautiful you are. Besides, they are two of the nicest young married women in town. They are just the kind of friends you should have." Though she and Knoxie still knew everybody and still clung to their antebellum status at the top of the social heap, their lives were too insular (what with all the men gone, not enough money left, and the neighborhood running down) for them to have a wide social circle or much social influence, which is what they now planned for Emily just as the family had once planned it for Knoxie.

"What difference does it make who serves the punch?" Emily must have asked herself. With Duke at her side, she was safe and whole and all she had to do was make Knoxie and Bessie happy one more time and then she'd be free to do as she pleased for the rest of her life.

She and Duke spent Christmas Day visiting both their families and looking so carefree and happy that, for at least that one day, no one objected to their love and nothing went wrong until they got out to the Depression-struck Ware plantation home of Knoxie's brother Boise and found Emily's eight-year-old cousin in tears because Santa hadn't brought the bicycle she asked for—whereupon Duke went to town, prevailed on a friend to open his sporting-goods store, and returned with a red bicycle in the backseat of his car. That wild gesture of sympathy, proficiency, and generosity seems to have erased all my mother's doubts about my father and may have had something to do with my conception.

Two weeks later, Emily wrote a friend of her plans to elope with Duke. "On Friday, January 24th," she said, "Duke and I are going to pack our suitcases and head for the Auburn dances. Saturday morning we are going to get an early start, get a marriage license and be married by Colonel Bruce McGhee in Opelika. Then we are going to strike out for Florida . . . we can't be stopped, darling. Oh, Genie, I'm so scared, I can't eat or sleep and will be nervous weeks before our wedding. I think we'll be very happy, though, because we love each other so much. Pray for me, Genie, as my family is going to expire!"

She signed the letter "Mrs. J. P. Paterson" and twice implored her friend not to tell anybody the news, because "Duke would kill me if he knew I had told."

39

The plans described in that letter were all Duke's—to be married among his friends by an old friend of his family and drive to Florida for a honeymoon that would include a visit with the only friends of Emily's he really liked. A week before the planned elopement, Emily got sick with the flu (or morning sickness) and they married a week later in a Baptist Church in Troy, Alabama, accompanied by my mother's friend Mel (not a favorite of Duke's) and her husband-to-be (whom he couldn't stand) and came home the same night to tell Knoxie and Bessie and Duke's mother.

Knoxie and Bessie did not expire. Bessie wept and said Emily was too young to marry anybody, and said it like a litany for the rest of her life. What she meant was "too young to marry" and "shouldn't have married Duke." I don't know what Knoxie said to them that night, but afterwards she said three things that nobody ever forgot.

"The only thing Duke and I have in common is Camel cigarettes" was the nicest of the three. The other two were references to her son-in-law's inferior social status: "I guess it will be good to have some shirtsleeves in the family"; and the much-quoted "We have sunk from the White House [alluding to Hal Walker's time there when his Uncle Polk was President] to the Greenhouse."

On the other hand, Ila, whom I call Gram, approved of Emily for Duke, perhaps because the younger woman's admiration seemed to steady her temperamental son, perhaps because it left a place for her own maternal strength in their lives, perhaps because Emily's family was still considered rather grand and people said Emily would have money (and Ila and her sons had never had that), perhaps because Gram had wanted a daughter when Duke was born and Emily at twenty still looked and acted like a beautiful child. Despite her sternness with her sons, my grandmother had an abiding weakness for true vulnerability in other people and seems to have loved my mother from the start.

In order to support his new wife, Duke sold his partnership in the gas station, gave up selling insurance, and went to work doing the thing he said he'd never do—managing the greenhouses with his cousin Bill. He was good at it; it was easy for him and it assured him a small but steady income.

My father loved all forms of work that combined the mental and the physical, and in that his work of growing things and building the environment in which they grew gave him great satisfaction all his life—and connected him to his family and to the memory of his father. What it didn't satisfy was an abiding sense of the wider horizons he had always intended to seek and the belief that he was supposed to have done something more important—and of more service to humanity—than he did.

It was those two urges—to adventure and service—that seem to have kindled his interest in going to Europe to fight for democracy long before most people thought what was going on "over there" had anything to do with us. By the time Duke and Emily married, Mussolini had seized Ethiopia, Spain was in chaos, Germany had occupied the Rhineland, and the Nazi persecution of the Jews was well under way. At home, most people were still fighting the Depression.

Duke never forgot the deprivation he saw in Alabama during those years and he never stopped trying to make up for his own comparative good fortune by hiring almost anybody who walked into the Greenhouse with a hard-luck story. If their need was great enough, he hired them. The financial shock that followed his father's death combined with the Depression and Gram's inbred fear of want left him with a lasting horror of being broke and poor himself. On the other hand, though he had expensive tastes in some things and was full of schemes for getting rich all his life, he had no instincts for making money and handled it impulsively and guiltily, as if he felt he had no right to what he had and feared it would be taken away.

Despite the differences in income and style of living and spending, Emily had grown up in households that were almost as cash-poor as Duke's and, I believe, even more anxiety-ridden. Though the money Jim Hillman's aunt left Knoxie and her children was more than sufficient for them to have lived well enough, Knoxie spent money compulsively and managed it not at all, so that in the end everything of hers that wasn't carefully protected was gone. The income the Walkers lived on at 410 was generated mainly by the sale and rental of land. When there was money, they spent it; when there wasn't, they charged and borrowed and talked constantly about the unfairness of it all.

My mother seems to have grown up thinking of money as a commodity that could be neither handled nor understood. Nothing she saw in her family would have led her to make any connection between wherewithal and her own endeavor. Money was simply a mystery, something that came in and went out in accordance with laws over which nobody—least of all herself—had any control. Though later in their marriage Emily would threaten to use her inheritance to leave Duke, in fact, as soon as her Aunt Emily's trustees turned it over to her, she turned it over to her husband and paid no more attention to it than if it had been solely his.

A few months after Duke and Emily were married, they borrowed against her inheritance (most of which would not come to her directly until she was twenty-five) and bought the sunlit, pecan-shaded, two-storied cottage on Narrow Lane Road where I was born. It was near the Rosemont Gardens greenhouses, near Gram's house, not far from the Alabama State College for Negroes.

Narrow Lane Road. Rosemont Gardens. Alabama State. A world so alive with Patersons that the streets themselves seemed to be ours. The house was also across the street from the Montgomery Country Club, to which (in one of the most astonishing acts of upward family mobility I ever heard of) all the Patersons now belonged. For a while, Emily played golf there with her friends, but Duke wanted her home any time he was there, and was from the beginning, I believe, jealous of the little group of five or six friends she loved. He didn't like the loud, silly way they talked. He didn't like their effusive fondness for one another. He didn't like feeling excluded the way he always did when Emily was with people she knew before she knew him.

Emily had, I suppose, assumed that married life would follow the pattern of her life with Knoxie and Bessie and that she would be free to come and go as she pleased and have plenty of time for her friends, who were, for the most part, different from the friends she shared with her husband. But Duke wanted her all to himself and wanted her home to prepare lunch for him and to be there to eat it with him and enjoy the break he took in the middle of a workday that began at six in the morning. That was the way it was done in his family. That was why he had wanted a house near the Greenhouse.

As it turned out, Emily had no proclivity for either housekeeping or cooking. In this she was more like her mother than like Bessie, who—though she usually had servants—liked to do those things. I suppose my father came home at noon every day and that they ate something, though I can't imagine what, since in the almost ten years I had with her I have not a single memory of my mother even so much as heating a bowl of soup or scrambling an egg. Emily's avoidance of the tasks of homemaking was so extreme that I am forced to wonder if she wasn't as phobic about failing in those duties as she had been about failing second-year Latin and algebra. There was, too, I believe, something of rebelliousness and arrogance in it—something that was there in her relationship with my father from the beginning. She was not a Paterson and had no intentions of turning into one just because she had married Duke. In that, too, she was more like her mother than she—or anyone else—ever admitted.

I know little else of the few months my parents had together before I was born, other than that they bought the house on Narrow

Lane Road and put a crib for me in a sunny corner of the room where they slept. And it was to that sunny room that I was brought after I was born on September 28, 1936, exactly eight months after my parents were married. Since I weighed eight pounds and my birth certificate says I was full-term, it seems safe to conclude that I was conceived around Christmas, a month before Duke and Emily married. Since my early conception was never discussed and never admitted, I have no way of knowing how disturbing it may have been to my parents or their parents; no way of knowing what reverberations there may have been with Emily's own un-settling beginnings. No idea to what extent either of them may have felt trapped into marrying the other.

Emily was a few weeks short of her twenty-second birthday. Duke was twenty-three. They had been brought together, in large part, I believe, by a desire to unbind the grief each identified (and identified with) in the other and seemed to envision a combined romantic and family life that would, by the very mystery and power of their attraction to each other, transcend and assuage all their wounds and failures. They were happy to be married to each other and glad that I had been born. My father didn't seem to hold it against me that I was not a boy—though, of course, he wanted a son next. And—although Knoxie was more interested in the love affair between Britain's King Edward and Wallis War-field Simpson than she was in having a third grandchild—the daughterless Ila and the childless Bessie were overjoyed that I was a girl and started to compete for my affections as soon as they saw me.

I was named Judith Hillman Paterson after the father Emily never saw and the lapsed Quaker who came to Alabama with slaves in 1822 and, when it was too late, regretted it. I doubt my mother knew anything about the Judith Anthony Ware whose name she gave me, except that her name was beautifully carved on the tall stone pyramid that marked her grave in the plantation cemetery at Wares Ferry. Though all my names derived from my mother's family, everybody said I looked like Gram and Duke. And as soon as I could stand on my own, it was plain to see that my compact body and earthbound feet belonged to that side of the family.

Though my mother was probably as thrilled by my birth as she said she was (now she would have a family like other people and nothing would ever be wrong again), she worried obsessively about my safety and grew so frightened of being alone with me that she hardly ever was. When a brown spot appeared in the gray-blue iris of my left eye, she decided I was going blind and didn't rest or sleep until Gram brought a registered nurse to the house to tell her my two-colored eye was just a birthmark and, she said, a good omen. After that, Emily said the brown spot proved I belonged to her, whose eyes were dark brown, as well as my father, whose eyes were a brighter blue than mine would ever be.

Though Emily's happiness over my birth must have been dampened by both her fears for me and her efforts not to drink, my earliest memories of her and of myself are marked by sunlight mixed with pride in my baby accomplishments. I categorize these images as my earliest memories, not because I know when they happened, but because of the shared quality of the way they come back to me.

In what must be the first of them, I bask in yellow sunlight, kicking uncovered on white sheets. A tall window sprinkles light to one side of me. A figure floats large and luminous on the other.

I am standing alone for the first time. Someone kneels to catch me if I fall. Her arms are brown and shiny. My mother is watching. My feet grip the hard floor beneath me. My arms are akimbo. I can do this.

I am seated on a child's potty seat strapped to the toilet. There is a green-and-blue duck's head in front of me. I am clinging to it. Emily is clapping. I let go of the duck's head and clap with her.

I am at the Greenhouse, squatting in a puddle of black mud. I have on white shoes and a dress. The place is misty with moisture and light. A black man picks me up. He smells like wood smoke, fertilized dirt, and tobacco. His hands are brown and dusty. He carries me in his arms to my father.

I am standing beside a goldfish pond built of stones in Gram's back yard. I am holding a green hose and shooting water into the pond. Red lights flash in the dark water. Gram is counting the fish and holding out her fingers. One fishie, two fishies, three fishies, four. I hold up my fingers.

I am in a dark room at 410, sitting in Knoxie's lap. She has on a big hat. A red flower blooms in the darkness. A red-and-green bird sits in a cage in a pool of bright sunlight, squawking, "*Em* a *liii* Goodbye *Em* a *liii*."

Emily and I stand in a hallway on cool, shiny floors. Duke comes with an armful of orange and yellow snapdragons wrapped in waxy-green florist paper. I hear it crackling in the kitchen . . . *kashuuuzzz . . . krrkkkssslllzzzz* . . . and think he has brought candy. Kan-uh-duh. Kanuhdii. Kandi. One magic word bubbling and burbling and babbling in my mouth, and three of us laughing and clapping and shouting for the glory of the first spoken word burbling and bubbling on my lips.

"Snap, snaaap," Duke says, making a poochie little mouth with the bright bloom of one of the flowers.

"Snnnn'pppp. Snaaaaaappp," I say, laughing and shouting, coughing up sounds and waving the flowers like flags. We are bubbling and babbling and laughing. Kana daaa . . . kandi . . . snaaaaap . . . snaaaappppp. Bright flowers. Green paper. Words in my mouth like candy.

Two anecdotes from the time when I think those things happened were told so often that (though they have none of the texture of the early images I call mine) I count them among my "memories" of my beginnings. Both pit Duke (who never told them) against Emily and her friends, who told them often and thought them hilarious.

So many of Emily's friends have married and moved away that when one comes home to visit they like to go out together without their husbands. Gene Daniel Bentley is home from Florida. I am still an infant. Duke agrees to stay with me so Emily can go out with her friends. I have a bowel movement, but every time Duke tries to change my diapers, he starts gagging and can't go through with it. Finally, he wraps me in a blanket and sits in a chair at the foot of my crib, drinking bourbon and waiting for my mother to come home.

As the story goes, I am perfectly happy; but by the time Emily and her friends arrive (later than they said they would), Duke is furious. Shame, rage, and resentment wash over his face every time they tell the story. The last time anybody told it in his presence, forty years had passed and he still didn't think it was funny.

Another friend, Mary Helen Scott—who had by then married her sweetheart, George Foster, and moved to California—comes to visit. They are playing with me in the yard. One of them says, "Damn it." I repeat it. They think it is funny and start teaching me to swear and set me up to do it when Duke gets home. I do it. He gets angry, because, he says, he doesn't want anybody teaching his little girl bad words. He hates it when Emily acts silly and raucous like that with her friends, and since that is what they like to do, soon they come only when they know he won't be home.

It was to Mary Helen that Emily had written in May to announce that she was pregnant again. "I can truly say my little muggin has given me more pleasure than anything in the world; she is so big and 'growny' now that you wouldn't recognize her. You know, though," she wrote her friend, who was also pregnant, "that I

47

never let you do anything without me; Dr. Harris's contraption did *not* work and the Patersons are going to have another addition to their family in October. I was fairly sick over the idea at first because Judy is so little, but it didn't take me long to get over that and now Duke and I both are thrilled to death over the new baby . . . Duke and I have bought a house up at the lake and after we get it all fixed up it is really going to be a peach . . . Duke also has bought a new Ford roadster (gray) that is really pretty . . . We are going to the auto races in Indianapolis, Indiana. Won't that be fun? Duke will kill me [driving fast] on the way home I'm afraid."

Duke has a boat that sits graceful as a seabird in the water, small and white, with an inboard motor. To make everything go faster, he takes the engine from a wrecked Cadillac and puts it in the Ford roadster and puts the roadster engine in the boat. Some people are afraid to ride with him. Not Emily. Not me.

The little boat is named for me and has JUDY written in tall black letters on the side. The three of us sit in it on the river. A grayish sky floats above us. Leaf-bare trees shimmer on the shore behind us. Emily's hair blows back and her face looks plump and young.

Duke poses ready to steer, his thick torso held militarily straight. He is powerfully built and deeply tanned. Azure eyes, thick brown hair, dimples, and perfect features make him movie-star handsome. I perch between them, leaning toward my father, wide-eyed, saluting the camera.

I remember not the boat and not the ride, but the sharp blowing wind and the icy wet kiss of the water. The soft, rocking sound . . . *schhhhhlurpurp* . . . *scchhhlurrrpop* . . . of the waves on the shore and the hull of the boat . . . *schhhhhlurpurp* . . . *scchhhlurrrpop*. We are love. We are love. We are bathed in sunlight and love.

My sister was born on September 30, 1937, two days after my first birthday, and was named Jane Ware for the Grandmother

Jane who saved the plantation. She is a cuddly, affectionate baby who matures slowly and is so attached to my mother that she seems hardly to be born at all. The main effect of her birth on me is that I begin a pattern of going to work with my father and spending the morning with him and Gram and returning at noon to spend the rest of the day with Momma and Jane. By then, a black high-school student named Mary Willie Jackson has been coming for months to help Emily after school. After Jane is born, she starts working for us full-time and soon becomes as much a companion to Emily (and a high-spirited, common-sense antidote to her fears) as a nurse to us.

Two important things happened in February 1938. Jane and I were christened at St. John's Episcopal Church, and our Uncle Sonny got married.

In marrying Catherine Lawrence Truby, Sonny picked a wife from among the aristocrats and gave Emily an ally in her battle with the Paterson way of doing things. Although the sandy-haired, freckle-faced Kitty lacked any claim to beauty, her every move bespoke sophistication and confidence. "Miss Kit," as my father always put it, "has style."

Though still in her early twenties, she was divorced, with a four-year-old daughter, Margaret, and already sterile from a hysterectomy, none of which sat well with Gram. She was also, I believe, to Gram's way of thinking, uppity. As for me, I was delighted to have inherited the clever, long-legged Margaret for a cousin and happier still when they moved down the street from us and added themselves to my circle of admirers.

Trouble was (and maybe Gram knew it), Sonny and Kitty drank the way Duke drank, and now Emily was under pressure to be with them almost every night, either at their house or at ours or across the street at the Country Club. Maybe the others could get by with it, but Emily couldn't. So sometimes she went with them and sometimes she didn't. And when she did, she almost always drank too much and the next day resolved never to do it again. January 1940 was unimaginably cold in Alabama. Snow fell north of us for weeks, icing Alabama like a cake. Though Montgomery was in the middle of the state and too warm for snow, one morning near the end of the month we woke to whiteness coming down in sheets and sticking in piles on the ground. Jimmie Haigler, my playmate from next door, is kneeling in it under the pecan trees and spooning it like whipped cream into a bucket. The world is new. I want to roll in it like a dog and stand still in it and spoon it into a bucket.

"It's too cold," Emily says. Her hands are shaking and sweating. Her mouth looks strange and her eyes float past me.

I have just looked out the window and seen the world more beautiful than any fairyland I could have imagined. My mother's eyes float past me. A *waaahhhhhhhhhuuuuuuup* rises inside me, stopped momentarily by an invisible fear, tightening and trapping a yell swelling and burning in my body. *Waaahuuuuuaaaa*, wild and total out of some primeval soul-urge and a child's inalienable right to walk in snow and spoon it like whipped cream into a bucket.

Blue rage lets loose in my throat like thunder. "Look at meeee," pounding and screaming, cracking the skies with my cries, my heart thumping like a drum in my chest . . . I waaaaaaant. Look at me. Look at meeeeeee. And suddenly, I don't know how, I realize that something is wrong with my mother.

Someone—maybe Gram, maybe Kitty—comes and takes me into the snow under the trees. Our feet make noise like the first sounds ever heard in the universe. *Kkhhrruuuuakkkkk . . . chkkkrrrchkk . . . kkhhrruuuuakkkkk,* krunching and kracking and klumphing where before there had been only silence. The snow is soft and smooth in my hands. I rub my face in it and lick it like a dog slurping water. It tastes cold and shines on top like sherbet.

Cold. Shiny. Like whipped cream, like sherbet. *Kkhhr-ruuuua-kkkkkk. Kkhhr-ruuuua-kkkkkk.* A child who has known only love and thinks the earth is heaven is learning to see, to think, and to suffer. Her mother's face is at the window. Something is wrong with her mother.

The only other thing I remember on Narrow Lane Road that happened the next summer: I am playing in the sandbox Duke has built near the back door. I am shoveling sand into a bucket and piling it around a big ball. A gray cat comes from somewhere and gets in the sandbox with me. I am playing with the cat. Sonny and Kitty come and sit with Duke and Emily in the yard. I know now they were drinking, though I wouldn't have understood what that meant at the time. The cat leaves. Kitty says we should get rid of the sandbox because the cat has been there and might give me ringworm and cause my hair to fall out.

What I know at the time is that I am in a trance of solitude and play when Momma comes and pulls me out of the sandbox. I think she is mad with me. She is, instead (or also), I now believe, beset with fear for my safety. I suppose, too, that she is well on her way to being drunk. "The cat's gone. The cat's gone," I yell, kicking and jerking out of her arms and reaching for the ball. "Nooooooooooooooooo."

Momma wants to let me back in the sandbox. The others say, "No. Ringworm is terrible. Her eyes could get infected." Duke and Emily start to fight in the strident, life-and-death way that I later associate with their drinking and the terrible discord between them.

Maybe it is the same night, maybe another one like it. Jane and I are asleep in the low beds we sleep in on separate sides of the same room. I wake up. Emily is sitting in a chair between the two beds, rocking back and forth like a child and moaning, "Noooo. Noooo," and "Please. Please."

I get out of the bed and move toward my mother, slow and held back like in a dream. Before I can get to her, she throws her head back and howls like a dog. The sound stops me where I stand and hurls a knife blade of fear into my body. I can only imagine what it does to my sister, who is not yet three years old and still doesn't know herself from our mother.

I associate that incident with the end of Emily's struggle not to drink and the beginning of my own fears and the birth of a baby conflict between wanting to stop my parents from suffering and wanting to do the things I want to do, like walk in snow and play with a cat and pile sand around a big ball. I am very young when I start to believe that the happiness and fate of our family depend on whether or not my parents drink, and only a little older when I start thinking my behavior has something to do with whether they do or they don't.

Wares Ferry

Sometime in the midst of it all, Aunt Bessie, who is in a constant state of grief because times are changing, decides that Jane and I are being deprived of an essential cultural experience because we have never traveled in style on a train the way people did before everybody had an automobile. And so she plans an excursion to take Emily and Jane and me on the train to Birmingham, to eat lunch in the dining car, see the sights in a bigger city, and come back to Montgomery the same afternoon.

Emily dresses us in pastel cotton dresses, bonnets, and high-topped white shoes. Knoxie comes to the depot to see us off and we ride the train to Birmingham like four children escaping the grownups. The memory is filled with yellow sunlight and an awareness of the marvelous that is beyond my adult ability to describe. It includes euphoria and a perfect communion with the universe and with some larger sense of who my mother is and how I am connected to her and to her family and to things that happened before I was born. In that moment, happiness is all that matters and we have no troubles.

We eat in the diner at a table covered with a white starched cloth and so tall that I have to sit on my knees to reach my food. I manage to get it across to Emily once and for all that I hate having anything tied under my chin, and she lets me take off the bonnet. We walk around downtown Birmingham and look in the window of a Chinese restaurant called Joy Young's, which Emily and Bessie think is very exotic and grand. On the way home, I sleep in Bessie's lap and Jane sleeps in Emily's, as happy as angels in the hand of God.

The next thing I remember about Knoxie and Bessie happened around the time of my fourth birthday, when they left 410 and moved down the street to an old apartment building called the Sophronia. Even in its prime, the Sophronia had been a plain, gawky old maid of a structure built with an eye more to utility than to either grace or beauty. Now it is old and running down, a maze of dusty, high-ceilinged, mothball-and-cooked-vegetable-smelling rooms inhabited mostly by women past all hope of happiness and love.

My cousin Jimmy Hillman is now ten years old, a winsome boy who likes to tease Jane and me by telling us things that aren't true. He hasn't seen his mother since she left for New York when he was three years old. His father has married again and has two more children, but Jimmy still lives with Knoxie, to whom the courts had given him on the condition that she stop drinking and smoking, which for a while she did.

Bessie says Jimmy is "running wild" and all he cares about is motorcycles and cars. In fact, he cares about any number of other things, including music and his grandmother—whom he wants to please and also to get away from. Bessie says Knoxie spends too much money, drinks too much, and smells up the house with the cigarettes she smokes and the animals she keeps. And so they are closing up 410 and taking two apartments in the Sophronia, one for Knoxie and Jimmy and one for Bessie.

Jane and I go with Emily to help them move out of 410. As soon as Emily sees Jimmy, she takes him into the bathroom and puts his head in the sink and washes his hair. Then we are sitting at a big, round dining-room table with nothing on it but some pieces of paper and three cups of coffee. The room is dark and crowded with furniture already draped in white sheets. Emily is helping Knoxie and Bessie decide what to take and what to leave. I get interested in a huge sideboard that has narrow top drawers lined with tin. Bessie says the sideboard belonged to her Grandmother Jane when they lived in an old-fashioned house with the kitchen and the bathroom outside. The drawers in the sideboard were lined with tin so the servants could bring the food into the house and put it in the drawers to keep it warm until the family came to the table. Grandmother Jane had a silver bell she rang to let the servants know the family was ready for its food. It was all very formal and grand, with china and heavy silver on the table and a butler standing ready to fetch whatever anybody wanted. I keep asking questions about the tin drawers.

"What kind of food did they put in them?" I ask.

"Well, pies, for instance," Bessie says. "Or vegetables."

"Why did they have the kitchen outdoors?"

"They didn't have safe stoves like we do now—or a fire department—and they didn't want the whole house to burn down."

"Why did they have so many servants?"

"Everybody did in those days."

"Were they rich?"

Bessie never said the word "slave" (she said either "servants" or "darkies") and I wouldn't have known what she meant if she had, but I hear something strange in her voice. Maybe that's it; maybe it is shame about taking another step down in their living quarters.

Emily says, "Judy, *please.*" Then she and Knoxie start to argue. I think maybe I caused it. The sun outside is very bright. The house is dark and cool. My mother is sad because they are leaving 410 and Knoxie and Bessie are getting old.

Duke brings some men and trucks from the Greenhouse to board up 410 and move Bessie and Knoxie's furniture to the Sophronia. My father sweats and moves things and loses his patience and wants Bessie and Knoxie to be perfectly satisfied with (and, if possible, grateful for) what he is doing. "Shirtsleeves, indeed," he says, as he always does at such times, in ironic reference to what Knoxie had said when her daughter married him.

I go with Emily to see Knoxie in her new apartment. We walk to the door of the strange new place. Knoxie's parrot, Polly, screeches, "Em a *li* Em a *li*," just like at 410. Jimmy's father, his stepmother, and their two small children have moved in with Knoxie and taken Jimmy's room. Jimmy sleeps on a little pallet in the hallway. Today his unmade pallet strikes me as just about the saddest sight I ever saw—as if my clever cousin were an orphaned child living among the cinders in a fairy tale. I think it must have bothered Emily, too, which may be why I noticed it. I don't remember.

What I do remember is that Emily and Knoxie engaged that day (or on another like it) in the only protracted argument I ever heard between them. Knoxie accuses Emily and her whole generation of being too public about sex, saying that whatever she herself had done, she had done circumspectly and in private. They argue for a long time about related things, some of them having to do with my father. Emily has had a miscarriage. Doesn't Duke know how frail she is? Are they both crazy? Their tones turn strident and out of control.

I go out on the porch. Orange geraniums bloom on the railing high above the street. Emily runs outside to warn me not to lean on the porch railing, which she says is too rickety to hold me.

She goes back into the room where Knoxie is sitting and says, "Well, Mother, Duke and I don't exactly do it in public, either." She is laughing. The argument is over. Emily pretends not to take her mother seriously, but she loves her and wants her approval and thinks it is impossible to get.

My sister and I go often to Bessie's apartment, which is very much like Knoxie's. Soon we will be spending nights there and going with her to movies, bookstores, fruit stands, bakeries, and restaurants downtown. Though we must have visited Knoxie on those occasions and we must have gone to see her sometimes with Emily, I have few memories of it, no memories of being with my grandmother alone as her grandchild, no memories of her coming to our house to visit.

Emily takes Jane and me to Wares Ferry, where our cousin Little Helen lives with her parents, Uncle Dan and Big Helen, in a cool country house built to catch the breezes in summer and hold the heat in winter. "In summer, it is too hot to move," they say. "In winter, too cold to move away from the fire."

We marvel at the blue-mottled stone that marks the grave of the Creek chieftain who said the place was his and refused to leave when the Wares came there, and stayed and worked for them and lived with the slaves until he died.

We want Little Helen to come out to play. She won't come. Emily goes inside. Jane and I stay outside and watch two bantam cocks fighting on a spot of bare earth not far from where Yankee soldiers had laid their tired, victorious heads in the spring of 1865. Red-and-yellow birds tumble and spin in a ball of white light, pummeling and flapping, gashing one another crimson with talons like knives.

"Sometimes we put the two together in a pit with steel spurs on their feet and let them fight till one or both are dead," Uncle Dan says, sliding the words together and emphasizing "ahhrr *deeaad.*"

A black man stands beside him. "Mr. Dan make a heap a money bettin' on them banty roosters," he says, poking Dan in the ribs to take the insult out of the words. "Bad luck if a hen crow," he adds, meaning "Get Emily's little girls away from here."

Uncle Dan is a bantam himself, small and even darker than Knoxie, so thin and narrow that, viewed from the side, he is almost invisible. His face is hard from the sun, bony as a skeleton, and decked with a soft, wispy mustache.

"Why do you make them do something that hurts so much?" I ask.

"Ahhhhh, Sugaahhh, weuulll . . ." He pauses, and I know there is something he doesn't want to tell me. "Well, it's natural . . . and we train them to do it," he says finally, gazing into the distance and rubbing my hair till the dust flies out of it.

"Why?" I ask again, meaning why on earth is it natural for chickens to fight like that and why in the world do they train them to do it.

"To see which one fights the best, Turkey Buzzard," Uncle Dan says with a sigh that tells me I've asked too much.

Uncle Dan put me on a horse when I was so young that all I remember is the feel of horsehide on my legs and my back against the coarseness of his shirt. He calls me Turkey Buzzard, and it becomes a private joke that lasts a lifetime, that his sister's coddled firstborn enjoys a country mockery likening her to the blackest and stinkingest of birds.

Emily loves her brother in the unexamined way she loves her whole family. All she wants is for everybody to be happy. My father condescends to him because, rather than work, he lives cheaply off what has been left him—and sharecrops the land and rises late and buys and sells livestock in a country way that produces almost nothing; and still somehow he lives. When he gambles, he gambles cautiously and makes money mostly by raising and selling gamecocks for other people to bet on.

Duke is fond of his brother-in-law but can't understand anybody who doesn't work. That Dan drinks too much and lives with little regard for himself or others goes unsaid. Of Emily's second brother, Jimmy's father, James H.—the most damaged of the damaged children of Knoxie Polk Walker and James Hoggatt Hillman— even less is said.

In truth, they had been taught by their mother and, no doubt, by Aunt Bessie, too, and perhaps by the example of half the people they knew, that it was beneath them to work or speak of money. A crippling set of attitudes and fears about money and, I believe, their own inadequacy seem to have come to them through a strange convergence of aristocratic pride (not to mention greed, envy, self-deception, and other traditional sins), the postbellum collapse of their fortunes, and a predisposition to addiction and despair. And so Dan clung to his money and drank and lost a wife and daughter he loved because of it; James H. threw his inheritance away at a rate of prodigality hard to imagine and lost two wives and three children because of it; and Emily turned everything over to a husband who had no experience with money and came from a clan of people who, though they loved work, seemed hardly to believe in money at all.

Whatever the concomitance was, it was so in place by the end of the Reconstruction that the heroic Grandmother Jane's only surviving son (a conscientious fellow who, after a year at the University of Virginia, went to work in the real-estate business in Birmingham and died there at thirty-seven of typhoid fever) could outline it all in a letter to his mother concerning her spoiled grandson Croom.

"Let him clerk," he wrote, "or do anything that is honest just so he does something . . . Give him money, if you must, but insist that he go to work like a man, as all young men of his age and prospects are now forced to do . . . He is acquiring habits of expenditure and idleness . . . and that is far more pernicious than you dream of."

Three generations later, I stand with my mother on a hill watching my cousin Helen playing under the trees beside a fish pond carpeted with lily pads. Emily calls down to her, "Come up here in the sun, baby, so I can take your picture." My cousin stays where she is in the shadows.

59

Big Helen is leaving because (I hear it whispered) Dan drinks, stays out all night, and knows nothing of love. He is tight with money, and now, Helen says, there are women. How can that be? She is so beautiful and Dan loves her so much.

Emily takes the picture in shadows. "Little Helen is going to live in town with her other grandmother," she says. "I'll take you to play with her there." I am eye-level with the hand holding the camera that has dropped to her side. Emily's fingers are square at the ends. Her nails are short, and she never polishes them.

Her brothers' early divorces break my mother's heart, this one especially. Helen had been like a sister to her; a sister would have made all the difference, she always thought. At twenty-five, Emily is already drinking like her mother (only worse), the way she said she never would, the way she never did until she married a drinker and started trying to get the love she always knew she wanted and thought she knew how to get and didn't.

The only other childhood memory I have of Little Helen is Bessie's too vivid description of how she got bitten by a mad dog and had to have shots injected into her stomach to keep her from dying. This was a few years later, but I hadn't forgotten her, and I don't think Emily ever stopped missing the two Helens, as she probably never stopped missing the father she never had or Sam or anybody else she ever lost. My mother was, I believe, a woman so terrified of losing that she could hardly bear to live.

One Sunday afternoon around the time Knoxie and Bessie move to the Sophronia and we go to Wares Ferry to tell Helen goodbye, Emily and Duke are driving down a country road when they are (as they always told it) "struck breathless" by the sudden grace and beauty of an oasis of woods and hills and tiny streams rising green and lush above the worn-out cotton fields south of the city, a solitary Camelot hardly changed since Hernando de Soto came through in 1540 looking for gold and finding death. Duke, who had always thought himself poor and always hated it, wants a life with some grace and beauty in it. Emily wants it, she says, if he wants it.

And so they sell the boat and the cabin by the lake and cash in some more of Emily's inheritance and buy forty acres outside the city and start to build a tall white house on a hill high above the road. And all the time my father is building the house of his dreams he is thinking about the fighting in Europe. The Germans have taken France and bombed Britain. America shouldn't sit by and do nothing.

Duke is twenty-seven years old. He knows Emily is in trouble and has no idea what to do about it. Although he knows sometimes he is at fault, he thinks most of the problems are hers. Off and on and for periods of time, he curtails his own drinking in order to cope with hers. Sometimes he wishes they had never married. Sometimes one of them threatens to leave the other.

And yet—mystery of mysteries—their souls are so entwined they hardly know themselves one from the other. Violently attracted and violently repelled, they lurch together and apart like coupling animals, mixing passion, despair, whiskey, rage, and tenderness together in a fateful potion. To drink it is to die. Not to drink it is not to live.

The Country

Duke stands in fading sunlight on a bare, round hill, smoking a cigarette, his hands on his hips. He looks like God to me, standing there smoking. The lump of land he stands on rises lush and green above a neglected expanse of orange dirt not good for much of anything, waiting—so it seems—for him to haul in enough good dirt to turn nature's little oasis into a paradise of pine and oak and beech trees, scuppernong and muscadine arbors, daffodils, azaleas, gardenias and camellias, wisteria and clematis vines twisting in lemony profusion wherever he put them. This is my first memory of the forty-acre piece of ground we called the country.

They bought the place from an old couple named Holt, who had lived on top of the hill since Reconstruction in a plain wooden, creosote-green farmhouse made graceful by a white railed porch stretched low across the front. In order to put our tall white house with bay windows and French doors where the Holt cottage had stood, some black men and some white men come from the Greenhouse and put the old house on a flatbed and pull it down the hill behind mules.

I stand, shoeless and shirtless, at a distance, expecting the house to collapse as soon as they pull. Instead, it slides slowly and smoothly down the hill, as if the earth has been greased for the deed. I think these men are geniuses and that I have seen something too miraculous to be believed even while I watch it. I remember nothing else until the house is there, an artful union of sunlit rooms and open spaces that manages somehow to be both comfortable and elegant at the same time—and is, in its own way, both a tribute and a monument to the deep oneness that still unites my parents. Though the house is wonderful to live in, it is nothing like as grand as it looks from a distance, perched like a nesting swan high and white above the road.

I know we are there by Christmas because Aunt Kitty, who writes the newspaper society column called "The Promenader," sends a photographer to take our picture. Jane and Emily and I sit on the spool bed that Gram has given Emily and Duke to sleep in. The rose-decorated wallpaper that shows behind us is so new it still smells like glue. We are a perfect picture of holiday happiness. Emily's hair is tied back with a ribbon; she is wearing a satin lounge coat and holding *The Night Before Christmas* as if she is reading to us. Jane and I sit beside her in flannel pajamas. Jane is pointing happily at something in the book and Emily is smiling at her. I pull away, looking stubborn and sullen. A certain slackness in my mother's expression highlights the unnaturalness of her smile, something not quite right that I think I must already have recognized.

It is Christmas Eve. A huge tree stands in the corner of the pine-paneled sun room with the French doors. Everything glows red. I walk into the cold fireplace and get soot all over me. Emily and Duke and Bessie leave brownies and Coca-Cola with whiskey in it on the mantel for Santa Claus and joke about putting switches and ashes in one another's stockings. I strain upward, baffled by nuances I don't understand. Switches. Santa Claus. Whiskey. My very existence seems to depend on understanding their words.

As soon as the house is finished, two men come with four yoked oxen hooked to crude plows and dig a blood-red hole in the back yard where the Holts had grown strawberries. Duke stands knee-deep in red mud and shouts orders and sweats. My cousin Jimmy Hillman stands skinny and white-headed beside him in the sun. The hole gets deeper and deeper; the men and Jimmy and the oxen look smaller and smaller.

They clean it up and pour concrete into a homemade wooden frame and make a small, rough swimming pool that is there for the rest of our lives, pale blue with ice-cold water from an underground spring, a little diamond surrounded by rose gardens, grape arbors, and daffodils. Men slide a house down a hill on a flatbed behind mules. A strawberry patch bleeds red and gives birth to a swimming pool. Those two miraculous deeds stand like beacons at the beginning of my remembered life in the country.

We spin on the hill in the twilight and throw rocks at bats, while Emily and Duke and their friends sit and talk on the knoll in front of the pine marsh where they put the Holts' house, in which an old black couple named Idabell and Jim Thomas now live with their children and grandchildren. Maybe it is one afternoon, the way I remembered it twenty years later. Maybe it is a hundred twilights merged into one.

Opposite the woods we call the pine woods stands a rough five-acre maze of meadows and knolls thick with sweet gums, red cedars, giant oaks, and much older pines. We call these the Indian woods and imagine them to be holy ground. Ancient trunks and long, sheltering limbs make a theater-in-the-round where we perform "Indian" rituals and act out stories we make up.

With childhood intuition we evoke the Creek warriors the Spaniards found building flat-roofed pyramids on the banks of the rivers, and attribute dull bits of pottery to a people who decorated giant burial urns with the round, red eye of the sun, whirling swastikas, crosses, and stars, worshipping wantonly everything that lived and everything that died. Though they have been gone a hundred years, we still hear them . . . *waaahuuuuuaaaa* . . . *waa-*

64

huuuuuaaaa . . . twirling and spinning, drinking the black drink, stomping the great dance in the round belly of our woods.

We squat in the ridges of the rough horse-path turned Federal Road that brought the British naturalist (and, some say, Tory spy) William Bartram there in 1776; and Aaron Burr on his way to Richmond to be tried for treason; and Andrew Jackson battling what was left of the Creek Nation; and then a stream of white settlers bringing horses and mules and cattle and kinsmen and African slaves to the new American South.

Unlike the Indian woods, which are dry and sunny, the little swamp we call the pine woods is riddled with the tiny tributaries of a shallow, slow-moving creek. The ground is cushiony with straw and mushrooms and low-growing foliage. Spanish moss hangs in the trees like dwarfs with long, straggly beards. No matter how hot it gets outside, the pine woods stay damp and cool.

We fish in the creek and Jim Thomas's granddaughter Hattie Jo catches a catfish as big as a rabbit. It thrashes around on the bank and tries to get back in the water with the hook still stuck in its mouth. Hattie Jo holds the pole with one hand and tries to pick it up with the other. It has whiskers like needles and looks so clear and white we think we can see through it. We lean over it and poke it with a stick. Hattie Jo's mother yells, "Catfish got whiskers sharp as blades," then cuts off its head with a pocket knife and puts it in a bag to take home and eat.

We play with the Thomas children almost every afternoon in the summer. If we walk far enough in the field behind their house and ours, we come to the sandy country road that goes all the way to town and becomes the Narrow Lane Road. A black man owns the field. Sometimes he and Duke talk about the crops and the weather and sometimes about some black person in the country who is sick or in trouble or needing to borrow some piece of equipment.

65

When the field is planted in cotton and corn, we have to walk carefully between the rows. When it is not, the ground is gray, dry, and full of stubble and we can play wherever we please.

Two huge oak trees and an old iron hand pump stand high in a clearing amid the stubble and the sometimes planted, sometimes unplanted rows. The pump is tall and hard to operate, but if we work at the handle long enough and hard enough, rusty water finally shoots out of it. If we keep pumping—two of us hanging on to the handle at once—we get beneath the rust to water that is blue and icy and tastes like nickels.

Hattie Jo says they put the hand pump in the field for slaves to drink out of and that—because of that—she can drink out of it and we can't. We drink the water anyway. It is only in public places that we don't drink after colored people, but I don't know that yet and don't remember how I finally learned it, though of course I did learn it.

The place we call the Greenhouse is now a large complex of glass greenhouses, outdoor gardens, supply sheds, and equipment shops. My father works mostly inside the greenhouses themselves, where all the men drink from all the hoses. The work is tedious and hot. They stop work when they are tired, pick up one of the gray-green watering tubes, and make an archway of water to put their mouths to. They drink and sometimes talk a little in the stylized shorthand that I never heard spoken anywhere else, and then walk back to their work and stay there until they are tired enough to drink again. They do it like a dance, working and walking and drinking and talking and walking and working for hours and days and years at a time.

I don't know what we think slaves are. I doubt Jim and Idabell Thomas were old enough to have been born slaves, though their parents undoubtedly were and would have been owned by planters like the Wares and remembered as slaves by their children. Hattie Jo says what she says as if it is something I have to keep to myself

66

so I can keep playing with her and drinking the water we pump. I have no idea what it means that they are black and we are white. No idea that my great-grandparents might have owned hers and worked them in just the kind of cotton field in which we stand. Sometimes we drink the metal-tasting water and sometimes we play in it. Hattie Jo likes the coppery taste of the red mud it makes. Her mother tells us not to eat it, but we do anyway, and squat in it and make pies with it and squish it between our toes. "Get up from there," Hattie Jo's mother says. "Y'all's as much pigs as Grits and Gravy."

Duke has bought two gigantic prize-winning hogs he named Grits and Gravy and put in a pen near the woods for the Thomases to feed and look after. They eat corn shucks and garbage and groan in the mud Jim Thomas lets us make with a hose. Their pig noses are huge, white, and flat as the bottom of a shoe. Their big, hoarse *RRRrrroinks* sound more like the barking of dogs than like the little *oinks* Bessie makes when she reads *The Three Little Pigs* to us. The woods around them take on the odor of the pen —intense, sweet, and comparable to nothing. We don't know this is supposed to be a bad smell until somebody tells us.

I climb the wide-spaced slats and hang my arms over the top. "Get down from there, girl," one of them says. "A hog that big'll eat you alive."

Duke and Emily bring their friends down the hill to admire Grits and Gravy in the twilight. They lean on the pen like members of a royal court surveying their kingdom. They drink whiskey and laugh and think up pig words: swinish, piggish, piggy, hoggy, hoggish, porky, oinky.

"Like a greased pig," somebody says. "Silk purse out of a sow's ear." "Independent as a hog on ice." "Happy as a pig in slop." "Go in pig; come out sausage."

Like a greased pig. Like a hog on ice. Like a pig in slop. The meaning of metaphor penetrates my skull like a live thing. I start to jump up and down. "Piggy went to market, piggy stayed home . . . To market, to market, to buy a fat pig."

The images darken. "Is all around a pig's ass pork? . . . Two things you can't wear out, a hog's nose and a woman's pussy."

"Watch your mouth," somebody says, glancing at me—standing on the slats, hanging on every word.

Emily snickers. Duke stiffens. They float up the hill, ice tinkling in their glasses, some talking, some not.

Emily says, "Duke's porked." Somebody starts to laugh and then stops. Nobody says anything after that. Heat. Dust. Pig smell.

A run-down old barn and two good milk cows came with the Holt place. Jim Thomas milks the cows into a tin bucket in the afternoon. A sharp stream hits the bottom and sides of the bucket . . . *zzzzt* . . . *zzzzt* . . . smelling warmer and sounding softer with each pull of the udder. The old man takes the softening teat in his worn brown hand and aims a stream of warm milk at Hattie Jo, who catches it in her mouth all the way across the barn.

"More," she yells. He squirts and she drinks in a series of perfect squirts and catches. No matter how often I try it, I end up with milk all over me. Hattie Jo says that when the milk tastes funny it is because the cows eat "bitterweed." Gram says it's true.

A little shed that looks like a dollhouse stands beside the well that provides water for the house and the barn. The well itself is covered by two heavy pieces of pink metal. One day Jane and I are squatting by the well, using the sun-heated metal to bake mud pies and dough we get from the kitchen. One of us drops a white milk-glass cup on the well cover. The cup shatters. I start across the hot metal on bare feet to pick up the pieces. A jagged piece of white glass looks up at me. The sun stings my eyes and something inside says, "You are going to step on it."

My right foot comes down on the edge of the cup, and I am frozen in the pure, painful pleasure of knowing I did it myself. I hear, "You did it on purpose," and I am gripped by shame and fear for what I have done.

The big-toe muscle is almost severed from the bone. Blood goes everywhere. I scream. Momma screams. The doctor wants to stitch it up. But because I cling to Momma and don't want anybody else to touch me, we go home without even a bandage.

The sore festers and clots and takes weeks to heal, and I refuse to walk for a long time, insisting on being carried around the house like a queen and saying "No" to every suggestion that I touch the damaged foot to the ground. Finally, Mary Willie tricks me into running to get something far away in the back yard. I remember that I wanted to have my own way and prove something by not walking on the injured foot. And—though I have forgotten what it was that I wanted to prove—I remember feeling defeated and ashamed, running painlessly across the back yard on my own two feet.

I can't remember a time before Mary Willie (Mamie) Jackson was part of our lives. She was still a girl herself—and playful as a child—when she started walking the few dusty miles from her school to our house on Narrow Lane Road to help Emily in the afternoons for little more than a tip. Though she wasn't tall, she was strong and shapely, with a handsome, high-boned face and shiny cordovan-colored skin, more burnt sienna than either black or brown. She almost surely had Indian blood in her veins and probably white blood, too. Part playmate, part sister, and part mother, she stayed with us more and more, and when we moved to the country, she went with us.

When Mary Willie wants to see her mother, Emily takes us across town in the car and leaves us at a little white-painted house that smells of ham and wood smoke even in summer and stands so close to the river and so high above its red banks that we think we will be washed away in it if we stand too long at the back door. Mamie introduces us to her mother, sitting alone like a queen in a high-backed chair, wizened and blue-black enough to have been among the first Africans tossed off French slavers onto the docks at Mobile in the 1720s before Alabama had a name or a history it remembers.

More likely, her ancestors came sooner, among the 10 million to 24 million West Africans handed over to European slave traders by native tribesmen swapping their enemies for rum, salt, and Spanish gold: among the 3 million who happened to make it to the east coast of North America, rather than the 2 million to 5 million who died below deck from starvation, suffocation, dysentery, or madness, or got sick enough to be thrown overboard or despairing enough to jump; brought unwillingly from Africa to Massachusetts or Virginia about the same time Duke's and Emily's forebears were coming of their own accord from Scotland, Ireland, England, Italy, and Holland. From there, they would have been carried (or sold) farther and farther south over generations, mixing black blood with white blood and red blood until they got to cotton-crazed Alabama, where no slave wanted to be, where some of them died and some ran away and some lost their minds and some lived humanely amid unthinkable sorrows.

Mary Willie loves jazz and show tunes and calls herself Mamie, after the early blues singer, Mamie Smith, whose strange, hollow-sounding "Crazy Blues" she plays on our Victrola at night when Emily and Duke are gone. But the Smith she really loves is Bessie . . . Saint Loueee woman with all her diiaaamuuuuund rings . . . man got a heart like a rock cast in the sea . . . ah waddle . . . de waddle da whoooooooooeeeeeeeee

Our days ring with it. Mamie working and playing and teaching us the words: "Once ain't for always, two ain't but twice . . . woke up this morning with the jinks around my bed . . . before I take your doggin' I'll eat grass like a Georgia mule"—and a many-versed folk ditty I never heard from anybody but her, about an old woman out to catch a young man . . . Old Lady Sally want to jumpty-jump, jumpty-jump. "Do 'Georgia Mule,' " we beg. "Do 'Jinks around My Bed.' Do 'Pigfoot.' Do 'Jumpty-jump.' " Our favorite is the decade-long hit "Blues in the Night" by Harold Arlen and Johnny Mercer, which we call "Ah Whooeee da Whooee" because of the way she sings it: A man is a two-face, a worrisome thing who'll leave ya ta sing the blues in the night . . . Ahhhh whoooeeeeeee da whoooeeeeeee ahhh click eh ty clack comes echoing back. Ah Whooeeeeeeeeee. Mamie is our jazz age, our wide, wide world. Because of her, we know there are big towns and big talk—Natchez and Memphis and St. Joe. We know there is a Chattanooga Choo Choo as well as a Little Red Caboose. Before we know there is a wide world, we know Mamie has been there. Life, as she sings it, is half joke and half tragedy. Maybe we understand it and maybe we don't.

When the mood is different, she mixes show tunes and jazz with sounds older than time . . . I know moonlight, I know starlight . . . Swing low sweet charioooooot . . . Take my hand, precious Lord hummmmmm huuu hummmmmm. Life is not a joke after all, and not a game.

71

Unborn Baby

Before we go barefoot outside for the first time in the spring, the Thomases dunk our feet in a tub of cold water, along with the feet of whatever children, grandchildren, nieces, and nephews happen to be at their house on the first warm day in April. Pink feet and brown feet kick and splash in a corrugated tub filled with water so cold we can hardly stand it. The Thomases say the foot dunking wards off illness sure to strike if winterized feet hit the cold earth unprepared. The practice has African roots, no doubt. To us, it means summer is coming.

Water, pools, and tubs figure prominently in my memory of that timeless time before I started to worry about my mother and feel fear as the bedrock of our lives. In the earliest of these memories, we haven't been in the country long. The downstairs bathroom still smells of plaster. Emily is in the tub. Jane and Mamie and I are in the bathroom talking to her and watching her bathe. Her white breasts float half in and half out of the water. Beads of moisture brighten the black-and-white tiles on the walls and the floor. Emily's hair dampens and curls in the steam. She is splashing water on her neck and saying she wishes she didn't have so many dark moles on her shoulders and chest.

Mamie says moles stand for beauty and men like them. Emily says, "Men are such fools . . ." And they laugh as if all women were equals and all men were jokes and there were no problems in all the world. Jane and I sit on the floor and play like cubs in a den.

One day, Hattie Jo and Jane and I find a huge toad stranded in a dry ditch between the Indian woods and the house. The creature is as big as a rabbit, heaving and moaning like death . . . *uuhuuoo . . . uuhuuoo . . .* Jane grabs it. It puffs up and groans again, deep and awful. She lets go. Jane likes toads and bugs and sometimes carries little tree frogs around in her hands for hours, but this gray, warty thing is too big and awful even for my sister, who is in many ways much braver than I am.

That night, we think we hear it splashing in some ditch or black pool far away in the dark, bellowing over long dewy fields . . . *ah-ghuuuut . . . splursshh . . . ah-ghuuuut . . .* Jane lies awake all night, thinking she has offended it, wounded it, perhaps mortally, with her touch.

I think she is silly to reach out to a toad. Sillier still to imagine it coming upstairs (or over the dew-gray yard and into the window) to get us, here, where we lie safe in our beds beneath the ceiling fan thumping and crooning . . . *thump . . . hummmmmmmm . . . thump . . . hummmmmmmm . . .* blowing the night air damp against our faces, swaying and humming . . . *thump . . . hummmmmmmmm . . . thump . . . hummmmmmmmm . . .* crickets and locusts soaking us in sound . . . *sssszzzzzz . . . sssszzzzz.*

Emily and Mamie bathe Jane and me in the tub upstairs every night. We splash and play and giggle like nymphs frolicking in a stream in some time before evil came into the world. We prize this playtime so much that we each use our continued participation as a bribe to make the other do what we want done.

I have something to tell that I don't want Jane to repeat. "I will tell you only if you promise not to tell anybody," I say. "If you tell, I will never bathe with you again."

A few nights later—our ritual complete—Emily gets Jane out

of the tub and starts drying her off with a towel. Jane shoots a sly look over her naked shoulder and whispers our secret to Momma. I cry and scream and kick in the water, as amazed as if a part of my own body had taken leave of my will and attacked me on its own. Emily and Mamie try to make me bathe with my sister after that, but I won't do it.

Though we are hardly more than babies, neither of us ever forgets it. Judy is stubborn, pensive, and cautious. Jane is odd, imaginative, and perfidious. Like a cell dividing, we are becoming our separate selves.

We haven't been in the country long when Mary Willie marries a stocky, powerful-looking, medium-colored soldier in training at the air base in Montgomery. He had a mustache, I think, and shoulders broad and thick enough to pop the buttons on his starched uniform, which was the only thing I ever saw him wear. I never heard him called anything but LeRoy; and although I only saw him a few times that I remember, he stood mythologically tall in our imaginations by virtue of the stories Mamie told about him, the songs she sang in his honor, and the dresses she wore to please him. A man might be a worrisome thing, but it was plain to see that LeRoy was a man worth singing the blues for.

I suppose it goes without saying that Duke couldn't stand LeRoy, a Northern Negro, a soldier, and a threat to our household. By then, urbanization and geographic and economic mobility had started changing things between black men like LeRoy and white men like Duke, even in Alabama. A new day for black people was written all over LeRoy—the way he carried himself, asserted his claim to Mamie, and called my father Mr. Paterson in a certain tone, rather than Mr. Duke in another.

When Mamie goes out with LeRoy, her preparations last all day long and the house smells steamy and flowery like a church. She rolls her hair on curling rods heated on the stove and presses her clothes with two thick black manual pressing irons heated the same way. One heats in the flames while she pounds and presses with the other, her shiny arms moving ceremoniously up and down . . . press . . . thump . . . press . . . thump . . . thump . . . thump in an elaborate celebratory ritual, singing and humming . . . Hear the crowing of the cock, still my man ain't come, got me goin', got me goin' . . . LeRoy comes at sundown and they leave, Mamie wearing a bright silky dress, high-heeled shoes, and sometimes a hat with a feather.

We have been in the country less than a year when Emily becomes pregnant with a baby that dies in the womb at three months. She knows it is dead long before her obstetrician, Dr. Ross, admits it. There is nothing for her to do, he says finally, but to wait for the fetus to deliver itself, however it can.

Dr. Ross prescribes phenobarbital for her nerves and morphine for the pain (real or imagined) in her head, her stomach, her back. She takes the pills, sleeps when she can, nearly goes crazy with grief, sleeplessness, and disgust for the thing rotting in her body, and waits for the dead baby to come out—which it finally does in a gangrenous purge that threatens her life and so terrifies her that she temporarily loses her eyesight and thinks she is losing her mind. She goes to the Catholic hospital and stays a long time.

Gram says, "Emily is so pale. There's no fight left in her."

Bessie says, "She is just too frail to be pregnant like this all the time. I don't know what she and Duke are thinking."

Then suddenly my mother is better. Her cheeks are getting pink, they say, and she has started to eat.

Gram takes us to the hospital and sneaks us past the nuns, who don't want children on the same floor with the babies. Emily's face looks plump and girlish. Her hair is tied back with a yellow ribbon. Duke stands beside the bed. The sun shines on their faces. She and Duke and Gram are so happy they laugh no matter what is said. Emily is safe and coming home.

I want to know why Momma is on the hospital floor with the

babies if she doesn't have one. They say she wanted a brother for me, but she didn't get one. Maybe next time.

The nuns catch us in the room and take us down the hall to look at the babies. Might as well, they say, since we are there already; but we mustn't come back. We think the nuns are nice. Gram thinks they knew we were there all along and let us in because our mother had been so sick. Gram thinks the Catholic religion is superstitious and impractical, and can't imagine why anybody would want to be a nun.

Gram and her friend, my godmother, whom we call Aunt Kate, teach Sunday School together in a long bare room full of tables and little chairs at the Highland Avenue Baptist Church. And because we often spend Saturday night with our grandmother, Jane and I start going there as soon as the two of us are old enough to sit still in the chairs.

Gram sits with us at one of the tables and reads about Jonah and the Whale, the Loaves and Fishes and the Lost Sheep from a big storybook with mauve-and-blue pictures in it. After that, we make whales and fishes and sheep with crayons on thin drawing paper. Then we pull the chairs into a circle around a faded linoleum rug and sing "Jesus Loves Me" and "Onward, Christian Soldiers" to Aunt Kate pounding a jazzy beat on a loose-keyed piano.

Aunt Bessie starts taking Jane and me to movies at the Paramount and the Empire theaters downtown long before we are old enough to know what we are seeing. With great fanfare and disturbance to the people who are already seated, she finds four seats in a row (one for each of us and one for her hat) close to the screen and tells everybody we are Emily's children—aren't we beautiful—and she herself bought the lovely dresses we are wearing; Emily lets us run wild in the country with no shoes and no shirts, but when we come to town with her, we are dressed like little princesses.

An affinity for plot lines in which good triumphs over evil and supernatural forces intervene at the last minute on behalf of the just, along with a few images from *The Wizard of Oz* and the earliest Disney cartoons, is all that sticks with me from my first exposure to animation and Technicolor. Bessie takes us to see Walt Disney, out of duty, I think, but what she really loves are the operettas of Jeanette MacDonald and Nelson Eddy. Though she took us to those, too, I remember almost nothing of the films themselves. What I remember is Bessie sitting beside me in a dark theater, humming and sighing and clasping her hands in rapturous response to the joys and sorrows unfolding before her.

For days afterwards, she dances and sings both parts of the famous duets. Though she can hardly carry a tune, she is light on her feet and a surprisingly graceful dancer. I see her still in the dull light of the high-ceilinged Sophronia, twirling with a broom or a saucepan in her arms, her sleeves rolled up to her chubby elbows, singing and humming. Ah, sweet mystery of life, at last I found thee.

One day, after the leaves start turning red, Duke comes home in the middle of the day and he and Emily argue so loud we can hear it in the kitchen. Emily storms out of their room with the keys to the car in her hand. "You can't stop me from doing *any*thing," she yells back at him. "This house is *my* house. God *knows* I wish it weren't. Stuck out here with you in the middle of nowhere, where my friends can't come and don't want to come anyway because of the way you act. L*ooo*rd God!"

She drives off fast, making the air brown with dust and gravel. Duke stays in the bedroom. I hardly have time to get used to what has happened when I see a tiny figure coming up the driveway, a half-human-looking creature with a dark face and the big bushy head of a lion. The creature is halfway up the hill in front of the house before Mary Willie yells and runs out the front door, and I see that the creature is my mother, her face discolored with blood and her hair sticking up all over her head.

77

In her anger (and perhaps intoxication), she had run the car into a tree a little distance from the house and bloodied her head on the windshield. The next day, she is sitting up in bed, happy as a child home from school with a chill. She looks like herself. People come to see her. Duke brings flowers.

I am glad she is safe and glad she is happy, but the image of her bloodied head and blood-matted hair sticks in my mind as a foreboding. I don't understand how she can look so strange and still be my mother. I don't understand how she can be so bloody and not be hurt. I don't understand how Duke can be so happy with her after the way she talked to him.

After that, my mother cries and stays in bed all the time and takes white pills to make her sleep. Everybody agrees the problem is the baby and the way she lost it—and now the pills—and everybody agrees something has to be done. Duke decides to take her to Florida on the train to visit a friend she hasn't seen for a long time. "No drinking on the trip," he says. "And no pills."

Gram takes Jane and me to the depot to see them off. Bessie and Knoxie arrive looking like a pair of mismatched sisters out of a Victorian novel. Bessie—short, wide, and firmly corseted—wears shoes made for walking and a dress that looks like every other dress she owns, plain-cut, with a deep V-neck to show off her fine chest and good skin, and hemmed just beneath her plump knees, regardless of style or season. Her dark, steel-streaked hair is piled loose under a broad-brimmed hat, and her cheeks and lips are rouged bright as a clown's.

Knoxie comes to see her sick daughter off on the train wearing a severely cut tea dress with a silver-fringed shawl and high-buttoned boots out of another era. The "large dark eyes, gold-brown tresses, aristocratic features, and complexion radiantly blending the rose and the lily" so ardently praised by turn-of-the-century society-page writers have not yet given way to the cadaverous face and the yellowing skin of an old woman who drinks too much and smokes too much and cares too little for the people around her. Her hair has gone from gold to brown, with only a little gray in it. Her famous dark eyes are as clear and engaging as ever. Her tawny skin still clings to the fine lines of her face and still glows a little. To me, she looks like a cunning old fox still plotting its escape from the zoo. Only she isn't cunning. She is simply determined (by habit and training) to hold her head high and do as she pleases. If she is full of woes, standing in the cavernous depot, watching the beginning of the end of her only daughter's life, it doesn't show. What shows is a determination not to be daunted, not to be mocked.

Her boots fascinate me. The heels are high and thick, and the leather looks as if it has been polished by fairy cobblers every day for a hundred years. My Grandmother Knoxie is an elegant stranger to me. Touching her boots seems out of the question.

Emily and Duke are going on this fabulous trip, she says. "The train is such a marvelous way to travel. Automobiles are so common. I wouldn't have one for anything."

Duke and Emily step onto the train. Fear goes off inside me like a bomb. Though I never call her that, *"Mootheer, Mooootheeeer"* roars out of some primordial place in the collective memory of children needing to be with their mothers in times of trouble. The depot is dark. Emily looks ghostly and white, standing on the train beside her husband.

I cry and scream and try to jump on the train. Gram holds me back. I think if I let my mother go without me, she will never come back. I sob in the backseat of Gram's car until my body seems turned to water.

While Emily is gone, Jimmie Haigler, the little girl who was my playmate on Narrow Lane Road, has a birthday party and Gram takes me there. By the time she gets back to pick me up, Jimmie has opened her presents and is having a tantrum because

79

she didn't get what she wanted. She is older than I am and seems almost as big as her mother, who is holding her arms down and trying to make her behave. Suddenly I am terribly afraid and homesick for my own mother, who, it seems to me, has—without explanation—gone away for good.

Emily breaks down completely on the trip. She neither eats nor sleeps. She is mentally ill with depression (postpartum perhaps, or some strain of the trouble her father and Grandfather Hillman endured), or the too sudden withdrawal from drugs and alcohol, or too many years of needing love to be easy and finding it hard, or all of it put together. She is too nervous and depressed, she says, to be anywhere except in her own bed in her own house.

Jane and Gram and I go back to meet them. The train fills the station with whistles and steam and the racket of steel on steel. Emily gets off the train and says, "Take me home." Had Knoxie been more of a mother to her, she might have said, "I want my mother." Instead, she says, "Take me home," and we take her to the only home she has.

As for me, I am glad to have her back and to know she is not a ghost. Her mothering may have been erratic and flawed, but it has been good enough to plant "I want my mother" deep in my heart.

A long and lonely time is going to pass before she is able to mother me again, and we will have moved a thousand miles away and back again before it happens. The important thing is that it happens.

Breaking Down

Sometimes Emily is like she was before she went to the hospital to have the baby that was never born. Sometimes she has headaches and can't sleep at night and can't get up in the morning and takes pills when no one is looking and drinks beer in the afternoon and wants somebody with her all the time.

Gram brings her niece Caroline (a tense, talkative young woman who has come to live at Gram's house and work in the city) to sit by the bed and talk and smoke and keep Emily company. Jane and I sit on the bed and rub Emily's head with Ben-Gay. The room smells like menthol, cigarettes, and powder, mixed with the smell of Momma's clothes.

Emily leans back on a pillow in the bed, smoking. Caroline, who is very flat-chested, says, "I'd give anything to have breasts as big and round as yours, Emily." Momma says big breasts just get in the way. She'd just as soon hers were smaller. Women with small breasts look so much better in their clothes.

"Men love them," says Caroline, who has come to Gram's in part to get over a breakdown caused by a failed romance. With that, they start joking about all the funny words for breasts. Bosoms . . . tits . . . titties . . . teats . . . boobs . . . bazooms . . . bazuuuuuums . . . jars . . . jugs . . . jams . . . mummies . . . mammies . . . boosummmms-boooobs-*tit*ties.

In addition to being flat-chested, the nineteen-year-old Caroline is very high-strung and afraid of birds and feathers. My grandmother loves birds and knows the habits and songs of all the ones that live around her house.

One day, when Jane and I are at her house, Gram comes into her bedroom keening the high-noted call of the Eastern phoebe, *fee-bee, feee-beee*, because she has found two of them building a nest on the ledge outside her bathroom window. For two days, Jane and I watch the little brown creatures create a lopsided oval of moss and twigs. Caroline closes her eyes when she goes to the bathroom, for fear of seeing the birds in their nest.

Soon the nest has three lightly dappled, cream-colored eggs in it. Gorgeous. Magic. We try to get Caroline to look. She won't. "I think I'll just be sick," she says, "if the eggs hatch where I can see them."

Gram tells us all about the eggs and calls Duke to bring us to her house the day they hatch. That night a blue jay kills them all, leaving only a few hairy morsels of the meal he has made of them.

Jane and I are horrified by the cannibalism. Gram says, "I could just kill that old devil," and tells us to leave the nest alone because sometimes (if nobody touches it) another bird—or even the same bird—will come back and use it again. Caroline says she hates the sight of anything with feathers and is glad the blue jay ate the newborns.

A few days later, Jane and I find a dead bird in Gram's yard and sneak around when Gram isn't looking and put it under the sheets in Caroline's bed. Night comes. Caroline goes to the front bedroom where she sleeps. We wait. She comes out screaming, running half naked in a mad circle in the round hall connecting the three bedrooms, until Gram catches her and holds her in her arms like a child, so skinny and frail she looks like some poor featherless fowl herself.

Gram is mad with us. We say we didn't know Caroline was

really afraid. We thought she was teasing. We thought Gram would think it was funny. Caroline shouldn't have said she was glad the blue jay ate our biddies.

Gram says Caroline has a nervous condition, that something is wrong with her, and we should have known better. I can't tell whether Gram is trying not to smile or whether she really thinks what we did was bad.

A few days later Duke brings us to Gram's with a present to give our high-strung cousin. We say we are sorry. Nobody smiles, but Caroline is hardly more than a child herself and soon we are friends again.

Caroline and Emily are friends because Caroline lives with Gram and also, I think, because so few of Emily's girlhood friends have remained in Montgomery. The woman I call Mel, who had accompanied my parents on their elopement, is one of the exceptions.

Mel brings her two sons to play with us in the country. The two mothers sit on a blanket in the yard and talk and smoke and drink beer. The more they drink, the more they laugh. After a while, the joking stops, and Mel starts crying and complaining about her husband.

"The only thing I remember about my honeymoon," she says, "is how *booor*-ing it was. Booor-in' . . . *Booor*-in'."

I don't know what sex is, but I know they are talking about it. I know that Emily and her friends think it is funny and that they don't talk about it in front of Duke or Gram. I know Jane and I are supposed to act like we don't hear them, the same way we pretend we don't know Emily drinks when Duke isn't there and tells her friends things she doesn't tell him.

In the middle of the tears, Mel and Emily start hooting and laughing. They hoot and laugh and pound on the ground till tears run down their faces. I don't like the way they are acting and start to cry.

Emily takes us inside and gives us ice cream in blue bowls.

Mamie says, "Judy, I could walk to town on your poked-out mouth," sticking her own raspberry lips out as far as they will go and thumping them with one finger.

Not long after that, another friend of Emily's brings her daughter Norma to spend the weekend with us so she can go on a trip with her husband. Norma and I are seesawing in the back yard. I push myself up high and come down hard. Norma goes up . . . up . . . and into the air and hits the ground with a thud. I think she is dead until she jumps up yelling and holding a broken arm. Emily calls Norma's grandmother to go with us to the doctor to get the arm set.

The next day, Emily and Duke take Norma and me to see puppeteers do *Cinderella* at the city kindergarten. The place is so crowded with children and parents that, after much discussion, they decide to let us sit in the audience alone and come back for us later.

Cinderella and the Prince float mysteriously across the stage. We know the strings are there, but we can't see them. White dress . . . round pumpkin . . . shiny slipper . . . Cinderella and the Prince swaying and floating. I am feeling very grownup and contented, sitting in the crowd, hearing the story and watching the magic, when suddenly Norma's parents appear out of nowhere and grab us and take us out.

"Momma and Daddy are coming back to get us," I say. "I want to stay."

"No," they say, sounding mad and upset. What are you doing in here alone? Who was watching Norma when she fell? Where are Emily and Duke? What were they thinking, leaving you here like this?

I see myself standing before them in the sun in a blue dress with tiny blue-and-green flowers on it. "I want to go back in and see the rest of it," I say. "I can go by myself." They don't say anything.

We stand outside a long time. Norma's parents are very angry. Emily and Duke are late and the implication is that they were drinking and not paying attention to us when Norma fell, and then left us alone at the kindergarten and forgot all about us and went off to do as they pleased. So the story ran when my father told it over the years in tones of righteous and amazed indignation. He and Emily were just doing her friends a favor and then they got all in a huff over an accident that could have happened anywhere. Of course they were watching us on the seesaw. Of course they were coming right back to get us.

But the story is told too many times. Guilt and embarrassment inflect the indignation, and the friendship is never patched. In memory, I stand outside the little recreational building on Fairview Avenue and sense for the first time that something has gone wrong in our whole family.

I am four and a half years old in the spring of 1941, and though I am still too young to have any understanding of our troubles, I am old enough to be bothered by some of the things that happen. In March, Emily's friend Mary Helen Scott, whose husband is in the Navy, comes to Montgomery to stay with her mother for a few months. We go to see her. Emily is especially fond of Mrs. Scott, who lives not far from Bessie in a house that reminds me of Gram's, dark and cottage-like inside, with a big front porch and concrete stoops in front.

Jane and Mary Helen's son George and I are playing at seeing who can jump the greatest distance off the stoops and into the grass in the front yard. The sun is bright. We are jumping into the grass. Momma looks out the door, says "Y'all be careful now," and goes back inside.

I think something is wrong and follow her inside. She is telling Mary Helen she is going to have another baby. She feels awful. She can't sleep. Her whole body aches. Duke drinks too much and they fight a lot. Duke wants a son. She already has her hands full with us. The Patersons are fine people, of course, but they are clannish and different from the people she is used to. She misses her old friends. She loves Duke as much as ever, but he is difficult and wants his own way all the time. Sometimes she is so lonely she thinks she will die of it.

Fear bites into my heart. If my mother has another baby, she will die. This time she will die.

Emily has a new friend, a nurse she met when she was in the hospital with the baby that died in the womb. Her name is Connie Turner. Connie has been so good to her. She is coming here today, to Mrs. Scott's, to bring her some medicine to help her sleep. Duke can't stand Connie. He thinks his wife ought to be perfectly happy to be with him and his family all the time. He would kill her if he knew how close she and her new friend have become.

Connie arrives with the medicine. She is tall, fortyish, and sandy-haired. By comparison to Emily's other friends (who still look and act like the girls they had always been together), Connie looks old to me, though even I can see that, in the plain, sensible way of women whose lives consist mainly of work, she is rather handsome. Emily meets her in the front yard by the street. They lean toward one another and talk. She gives Emily a package and leaves.

Emily stops by the stoop and says, "Judy, don't tell Daddy we saw Connie. He doesn't like her."

Emily decides it is time we started going to Sunday School at St. John's and gets up early one Sunday and takes us. We walk up the steps and into the parish house. It is too early. The hallway is dark and we seem to be the only people there. Emily looks around as frantically as if she were lost in a foreign country. I feel fear in her hand clutching mine. A lady comes and takes Jane with her and shows Emily where to take me.

I sit at a low table with a few other children. There is no piano and no marching, and we don't know the teachers, but the pictures in the books are just like the ones at Gram's church. Baby Jesus in the manger. A shepherd carrying a sheep in his arms. Jesus and the Disciples facing a high wind in a boat.

The air is dusty and smells like cinnamon. We eat cookies, make a church with our fingers, and chant, "Here's the church . . . and here's the steeple . . . [then, turning our hands inside out] Open the doors and here are the people."

Emily sits by the door in a child's chair. Her eyes and face have lost all expression. Her body slumps in on itself like a balloon leaking air. Whatever the urge was that got her up early enough to dress herself and us and drive to town is washed away in whatever the terror is that shows in her face.

I am torn between wanting to keep my mother in view and wishing she would leave so I can pay attention to the stories, smell the cinnamon, and learn to turn my hands inside out so my fingers are in the right place when we shout, "Open the doors and here are the people!"

She sits there the whole time and takes us into the church afterwards and sits with us in a pew near the back. We are the only people there. It's dark except for the dim-hued light coming in the stained-glass windows. The ceiling is the bluest blue I ever saw. Emily kneels on a prayer cushion and sobs into her hands. I am afraid to touch her. I start kicking the back of the pew in front of us. I want her to stop crying.

"God help me," she says. "God help me."

I think now that she must have been praying for strength to bear her life and to stop drinking and to be able to care for us and to cope with the trouble in her marriage. I see, too, that the battle she was waging was probably already lost, and ask myself if it doesn't perhaps take as much, or more, courage to wage a battle that is lost than to fight with hope for something that might be won.

That was the last time I remember seeing my mother in St.

John's. After that, Duke takes us there to Sunday School and leaves us while he visits with his brother and cousins at the Rosemont store, the new one built on Perry Street in 1940, with a pine-paneled showroom and a forty-foot picture window across the front, beautiful at all times, breathtaking on holidays. After Sunday School, we go back to the store to play with our cousins in the storage room or watch the women making bouquets and corsages at long tables in the workroom. Our cousin Elsie (who is as white-skinned and black-haired as Snow-White) teaches us to make dolls out of wrapping paper, pipe cleaners, and sticky green tape.

On the way home, we stop at Shulman's Bakery on Court Street, near Bessie's house. On Sundays, the whole block smells of hot bread and vanilla icing. We buy the same thing every week— little square devil's food cakes covered with shiny black icing, crescent rolls, and a braided loaf of challah just out of the oven.

In those days, downtown was as safe for children as a neighborhood park. When Duke is late, we wait without fear on a stone bench by the street. My first gift from a boy is received there, a box of candy from Thornton Clark for Jane and me together because both our birthdays are in September. We sit stiffly with it between us, not knowing how to act with a grownup-looking box secured with gold ribbon.

Thornton's mother says, "Is your mother coming to get you?"

"Not Momma," I say. "Daddy."

She says, "I want to take you to Oak Park next Sunday."

People who know about Emily's illness are sometimes nice to us because of it. Duke doesn't like it, because the people who "go out of their way like that" are usually people who had known Emily before they married, and he thinks their kindness implies criticism of him. How much her friends blamed him, I only knew afterwards. Jane and I are timid about going places with people we don't know, but I know we went to Oak Park with Thornton and his mother that time, because Duke and Emily argued about it beforehand and I worried about it at the park.

I associate the candy Thornton gave us and the afternoon at Oak Park with my first memory of being switched by my mother. Jane and Emily and Mamie and I are in the sun room. I don't remember what I did wrong. What I remember is that I won't say I'm sorry and am switched for that rather than for the original crime.

Emily switches harder and harder, trying to get me to say it. I refuse and put my hands behind me where she is hitting. When she finally stops, my hands have big welts all over them, and Emily is horrified. I don't remember feeling either emotionally or physically harmed by the switching. What I remember is feeling wronged by the punishment and disturbed by how unsure of herself, embarrassed, and remorseful my mother was after she saw the welts on my hands. How she joked self-consciously with Mary Willie about her ineptitude as a disciplinarian (and a mother) and then went and got Thornton's candy and let me eat as much of it as I wanted, to make up for what she had done. Emily's seeming mockery of herself (and somehow, by extension, of me and of everything that mattered between us) is what I remember as painful—that and the unfairness of being rewarded with candy that had been mine in the first place and had been kept from me so long I had forgotten it existed.

A second, more intensely felt incident bears the same message and must have happened around the same time. Duke had built a two-room playhouse for us out of scraps from the house and put a sandbox and a tall steel sliding board in the back yard near the seesaw. The sliding board looks so high to Jane and me that at first we are afraid to climb up the steps, not knowing which is the scariest, being stuck at the top or going down the slope in terror. Finally, I get up the nerve.

Up . . . up . . . one step at a time, my heart in my mouth, until I get to the top and look down at the distance and wait for desire greater than fear to grab me and hurl me to the bottom. AAAAAAhh, one long, terrified gulp of air then bump . . . down . . . *yeeeeeeee* . . . down like an elevator . . . my heart in my stomach . . . I am speed . . . I am light . . . I am a *biiiird* with wings.

Around . . . up . . . down . . . around . . . up . . . down. Up-up-up-bump-down-*zooooooooosh*-*yeeeeeeeee*-up-up-up-bump-down-*zooooooooosh*-*yeeeeeeeee*, and then Jane goes down and my doll Suzie and buckets and shovels and shoes, again and again and again—until we are drunk with the speed of our running-sliding bodies and girls-doll-buckets-shovels-shoes-slide-dust-sunshine-grass meld together in a single streak of golden light. We are speed. We are birds *zooooooooosh-ing* and *yeeeeeeeee*-ing in the light.

A door slams and our dog, Shag, gets out of a car. Only he doesn't look like Shag, who went to the vet for mange looking like himself and has come back shorn of his white fluff and painted with gentian violet so that he looks like something out of a cartoon or a dream, a strange amalgamated creature, part horse and part dog, with a slick purple body, white ears, and a bushy white tail.

"It's Shag," Emily yells from the house. I keep sliding. "Don't stop. Jane! Your turn!" We are birds, air, streaks of light. *Zooooooooosh*. I think I will die if it stops.

Jane gets to the top and stops, too scared of the purple creature getting out of the car to come down, she says. I think she knows it's Shag and is just trying to ruin everything and get attention from Emily by acting helpless and stupid.

Jane . . . please . . . *zooooooooosh-yeeeeeeeee* . . . can't you see . . . we are air . . . we are speed . . . we are light. But the light is fading. I've got to make her come down.

"It's Shag," I yell, "Shag with medicine on him. *Stuuuuuu*-pid, *Stuuuuuu*-pid. Come down. You aren't really scared. It's not fair. It's *my* turn. Damn it, Jane. You *know* it's Shag."

Jane just stands there with the fingers of both hands in her mouth, looking toward the house, whimpering and watching for Momma.

"You can sleep with Suzie," I wheedle. "You can go two times in a row, three times. Come down, *I said*. You *know* it is my turn. You *know* it is *just* Shag." Jane ruins everything. I don't want to look after my whiny sister. I want to do what I want to do. I am a bird . . . I am light.

"Cry, baby, cry . . . stick your finger in your eye . . . if you don't come down from there, I'm going to sic Shag on you and you'll have to stay up there forever."

I feel Emily and Mamie at the window, a white presence and a black one, watching for me to do what I am doing, almost willing it (so it seems to me when I remember it). Not that I could have stopped myself even if I had known what was coming. I have to make my sister take her turn, so I can take mine, and we can get back to doing what we are supposed to be doing.

"Shag's gonna getchooooooo . . . Shag's gonna getchooooooooooooo. Sic'er. Sic'er."

My sister says she is not coming down because she is scared of the purple Shag. I say if she doesn't come down I'll see to it that her worst fears are realized. My childish logic is, to say the least, flawed.

Wr-RRU-ufff WrRRU-uff roars out of my chest. I didn't know I could sound so much like a dog. I am a dog. I am Shag. I'm going to bite that stupid Jane. COME DOWN! Damn it, Jane. You *come down* from there. The purple phantom glides toward us. Jane yells and looks toward the house.

Suddenly Emily and Mamie fly out of the back door, running and flapping their arms like bats. I think they are coming to play with us, until Emily starts soothing Jane as if she were some sort of helpless fool, instead of just plain contrary and perfectly capable of looking after herself, and a big liar besides.

I ignore the tiny flag of fear going up inside me and keep barking

91

and roaring out the side of my mouth and trying to explain at the same time. "Not fair . . . my turn . . . she knows good and well it's Shag."

I don't want to look after my sister and hold myself back to her babyish pace. I want to *zooooooosh* in the light and fly like a bird. Wr-RRU-ufff . . . grrrURfff . . . Shag's gonna getchooooooo . . . Shag's gonna . . .

"Stop that, Judy," Emily says, holding Jane in her arms, not listening to me, not meeting my eyes.

"She's not scared. She's just lying and ruining our game . . . Li-ar. Li-ar."

Either I don't know I'm in trouble or I think I can get out of it.

Mamie picks a switch off a bush and hands it to Emily. "Don't you *dare* call your sister a liar," Emily says, taking the switch.

I keep yelling, "She is *not* scared. She *knows* it is Shag. That makes her a liar. Li-ar! Li-ar!"

Not matter how hard Emily switches, I keep barking . . . WRRRUFFf . . . GRRR . . . and yelling . . . LI-AR, LI-AR . . . out of some innate sense of my right to tell the truth as I see it and to bark like a dog and *zooooooosh* like a bird in the light.

Pee runs hot and sticky down my legs; my teeth clamp together so hard I think my jaw will break, but I don't stop yelling . . . No . . . Nooooooooo . . . Not fair . . . I am Shag . . . Jane's the biggest liar there ever was and tattles and whines and breaks her promises . . . I was being a bird.

Emily and Mamie carry me inside, turn the cold water on in the shower, and shove me under it, still kicking, still barking, still flapping my wings. Emily says, "This is what Helen does when Little Helen has a tantrum."

The water hits my head like cold rocks. Wrong. Not fair. What's Little Helen got to do with it anyway. What about me?

I am a giant red dog inside the water. I will NOT stop. My breath stops. My body stiffens to a rigor and my neck wrenches as far back and to one side as it can go without popping. I would stop the words and noises if I could, but something inside me won't do it. Red rage turns to terror. I can't stop what I am doing, and I can't stop being afraid.

The world goes black with a blackness I can't possibly understand or verbalize, not knowing that alcoholism and the untended wounds of their own childhoods have all but demolished the dreams, though not the passions, that had drawn my parents together like polarized magnets, not knowing that what's left of their love now hangs on the hope that the child my mother carries will be the son my father thinks will make him all the things he thinks he isn't, not knowing that my mother suspects her drinking (or some other unmotherly sin) to be the cause of my sister's unreliability, poor vision and inattentiveness, not knowing that Emily already spends too many nights drinking and longing for she-knows-not-what from Duke, who shares both the longing and the unfulfillment, not knowing that the sometimes cruel, jesting edge to her treatment of us mirrors her own mother's heartless mockery, not knowing that Emily already has more children than she can properly mother.

What I do know is that my mother identifies with a real or imagined fragility in my sister that assigns Jane a strange combination of inferiority and special value and vests me with more maturity than I can sometimes muster and more responsibility than I am ready for. What I know in that moment is that I am mocked, humiliated, and tossed into darkness, tumbling and spinning like a star falling to earth. I don't want to look after my sister; I want my mother to look after me.

I go calm and step out of the tub . . . i am a bird . . . i am light . . . i am me. I am big. BIG. Emily and Mamie are little and I am a big, fiery giant inside the water. And then I am little again. But when I am big, really big, I will go where I please and tell the truth as I see it and *zoooooooosh* in the light to my heart's content and never be lonely again.

The memory is painful and humiliating out of all proportion to what happened, marking for me the betrayal (which I suppose comes in all but the most blissful of childhoods) of the promise that because my parents loved me I would always be safe and cared for and happy. I don't know what happened next, except that my mother probably tried to make it up to me and that, in some black corner of my heart, I didn't forgive her.

I go to Gram's and the Greenhouse with my father more and more after that. Duke puts Jane in the bed with Emily in the mornings when we leave, or they stand at the door in their pajamas and wave. I go with him and Gram into places I have never been, streets and fields and strange new houses. I want also, but not as much, to stay with Emily and Jane in the bed, in the warm smells and deep darkness of home, where all we do is wait and where what our mother does is all that matters.

I will be five in September and want to go to kindergarten in town with my Paterson cousins, who go every day and sit at round tables and draw pictures and write their names on lined paper. Gram takes me to the city kindergarten where Norma and I saw *Cinderella*, to see how I like it. Emily wants me to go to Mrs. Helen Cottingham's private kindergarten with the children of her friends, but Gram says this one costs less, is just as good and closer to her house.

They give us apple juice in little white cups. The yellow juice tastes sweet and sharp at the same time and not at all like apples. The puppeteers do *Little Red Ridinghood*. Afterwards, the actors come out and let us pull the strings on the puppets. I pull the strings on the Bad Wolf and make his long red mouth open and shut like a crocodile's.

Pull . . . "What big teeth you have, Mr. Wolf." Pull . . . "The better to *eat* you with, my dear" . . . shut. I go suddenly timid at my success and hide behind Gram.

She says, "That's not *my* girl acting so shamefaced, is it? I thought you said you wanted to come here every day. You'll have to be a big girl to do that."

Despite being momentarily shy, I want to come here every day more than I have ever wanted anything in my life.

A Son Is Born

 The summer of 1941 stands in my mind as the end of that time in childhood when we remember "what happened" mostly as a series of loosely connected events linked by themes and images rather than by logic, cause and effect, and the passage of time. My first inkling (and dread) of the future implications of the present seems to have come to me by way of a precocious inclination to worry about my mother.

Though I pinpoint my fifth summer as the beginning of a compulsive, lifelong tendency to anticipate and visualize the worse possible outcome of a given set of circumstances, I cannot say exactly when my ravenous involvement with the pleasures of the moment began to be mingled with a sense of impending doom.

Yet I think I did know, in some way, by the time that summer began that if my mother kept doing the things she was doing, "something bad" was going to happen to her; and if something bad happened to her, something bad might happen to me. What I did not know was that the shattering of whatever chance my parents still had of creating a stable family had already begun, along with whatever chance my mother had of living a long life, whatever chance my father had of thinking himself worthy of his heritage, whatever chance my sister and I had of being unharmed by their troubles. Unlike the five years that precede them, the next twelve months are packed with memories easily fixed in time.

By the middle of July, Emily is seven months pregnant, drinking heavily, agitated in the daytime, sleepless at night, fighting with Duke, taking sleeping pills, pain pills, Stanbacks, whatever she can get her hands on to keep her body from aching and herself from being herself.

One day Duke comes home in the middle of the afternoon and comes upstairs to help Mary Willie pack our suitcases to go to Gram's. His sun-darkened face looks drained and stiff as a statue's. He doesn't come upstairs very often. I have never seen him help Mary Willie before.

We go to Gram's. Duke comes back two or three times. He and Gram sit in her bedroom in front of a little fan that whirs. He looks like he wants to cry in her arms. Gram rocks back and forth, back and forth in her chair. He sits still as a stone, then jumps up and leaves. He comes back. He sits down. He gets up and leaves.

I have a brother in the hospital. He is tiny and weak. He has been named James Porter, like Duke's father and grandfather. The name is given, not for the grandfather, whose Yankee existence is never acknowledged, but for the beloved father, whose death left a hole in Duke's manhood that he thinks only a son (and what a son it will have to be) can fill.

Duke comes back again before dawn on the second day. The wheels of the car stop in the dirt by the back door. The screen door klaa-*popps* behind him. Gram says, "What happened?"

They walk close together and slowly, as if something invisible was passing between them. Jane and I stand against the wall like shadows. My father looks like he is going to throw his head back and howl. Instead, he stands so still he seems hardly to be breathing at all.

"The baby died, Mother," he says in a voice that is more growl

97

than speech. A ball of horror leaps from his body to mine. All I know is that we are swallowed up in suffering and my brother has died a terrible, shameful death.

"Damn that Dr. Ross," Gram says. "I never could *stand* that man." The baby would have been her first grandson, named for the only man she ever loved.

Jane cries to go with Duke. He takes her. I go back to bed with Gram. Her body is warm and smells like milk. Sometimes we lie in bed together and put ourselves to sleep making up stories about the shadows the trees make on the side of the Greenhouse, but not this time.

What Duke and Gram know that I don't know is that Emily had talked her obstetrician, Dr. Ross, into inducing labor two months before the baby was due. Big, awkward, and potbellied, with a round, pockmarked face and a balding head, the man I call Dr. Ross stands in my mind as a figure of the Devil and the most repulsive-looking man I ever saw. He was also unprincipled, foul-mouthed, weak-willed, and alcoholic himself.

Emily tells him she is too depressed and nervous to stand the pregnancy another day. She is in pain, unable to sleep, sick to death of Duke, sick of trying to bear him a son she doesn't particularly want. By then she is addicted to both alcohol and the barbiturates she gets from Dr. Ross and her nurse friend, Connie, who is also a friend of Dr. Ross's. She had rather be dead than be pregnant another minute. She will kill herself, she says, unless he gets the baby out of her body.

"Women either love Dr. Ross or hate him," people say. Emily is one of those who love him. Gram hates him first for the crude, blasphemous speech he uses and after that for what happened to Emily and, most of all, in the end, because she can't get Duke to make Emily leave him. I know now that my mother could no more leave the source of her drugs than she could stop drinking and that the only thing my father could have done that might have helped was to stop drinking himself, which he also couldn't (in any case, didn't) do.

Gram (who could never blame Emily for anything) blames Dr. Ross. Duke blames Emily. She killed his son. She is crazy. A murderer. Better for *her* to have died than his boy. Emily blames Duke. He is driving her crazy. All he wants her for is to have children. She's already given him two girls and had two terrible pregnancies after that. She doesn't care if he *never* has a son. She doesn't *want* any more children.

I don't know to what extent the charges of infanticide and betrayal struck me as personally dangerous and raised questions of my own mortality and vulnerability. If my brother was dead —killed by my mother—then did parents just kill their children, and would Jane and I be next? If my father was a monster and my mother insane, who would look after us?

I have no memory of such thoughts, but—given how deeply abandoned I have sometimes felt and how easy it still is for me to feel cast out and endangered—I imagine they were there, no less (and perhaps more) real and horrifying for being suppressed. What I remember is the deep thrust of a new level of anxiety about Emily's safety, and an abiding conflict between wanting to know where my mother is and not wanting to be alone with her or to see her suffer.

Connie Turner visits Emily in the hospital and hovers over her like a mother over a dying child. What she did wasn't so bad. She has seen women do much worse than that. Emily will be all right. She can have other children if she wants to. Duke will get over it. Soon everybody will have forgotten.

Emily says she is too weak and anxious to be alone and wants to pay Connie her full salary to go home with her. Duke doesn't like the idea. Mary Willie can look after everything, the way she always has. Emily says, "I need her. It's my money, I'll do what I please with it." Dr. Ross agrees with Emily, and Connie comes home with her.

My mother is twenty-six years old, alcoholic, addicted to sleeping pills, and terrified of being alone. She is also, no doubt, suffering from some combination of the depressive illnesses that I believe ran in the family of her mother as well as her father.

Emily lies in bed and Connie sits in a chair beside her, sometimes talking, sometimes reading or knitting in silence. In the only conversation I remember between her and my mother, Connie says she has been with us long enough, that she doesn't like just sitting around our house doing nothing, wasting Emily's money.

"What do *you* care?" Emily asks in a voice filled with venom, her eyes bright with barbiturates. "It's *my* money."

"All right then, Emily," Connie says, and leaves the room, looking hurt.

For the most part, my life remains the same. I still go to Gram's and the Greenhouse with Duke. Jane and I still go to town with Bessie. We still play with Hattie Jo and interesting things still happen at home.

The arrival of a tall, young mulatto cook named Eugene is one of the interesting things that happen. Eugene is very flamboyant and theatrical-looking and doesn't act like any colored person I have ever seen before. He and Mamie gossip and flirt and sing and pretend to be movie stars in the kitchen. Every week Eugene cooks a turkey and a yellow custard that stands up round in the dish and makes the whole house smell like vanilla. I like to watch him and Mamie in the kitchen. Sometimes he cooks fast and with concentration. Sometimes he lets me stand on a chair and stir things on the stove.

In addition to cooking, Eugene runs errands for Duke in return for getting to do a few errands of his own in the Ford roadster with the Cadillac engine. Once, when Emily was sick and Connie was there, he took Jane and me to Gram's to spend Saturday night and had to make the trip twice because we forgot our suitcases.

On the way back to town the second time, he ran the car off a wooden bridge and into the stream beneath it and "climbed out without a scratch," so the story goes, and walked back to the house "speckled like a clown" with the spillage from a bucket of green paint that had been riding in the backseat.

I don't know what caused the accident, but Duke always told it as a celebration of Eugene's survival and the fact that Jane and I were not in the car when it happened. Eventually, it took only a phrase—"Eugene's bridge" or "paint everywhere" or "what good luck it was"—to evoke a story that, for my father, had overtones of the miraculous, though it ended the career of the customized roadster.

One day, Jane and Hattie Jo and I are in the kitchen with Eugene. He is opening a can of popcorn with a can opener. It is three-quarters open when the can opener breaks. Jane is sitting on the kitchen counter watching Eugene. Hattie Jo and I are standing beside him. We have never had popcorn at home before.

"I'll be right back," he says, leaving to look for something to finish opening the can with. "Don't touch that can. It'll cut you."

As soon as he is out of the room, Jane reaches inside the can like a bear cub going after honey and gets her hand stuck. Every time she tries to pull her hand out, the jagged edges cut into her wrist.

Hattie Jo says, "Go get Eugene."

By the time I get back with Eugene, Hattie Jo has taken a pencil and pushed the half-cut lid far enough down into the can for Jane to get her hand out. I have never seen an act of ingenuity and quick thinking as impressive as that. Hattie Jo is a hero. We talk and talk about it. Jane's hand is barely scratched and everybody is happy.

On a similar morning that same summer, Mamie and Eugene

are dancing and singing like Nelson Eddy and Jeanette MacDonald in the kitchen . . . Ah, sweet mystery da da da da da da . . .

Emily appears in the doorway, wearing a white, flapperish tennis dress. Her hair is still wet from her bath. Her mouth is a dark, unblotted smudge of red. The half smile, half sneer on her face tells me she is already intoxicated.

She joins the singing and waltzes around the kitchen with Mary Willie. Eugene grabs my hand and Emily's and the four of us dance and whoop in a circle like Indians around a campfire. Our hands are like different-colored links in a chain. Emily's hands are pink. Mine are brownish from the sun. Eugene's are a little browner. Mamie's are the color of wood. My mother's boyish, blunt-fingered hands are the only part of her body that has not grown frail and strange to look at.

Two dark spots of menstrual blood appear on the floor beneath Emily. She and Mamie scurry to clean it up, joking and laughing and pretending they are the only ones who know what has happened. Eugene turns toward the sink, cutting his eyes back at Mamie. Someone is being made fun of. Maybe Emily. Maybe Duke, whose car has just entered the driveway.

I know what menstrual blood is; I know everybody is pretending Eugene doesn't know what is going on; I know everybody knows he knows. I understand the joking and pretending about the blood. I don't understand the wildness that precedes it or the mockery that follows.

They keep laughing and joking until Duke gets to the back door. I know he won't like what they are doing, and run to the door to distract him. Sex, drink, and racial taboos mingle with mockery and wildness in my mind. They are playing a game that excludes me and reddens my face.

On another such day, Duke comes home and goes to the back of the house. Emily is in the bed. Connie is sitting by the bed in a chair. He leaves the room in a hurry and goes outside to get on the tractor to cut the grass. I talk him into letting me sit in his lap and ride with him and put my hands on the steering wheel with his. I know he doesn't want me to go, but I think if he takes me he might get in a better humor and stop looking mad.

This is one of the special things we do. I sit in front of him like a possum in its mother's pouch and we ride and steer and talk. He tells me about trees and plants and the weather. I feel his chest and his stomach rising and falling against my back. Sometimes I steer alone and he tells me how smart and big I am.

Today he is angry with Emily and nothing I do changes his mood, though I keep trying. Finally, he says, "Get down, Judy, and go up to the house and get me a glass of water with some ice in it. You're big enough to do that, aren't you?"

It's a long walk up the hill to the house. The sun is bright in my eyes. Mamie is in the kitchen talking to Eugene. It takes her a long time to understand what I want.

"He's too far down there, baby," she says finally. "You stay here. I'll take it."

"No," I say. "I can do it. He said for me to."

She puts water and lots of ice in a tall glass, and I head down the hill with it. I walk and walk, sipping the water and watching the sun make diamonds on the ice.

The sun is behind Duke's head. His face looks sad and mad at the same time.

"I drank a little of the water on the way," I say, holding the glass up to him, ignoring the tiny fear flickering in my chest.

He takes the glass, sips, and lets out a sound I have never forgotten, which can only be described as a howl . . . *eeaaaaagh . . . You drank it . . . The glass is empty . . . You took too long . . .* Suddenly all the pent-up fury that should have been aimed at himself, Emily, Dr. Ross, and the strange woman in our house lands on the unhappy head of the five-year-old bearer of a half-empty glass of water. A stream of vituperation halts whatever defense I have as palpably as if he had stuffed my throat with sand.

I don't remember the words he said. What I remember is the feelings that go with *stupid . . . bad . . . wrong*, and the terror of seeing my protector turned into a demented giant.

I might have felt outraged myself, I suppose. After all, I was trying very hard to do something for him that I wasn't quite old enough to do. The hill was steep, the sun was hot, and my legs were very short. I didn't know he was all that thirsty and I had never before been assigned a task the outcome of which made that much difference to somebody else. I was too surprised for outrage, too hurt to defend myself.

We go back to the house on the tractor. He gets off and heads for the kitchen bellowing for water. I follow on inadequate legs braced against the firebombs of rage still falling on my body.

Shame and self-disgust sink into the soft tissue of my heart like burning rocks. I drank the water. I took too long. I am nothing to the person I love the most in all the world.

Mamie gives Duke a glass of water and stands there watching him drink it with her hands on her hips and her mouth clamped shut and twisted to one side. He hands the glass back to her and turns toward the tractor in the yard. Mamie mutters something I don't hear and takes me upstairs in her arms.

Not long after that, Jane and I are in the backseat of the car. Duke is driving. Emily sits beside him, trying to talk him into seeing something her way or letting her do something she wants to do that he is against.

"You don't even *try* to understand," she says. "You are too *stubborn* to listen to anybody else. All you care about is having your own way. Your *own way*." He sits stiff as a military guard, staring ahead at the road.

Coming down the road toward us is an old black woman sitting alone on the wooden seat of a flat wagon pulled by a mule and piled high with hay. The woman, who is as dark and tiny as a cricket, holds the reins loose in her hands and sits regal as a queen amid the billows of a big skirt that is brown like her skin and the hide of the mule and the wood of the wagon.

I start jumping up and down, shouting, "*Look* at that lady! Look at that *laaady!*"

My father and mother keep arguing. I keep pointing and shouting and bouncing up and down behind them. I have never seen a woman driving a wagon before. I want them to see what I have seen. I also want them to stop yelling at each other.

Instead, Duke spins around in the seat and yells, "Don't call a *nigger* a lady. *Don't you ever do that again.*"

Emily says, "Don't yell at her like that, Duke. And don't say 'nigger' in front of my children. What do you want them to grow up to be?"

The sun shines on her face. She is wearing shorts and a bright flowered shirt. Her hair seems longer than usual and she looks bigger than she is. The more she talks, the more agitated she becomes. My father sits stony, a hint of contempt curling his lips. He says what suits him. He does what he pleases.

Although I have never heard the word "nigger" said in my family before, I know what it means and sense more of the implications of what my father has said than a child my age could possibly have understood consciously. I know it insults Mamie and the Thomases because of the color of their skin. I know that, by breaking one of the rules of our family, my father insults both my mother and me and puts each of us in our place. That I have been accused of making another terrible and inadvertent mistake I understand perfectly well.

Shame pours into me like steam. Only this time the shame is mixed with anger. Anger at the senseless abuse being heaped on my head. Anger at the constraints my father is putting on what I can see and say. Anger at what "nigger" says about Mamie. Anger at both my parents for spewing their fury against each other all over me.

Connie stays. Emily and Duke get drunk and have a fight that Mamie gets drawn into. Duke insults her. LeRoy comes and gets her and says she's not coming back. Daddy and I go to her mother's house by the river to look for her. It must be Sunday. I have on a yellow cotton dress, smocked in front and soft as silk. An old man in the yard says he doesn't know anybody named Mary Willie, but finally Mamie comes out on the porch and says something to Duke.

He stands in the yard at a distance and shouts, "Damn it, Mary Willie, I'm offering you the moon, I'm offering you the moon." His face is red and his voice has tears in it, but I think he must be joking, calling Mamie "Mary Willie" like that and offering her the moon . . . Hey diddle diddle, the cat and the fiddle . . .

"Don't you cuss me, Mr. Duke," she says, slurring "mister" and spitting "Duke" out in two hard syllables so it sounds like she has called him by his first name. "Don't you cuss me, mms*Duu*ke," she says again, slow and mad, standing on the plain bare porch in a faded blue dress with her arms crossed in front of her like a statue.

Duke says, "Good God A'mighty," and drives off fast and mad. I don't yet know what it means for someone to leave and not come back. I don't know how little power any of us has over the things that are happening. After a few days, Mamie comes back.

Somehow—I can't imagine how—Emily and Duke and Dr. and Mrs. Ross have become close friends. "Thick as thieves," says Gram, who must by then have begun to realize the role her son's drinking is playing in our troubles.

The Rosses come to our house and swim and sit by the pool. They come by themselves and they come with other people. Eventually, they have a baby boy and he comes with them. Mrs. Ross is a quiet, sullen woman who drinks hardly at all. Dr. Ross is just the opposite.

One day they are there a long time. Duke and Emily and Dr. Ross are swimming and drinking and laughing by the pool. Mrs. Ross sits in a chair on the grass. Some other people are there, too. I walk out the back door and head for the pool, thinking my mother will pick me up and take me into the water with her friends.

What I see stops me in my tracks and I watch for a long time, a tiny troll of a creature turning from happiness to misery in the shadow of a corner of the house that seems to grow darker with every minute I watch. I don't know how long I stand there or what, exactly, I see.

My parents and Dr. Ross and some people whose faces have left me cavort like mythological madmen around a black pond in some jungle somewhere. It is late afternoon. The day grows dark. Words seem out of sync with gestures. Laughter that should sound happy sounds harsh and mean.

Emily totters toward the house in her bathing suit, a beer in one hand, a cigarette in the other, almost too wobbly to walk. Drunk, with his big belly hanging over the top of his trunks, a lone lock of hair falling into his face and beads of water standing on his skin like sweat, Dr. Ross follows her toward the house.

I run toward my mother. She looks strange. Her eyes shrink to slits and her face goes murderous at the sight of me.

"What are you doing out here, *Judy?*" she asks, stressing my name like a dirty word.

"I want to swim."

"Get back in the house where you belong."

I stand in memory, a small child wearing only her underpants, waiting to be taken in her mother's arms. A woman stands before me, slinging her head from side to side like a colt in a burning barn. Her skin is blue-white. She is both my mother and not my mother. The figure of a man looms over her from behind. Drops of water pebble his arms. I stand in their path, absorbing evil as palpable as if it rose from the rotting earth.

"Don't touch me. Don't touch me," roars out of my throat. "*Stop it. Stop it.*" I want my parents to stop turning into monsters. I want their blackness to stop pouring into my body like fumes.

I fall down and kick and scream in the dirt. Grass prickles my skin. Dust and sunlight sting my eyes. *Stop it. Don't tooouch meee.*

A World of Trouble

 By the end of the summer, it should have been clear to everyone that Emily was genuinely ill. Perhaps little more could have been done for her at that point. Perhaps not. In any case, addressing her illness would have required that both Gram and Duke admit the role my father's addiction to alcohol was playing in their troubles; since nobody wanted to do that, for a while things went on as they were.

Jane and I began spending whole weekends with Bessie, and I came to love Bessie's downtown world as much as I loved my home-away-from-home at Gram's and the Greenhouse. At Bessie's we followed a routine of setting out on foot for town in the late afternoon and eating an early supper, usually at a bar-diner called the Tavern, a place frequented only by people Bessie knew (or so it seemed to me) and run by a clan of Sephardic Jews named Franco. The Francos had taken Bessie and Knoxie into the bosom of a family of kinsmen and customers who gathered there almost nightly to eat and drink and talk about the disasters befalling their aging friends.

Occasionally, we went instead to the Pickwick Café, a sedate place with white linen tablecloths and thick, starched napkins on the tables and a hushed atmosphere, where we ate fish or chicken and baked potatoes and chunks of lettuce with red dressing, like grownups. The waiters were all white-jacketed black men who seemed to have known Bessie (and she them) since childhood, but she always requested the same one, a handsome man named Henry, who stood over our table and reminisced with her about her father, the General, who never met a stranger, colored or white. Things (meaning relations between the races), they agreed, were not what they had been when everybody knew one another and got along.

Bessie's beau, a man I never heard called anything but Judge Stone, sometimes went with us. Judge Stone was shaped just like Bessie and had graying hair and a short white beard and seemed perfectly suited to her. He liked the Tavern and the Pickwick. He liked Jeanette MacDonald and Nelson Eddy, and—like Bessie— he loved to talk. They talked gleefully and constantly about old times and how things had changed for the worse.

Winter and summer, Judge Stone wore a three-piece tweed suit that seemed form-fitted to his stout, square body. After the movie, whether Judge Stone was with us or not, we stopped at the fruit stand next to the Tavern and bought perfectly ripened apples and oranges and pears from a bald-headed, bent-over man named Simato, who chose our fruit and wrapped it in pastel tissue like a jeweler picking gems for the bracelet of a queen. He wiped his hands on his long white butcher's apron and showed us fruits we'd never seen before—pomegranates, kumquats, and red pears—and told us about the faraway places they came from.

Sometimes we stopped and talked to a gypsy fortune-teller who sat in a tiny golden tent on the sidewalk between the fruit market and the stand where we caught the Yellow Cab that took us home. Judge Stone sometimes saw us to the door of the Sophronia, before getting into the cab and going to wherever he lived.

Once we were inside, Bessie always said the same thing, "You don't have to worry about me marrying Judge Stone. I love you children and your mother too much to marry anybody." And then: "Your Grandfather Jim Hillman was the loveliest, wittiest, most patient [with the scatterbrained Knoxie was what she meant] man who ever lived—and the only man I ever loved." Because of the playful way she put it, I always doubted the seriousness (or even the truth) of what she said about her feelings for her sister's husband, though I believe it was true that he courted her a little before being swept off his feet by the sister she often referred to as "the celebrated Miss Knoxie."

Except for a few photographs of a handsome man with thin blond hair, regular features, a head a little too big for his compact body, and a bland, solemn look on his face, Bessie's idealized picture of her long-suffering brother-in-law is the only image I had of Jim Hillman. It was also, I suspect, one of the few images my mother had of him. She mentioned him in my presence only once that I remember, and that was because I asked.

As I recall it, Jane and I are in the backseat of the car. Emily and Gram are in the front. They are talking about Duke's father and how he died. I ask Emily what happened to her father.

"He died, too, when I was little" is all she says. Something in her tone tells me not to ask again, and for many years I didn't, though I never passed the corner we were turning when I asked it without remembering what she said and the lonely little girl's voice in which she said it.

Bessie gets up very early when we spend the night with her and makes a huge breakfast of bacon, baked potatoes and bread from the bakery. Because her arms are often covered with an itchy red rash she blames on an allergic reaction to white flour, she cuts at least two kinds of bread (French and either whole wheat or rye) into big chunks and butters and heats them until they are almost all crust—a fine breakfast, indeed, by modern standards, Bessie says, though she likes to remember when fires roared before daybreak and breakfast included roe cakes, fried apples, corn bread, and homemade biscuits.

One Saturday I am at Bessie's alone, enjoying her undivided

attention and expecting to stay the rest of the day. Duke calls and says he is sending somebody in a Rosemont delivery truck to pick me up and take me to the Greenhouse so I can go home. The truck is white, with green writing on the side. Inside, it smells like flowers and green floral paper.

When we get to the Greenhouse, Duke says, "You have to go home. Your momma misses you." My stomach is full of Bessie's breakfast. I'm sleepy. Somebody takes me home.

I go to my mother's room. The nurse Connie lies beside her on the bed. Emily has on a gown and looks as white as the sheets. Connie is holding her in her arms like a man. Her hands are all over my mother, who is sobbing and gulping air like the catfish we saw on the bank of the creek in the pine woods. Though I may have seen more, that is all I remember.

I stand at the door. Everything goes white. The women look like ghosts entwined on the bed. I open my mouth to scream but nothing comes out.

I go to the kitchen to get Mamie. "What's wrong, baby?" she asks.

My mother is in danger. My mother is a ghost. The words "Don't tell" strike my ears like a voice from above. If I tried to tell, I don't remember it. What I remember is "Don't tell" and despair as deep as a well.

Pretend it didn't happen, the way Bessie says *Hansel and Gretel* never happened, because children don't get lost in the woods in real life. It didn't happen. I didn't see it. Nothing bad is going to happen to anybody.

Not long after that, Emily wants Connie to drive her to Birmingham so she can eat at Joy Young's Chinese Restaurant—both to remind Duke of how much grander her life was before she married him and to get out of the house with her friend. Duke thinks it is a terrible idea but finally agrees to it on the condition that Uncle Dan's second wife, my new Aunt Mary Lou, go with them.

Mary Lou is a vivacious, plainspoken woman with huge brown eyes and a nice figure. She wants nothing so much as to be part of our family. Some of my other aunts and cousins are already worried about what's going on between Emily and Connie but are afraid to say anything to Duke. They don't want to make him angry. Maybe he wouldn't believe it anyway. And why can't he see for himself what is right under his nose?

Mary Lou sits in the backseat. Connie and Emily sit in the front. There is no doubt in Mary Lou's mind about what she is seeing. Connie and Emily are flirting and sitting close and touching each other's breasts with their hands. Something is definitely going on between them.

They have a high-spirited lunch at Joy Young's and get home before dark, as they had promised they would. That night Mary Lou tells Dan everything. They think Duke might not believe her because she is new to the family. No telling what he will do if he does believe her.

In the end, Mary Lou tells Gram, and Gram tells Duke that Connie is giving Emily drugs in exchange for sex. Emily says it's not true and begs him to let Connie stay. She is paying Connie with her own money. She isn't well enough to be alone. Connie looked after her when nobody else did. They are friends. That's all. She's sick to death of Duke *and* his mother.

What happened next freezes in my mind forever and replays itself for the rest of my life like the fragment of an old movie that pops to the screen whenever it pleases, regardless of what may already be playing there. Connie has left. Jane and I are standing upstairs in our room under the fan. Mamie is talking to Gram in a low, solemn voice. I don't know how I know what sex is, but I know what they are saying has something to do with it. I remember the time Momma and Mel laughed and hooted about their honeymoons and I felt ashamed. I remember the black rotten feeling inside me the day Dr. Ross followed Emily to the house from the pool. I remember what I saw Emily and Connie doing in the bed. Maybe I should have told and didn't. Maybe I shouldn't have told and did. Maybe just my seeing it was enough to cause the terrible danger I sense in what Gram and Mary Willie are saying to each other.

"I was afraid he would kill her, if he knew," Mamie says.

Gram takes off her glasses, rubs her eyes with both hands and says, "It may be the death of us all, anyway."

The next day or the next, Jane and I walk up behind Mamie, who stands at the door of Emily's room, and see our mother's nightgowned body hurtling up and down on the bed like a circus clown on a trampoline. Her back arches so high when she goes up that I think her neck will break every time she comes down.

Gram, Bessie, Duke, and someone else stand at the four corners of the bed like figures in a dream. She needs medical attention, they say. No, she can't have any more pills. No, Connie can't come back.

The sheets on the bed are shiny white, Emily's gown is white, and her body shines incandescent in the dull light from a fixture in the ceiling. The only color I see is the tobacco-brown of her hair hitting the mattress. Up . . . Down . . . Crash. Up . . . Down . . . Crash, like a child in a tantrum, like a star falling to earth.

Jane and I start to laugh hysterically, not because what we see is funny, but because it is impossible to believe, impossible to endure. "Stop that," Mary Willie says in a tone so harsh I can't believe that either. "Don't you know your mother is *sick*."

I don't hear "addicted" or "crazy" or "drunk" or "bad." I hear "sick" and see my mother's body floating off the end of the bed like a ghost in a cartoon and know they are going to take her away again and think, "This time she will die," which is what I am going to think every time something frightening and unforeseen happens to her, or anybody else I love, for the rest of my life. My own body seems to leave the room with her ghost. Freeze. Shut your eyes. Pretend. Forget.

Bessie gets a robe out of the closet. She and Duke prop Emily up between them and take her to the car, struggling and squalling like a baby. Jane goes to the car with them.

Nobody says anything to me. It's like I'm not there. I wish somebody would tell me what is happening to us and where my mother is going.

She goes to a hospital in Virginia. Jane and I stay at home with Mamie or go to Gram's and the Greenhouse or Bessie's. Emily is gone six weeks. Not long enough, everybody says. She says she misses Jane and me too much. When Duke goes to get her, they tell him it is too soon for Emily to come home, that if she doesn't stop drinking she will die. She can't do it by herself—she isn't a strong person—he will have to stop, too. He says he will see to it that she doesn't drink and he won't drink either.

Within a few weeks they are both drinking again, and Emily is calling Connie for pills. "I can't stand it," she cries into the phone in her bedroom.

Silence.

"What about your sister's Nembutal?"

More tears.

"To hell with you."

Blam! The phone hits the receiver.

Someone calls Gram and tells her Emily is drunk at a motel out on the highway with a man she and Duke both know, another alcoholic. Gram calls Aunt Kate, and the two prim, gray-haired ladies in starched cotton dresses and sensible shoes drive out to this place "below town" and find her and lecture the man and bring my mother home.

Emily gets out of the car crying and so drunk she can hardly stand up. Her face looks twisted and strange, the way it looked the day she bloodied her head on the windshield and walked home.

Gram tells Mamie what happened and says, "No need to tell Duke."

Mamie says, "Yes'm, Miss Ila," with a blank face. Doesn't Gram know she knows better than that? Mamie looks like she's thinking about leaving again.

Emily goes to California to visit her friend Mary Helen and calls Connie every day and talks about leaving Duke. "All he wants," she says, "is to get his own way and make me suffer as much as possible. If I could stand being away from my children, I would never go back."

By the time she gets back, the leaves have started turning yellow on the trees. I stand on a chair by the stove, stirring custard with Eugene. The custard smells like vanilla and eggs. Emily is down by the pool, with her head in her hands on the fence. Duke follows her. As surely as if I could see through the walls, I know something is happening and get down from the chair to go see what it is.

Emily cries soft child-sobs into her hands. Her face is as soft and still as the face of a saint. She looks real to me for the first time in a long time. I want to touch her and stop her from crying.

"I want to take Judy and Jane and go back to 410 with Bessie," she says.

I see the muscle jerking in my father's jaw. "You can go," he says, "but I won't let you take them. I won't let them live that way."

Momma's hands hang limp at her sides. The air is perfectly still. I stand close to her, waiting . . . waiting . . . waiting for her to speak. She doesn't. Duke puts his hand on my shoulder. I pull away and walk toward the house with my mother. My father stands for a long time looking into the distance, with his shoulders hunched and his elbows on the fence. The suffering of my parents goes into me like something I have swallowed.

Pearl Harbor

Somehow, they decided to patch it up. Or, rather, sewed a patch over it. Duke was going to stop losing his temper, stop trying to make Emily do things she didn't want to do, stop blaming her for the death of their son. Emily would stop taking pills, do all the sensible things Gram and Duke told her to do, and (I heard it whispered) try to have another baby to make up for the one that had died. They were both going to stop drinking so much.

Emily starts getting out of bed in the mornings and taking us places like she used to. Her friends come to visit and sit in the yard. Mary Helen's mother—a calm, sweet-faced woman whom my mother loves—brings samples of cloth and wallpaper to help us decorate the house and stays a long time and talks to Emily about old times. Old times when she and Mary Helen were young and had no troubles and no one talked of war.

Duke wants to enlist, Emily says. Can you imagine? Why would a family man close to thirty years old want to risk his life for things that have nothing to do with him? "He can talk of *nothing* else," Emily says in the overly gay, overly inflected tones she and her friends cultivated as girls and still use among themselves. I stand between them at the front door in the almost visible stream of love that flows between my fragile mother and this sturdy, dark-haired woman who looks, to me, like somebody's fairy godmother.

Suddenly the tone of the conversation shifts and I hear something sharp in Emily's voice. "Things have been terrible for Duke and me, but they are better now. I think I'll die if he leaves me." She never had a father. She barely had a mother. She is terrified of being separated from her husband. She knew, of course, as everyone else did, that the United States would soon join the Allies in Europe, that there would be a draft, and that even men with children could go if they wanted to. Some people said they would take a man with two children but not three.

Time passes. Cold weather comes. On the weekends we listen to football games on the radio with Gram and Aunt Kate and wait for Duke to come back from Wilcox County with a sackful of doves and quail. He is such a good shot that he sometimes hits a bird right in the eye, or hits the same bird twice. We say, "Oh, the poor little things," and unload the warm pockets of his wet-smelling coat, which is always filled with the dead, warm-smelling, floppy-headed creatures. We go with our father from house to house, standing in the yards of black people and white people, giving the birds away, or Gram cooks them and there is a banquet of birds and grits and gravy, with much debate about which is best, the dark flesh of the dove or the delicate white meat and tiny bones of the quail.

Duke brings home a dozen wild ducks and keeps them with the roses in the icehouse at the Greenhouse. Gram gets out the white china and plated silver she and Jim had scrimped to buy, and for days there is talk of ways to get the "wild taste" out of the meat. Duke brings rough wooden tables from the Greenhouse and covers them with white tablecloths and napkins from our house, until the long field between Gram's house and Carter Hill Road looks like the setting for a biblical feast.

My father's prowess as a huntsman is celebrated by his Watson cousins and uncles (those expert countrymen) as well as the Patersons, most of whom say they know more about growing flowers than killing animals, not that they mind eating them or think anything is wrong with killing for food. For once, Duke is more important than all the rest, and he and Gram are together in a way I saw only a few times in my life, except when there was trouble.

Emily comes late and brings Bessie. It was one of the few times I ever saw Bessie (and never Knoxie) with that side of my family in that way. She is the only woman there wearing a hat and seems perfectly at home.

I watch from the porch, where I am playing with one of my cousins. We are using the window ledge and the burglar bars between the living room and the front porch as a counter from which to play "drugstore" with the glass medicine bottles Gram saves for us. The little chunks of amber, red, and blue look like the windows of a church shining in the sun.

I say, "I'm going to kindergarten this year," not knowing that the yellow leaves and the cool air mean another school year has started without me. My cousin is more interested in telling her customer that the product she has requested is "out for the duration" than in talking about school.

At 7:55 on Sunday morning, December 7, Japanese bombers attack the U.S. naval base at Pearl Harbor in Hawaii. By late afternoon, Duke has heard it on the radio and talked to everybody he knows on the phone. We go to Knoxie's apartment. People keep coming. Bessie orders spaghetti, garlic bread, and salad from the Tavern. Knoxie is exhilarated. This is the way her life should be, only isn't it terrible, all the men are going to war.

Duke says he is going as soon as the President calls for troops. He's able-bodied. He knows how to get things done. He can be of use, and he is not afraid. Hitler has already taken half the world, and the Japs want the rest. It wouldn't be right for him not to go, even if he could get out of it, which—with a family business, a sick wife, and two children—everyone knows he can. It goes without saying that, when there is something to be fought for, the Patersons fight.

Within a few days, the country is officially at war with Germany and Italy as well as Japan. By the end of the month, Duke has registered for the draft. Sonny is about to join General George Patton's Third Army in Europe and become a hero commanding a tank destroyer company in some of the fiercest fighting of the war. Mamie's LeRoy is going to be transferred to who-knows-where. Eugene signs up one day and leaves the next, headed—he says—for Paareee. Emily and Gram agree. Duke should stay home.

Gram knew there was no stopping Sonny, but she didn't think a widow who has lived her whole life on a pittance and never asked anything for herself ought to have to risk both her sons. She was also the only person I knew at that time who didn't share the country's enthusiasm for the war. "Maybe, even though the Bible says not to do it, people have to kill sometimes," she'd say, "but they don't have to act so happy about it."

Elliott Cobb, the son of a sister of Gram's who had died when the boy was young, is the one man in my grandmother's life who seems sure to stay home. Cobbie, as he was always called, had practically grown up at Gram's house with her sons and still lives there off and on. He is a graceful young man with dark curly hair who suffers from tuberculosis exacerbated by alcoholism; but when he is well enough, he works either at the Greenhouse or in an office downtown.

When he gets either too troublesome or too ill, Duke and Sonny come get him and take him back to his family in Wilcox County or out to the tuberculosis sanatorium they call the "fresh-air camp." When he comes back, everybody talks about how wonderful he looks, fat, rosy-cheeked, and (though they don't say it) sober. With every return, Gram—who loves her charming, immature nephew with an indulgence completely void of the strict standards she sets for her own sons—seems perfectly confident that this time her ministrations will restore her nephew to permanent health and sobriety.

Christmas comes. I go with Sonny and Gram to the fresh-air camp to take Cobbie his presents and a little pine tree decorated at the Greenhouse. We walk up a hill in cold air and find Cobbie standing in darkness on the screened porch of the rough little cabin where he lives. He is wearing a dark bathrobe that is too big for him. We stand outside. He wants us to come in. A nurse in a uniform takes the presents and tells us we can't go in because Cobbie is infected. Cobbie looks old and strange and starts to cry.

In memory I see a small child walking down a hill with two adults in bright sunshine. The woman has gray hair and thick glasses. She is starting to stoop; when she is tired, one of her eyes has a cast to it. The man is young and straight-backed, with a strawberry-blond mustache and a carnation in his lapel.

On the way back to town, Sonny tells the old story of how—when he was in college—he talked his country cousin into driving across country with him to California to see the Pacific Ocean. Pulling up to the beach at Santa Monica after many days on the road, they get out of the car and walk down to the ocean. "You know," Cobbie says, "I thought it would be bigger."

Sonny laughs. Gram shakes her head. "Thaaat *Cob*bie," she says. Love and sadness fill the car.

The new year brings more talk of the war in Europe. On February 9, Sonny takes Jane and me to Alabama State College for the Founder's Day celebration that is held every year on William Burns Paterson's birthday. We sit in a room full of colored people. All the men have on suits and the women wear hats and gloves. They read our ancestor's favorite poem in unison and sing "The Bluebells of Scotland." A man stands up and tells how he arrived at the college with just the clothes on his back and a few things in a "gunnysack" and Professor Paterson found him a job so he could learn to be a teacher. Now he is a professor himself, up North. Ahhh-men. Ahhh-men.

We are the only white people there: a small, Irish-looking man with a light-colored mustache and two towheaded children. The Patersons live by a great myth that both simplifies and complicates their lives and, in moments like this, transcends the terrible realities of race, class, and history by which we live.

Sonny tells the men who gather around him and shake his hand (only here do white men and black men shake one another's hands) that he is going to war. If they need anything, they should call his Uncle Will. They nod, because they already know this. My Great-uncle Will is on the Board of Education and is a friend of black education like his parents. Many of these people have known him since he was a little boy and lived on the campus, where Sonny himself had been born. They reminisce some more, and then we leave.

"What's a gunnysack?" I ask.

"Same as a croker sack," Sonny says.

Though I see that the talk of war is cause for excitement, I have no idea what it means. I don't know that people I love may be gone for a long time and may not come back. I have no idea that our lives are about to change forever.

By now, the Navy has begun recruiting the men who will become the Navy's construction battalions, otherwise known as the Seabees. As soon as he hears of it, Duke knows he wants to join the Navy's "Can-Do" battalions—"to carve roads and airstrips out of steaming jungles and frozen tundra; to drive a million pilings; to bulldoze mountains and bridge rivers; to assemble Quonset huts by the thousands; to hit beaches with Marines and soldiers and then bring the stuff ashore; to endure mud and rain and loneliness and death, yet always be ready to drop the work and grab guns."

He knows how to build things and he knows how to work men and he hates to be idle. He hates to sit by. Sometimes it seems as if all he has done since the day he married Emily is "sit by."

By the time he finds out how to get in the Seabees, Emily is pregnant again, trying to gain weight, stay healthy for the baby, and do whatever else she can to keep Duke from leaving. He agrees to wait until the baby is born. But after that, he is going, he says, if there is still a war to go to.

Summer comes. Emily is nearly manic with enthusiasm for the pregnancy and her new health regime, doing everything the doctor tells her to do and obeying all the old wives' tales she hears. They say drink buttermilk, she drinks the terrible stuff. They say gain weight, she eats constantly.

"Soon I'll be all belly, like the Little King in the cartoon," she says, patting her stomach. She doesn't say, "I'm not drinking at all," but I know that is what her resolutions mean—and know by now how unlikely they are to be kept. I watch her standing in the sunlight in the back doorway patting her stomach. A hard, chest-shattering anger battles with the hope I have to keep hoping in order to live. Another big belly. Another baby. More sickness. More fear. More drinking. And then: Why can't she just act right and look after me? Why can't she be like Gram? Why can't somebody else be my mother?

If the anger was followed by fear of retribution, I don't remember it. What I remember is the false timbre of Emily's gaiety and the image of her belly like a ball under the red-and-blue fabric of her skirt, and the force of my anger followed by the hopelessness that accompanied it and a deeper loneliness than I knew existed. I want my mother to mother me. I want our suffering to stop.

James H.'s wife, Evelyn, comes and sits outside with Emily. Jane and I play in the shallow end of the pool with our cousins Anne and Melbourne for a long time and nobody makes us get out. Evelyn is leaving James H. and going to work as a secretary at the air base. All the money is gone. She doesn't know how she will manage.

After they leave, Emily starts talking to Duke about adopting our cousins. She talks and talks. She is so happy. She is feeling so good. She is going to call Gram and tell her. After all, they are her own brother's children. She always wanted a big family. The bigger the better.

The look on my father's face is pure horror. Gram comes and they talk Emily out of it. Our cousins move away and we don't see them again for a very long time.

We go with Emily and Gram to the drugstore across from Cloverdale School and sit at a round table in bentwood chairs and drink chocolate malted milk shakes made at a lunch counter that serves everything from cherry Cokes to homemade vegetable soup. Jane and I are drinking our drinks and looking at a box of squashy plastic balls full of bubble bath. Emily gets up to go to the back of the store to talk to the pharmacist.

I can tell by the jerky way she walks that—even though it is still morning—she is already inebriated. My heart sinks. I start to squirm in my chair and kick one foot on the base of the table. Maybe I'm wrong. Maybe if I don't say anything it won't be true. My throat fills with cotton. Don't scream. Don't speak. Don't breathe.

"Don't do anything to make it worse" freezes me in my seat and sets my heart thumping.

Gram, of course, already knows. She takes us to the car and goes back to get Emily. They come out with the pharmacist.

Emily is crying. The pharmacist says, "Dr. Ross told me to give Connie whatever she wanted for Emily, but not to give anything to Emily herself. But she was so pitiful I did it a few times anyway. I can't do it again."

"Well, I should think *not*," Gram says, as if it were that simple, which I can see from the look in her eyes she knows it isn't. Her

125

common-sense solutions have met their match. Who in the name of thunder is to blame for all this trouble, and where in the world will it end?

The sight of an old-fashioned food counter or the taste of malt on my tongue always brings the moment back. My addicted mother. My helpless grandmother. My throat clogged with cotton.

For whatever reason (something that was said that day? the proximity of the pharmacy to the city kindergarten or the school I later attended? a slant of light in one memory evoking another?), I associate that morning with my belated realization that my cousins have started another year of kindergarten without me. Duke and Gram say I have to wait until Jane is old enough to go with me. Emily needs me at home with her and my sister.

Jane's a whiny baby. I'm old enough. She's not. They promised. "My mother doesn't love me" digs into my heart like a spade in soft dirt. If she loved me, she would stop drinking and having babies and start paying attention to me and people would stop breaking their promises.

In memory I stand forever motionless on the sidewalk in front of the Cloverdale Pharmacy and wait for the day to come when my mother will love me again the way she did (or so it seems to me) before the babies started dying and new addictions planted new troubles between her and my father and heightened their obsession with each other and their inattention to me and my sister.

In that moment, waiting (waiting to go to kindergarten, waiting for Emily to stop drinking and taking drugs, waiting to feel safe with her again) becomes forever linked in my mind to being unloved by my mother—both not having her love and not being entitled to it, a set of feelings that came in part, I believe, from the events of those years and in part from a sense of hopelessness so deep in her that it seems to have passed from her to me by a transfer of emotion as palpable as a blood transfusion.

I loved my troubled mother with a tenderness and a need that is hard to describe, though it has become easy to remember. I wanted to be near her, to touch her, to belong to her. Almost as much as I wanted her to look after me and my sister, I wanted to be able to look after her—to do for her (and perhaps, by extension, for myself) what she was no longer able to do for either herself or us. If I could have, I would have followed her even into the blackness into which she was sinking.

Sheeps and Goats

Bessie and I are home at her house for the night, sitting propped up on pillows at the head of the rose-canopied bed that had been too short for Prince Albert. Bessie is wearing a cheap terry-cloth robe and cloth slippers run over at the sides. Her graying hair hangs loose on her neck and her upper lip is almost as whiskery as a man's. She smells like talcum powder, Listerine, and lavender cologne and perches her half glasses so low on her nose that she has to breathe through her mouth to read from the big illustrated copy of *The Three Billy Goats Gruff* she holds in her lap.

Reading in the methodical manner of her ancestors sitting in their parlors taking turns with a Greek play or a Victorian novel, Bessie gives each character a different voice and brings all the drama of a Shakespearean chronicle to the little saga of goats and trolls. I listen as expectantly as if the wisdom of the ages is falling on my ears, which perhaps it is. After all, the goats set out on a quest and brave danger and terror and learn a thing or two and get what they want—though it is clear enough that they might just as easily have been mauled or eaten alive.

The pages are big, with pink-and-blue pictures, and only a few words on each page. After I recognize the word "trip" (as in "trip-trap," which Bessie delivers in a prolonged, phonetic drawl . . . tuuuuu*rrr*ip . . . tuuuuu*rrrra*p), she starts teaching me to read and spell, casually and unsystematically, to be sure, since we are both more interested in the goats getting over the bridge than in anything else.

"Do you want to hear about Queen Victoria and Prince Albert?" she asks. "Do you want to hear about Grandmother Jane and the Yankees?"

"No," I say. "Read."

Sometimes I sit in Duke's lap at home and he reads *Little Orphan Annie* to me out of the newspaper. I don't understand it at all, but I like to sit there and I like the scholarly tone of his reading voice—learned, I like to imagine, from his father, who may have learned it from his father, the old professor, who taught it to himself sitting on a dirt floor in front of a peat fire in a peasant's cottage at the foot of the Highlands in Scotland. I hear Duke intoning to Emily in bed on nights when she can't sleep and hear the library-book cellophane crinkling in his hands.

Some time after Pearl Harbor, while men all around him go to war (men ten years younger than he, without responsibilities, Emily with her growing belly keeps reminding him), Duke buys fifty sheep to graze in the country, thinking they will keep the grass cropped in front of the house and he can contribute to the war effort and make money selling wool to the government and lambs to the butcher. Jane and I are only mildly interested in the sheep that now occupy our long front yard—stupid-looking, oily-smelling creatures with fat, matronly bodies and pink eyes set so far apart on their heads that we marvel they can see in front of themselves at all.

We are very interested in the sheep-wisdom that prevents the creatures (not as stupid, maybe, as they look) from putting their feet on the cattle gap Duke builds at the entrance to the driveway to keep them from getting out. Sometimes Shag chases them and they look like fat ladies running in high heels.

Along with the sheep come two other creatures that are of much greater interest to us: a pet goat named Lambie-Pie and a black-and-brown sheepdog puppy we name Martha. Lambie-Pie lives in a shed on the edge of the pasture behind the house and eats anything we feed him, from table scraps to old rags and newspapers. We try to get him to eat other things, like wood and pieces of metal, which he won't do. Hattie Jo tries to ride his bony back but gets bucked off. She says I should try it because I am so small he might not mind. Mary Willie saves me the humiliation of admitting I am scared to try it by telling me not to do it.

Martha sleeps with Jane one night and me the next and demonstrates absolutely no interest in the sheep. Emily thinks this is funny. Duke says he is going to find somebody to train her. He likes Lambie-Pie a lot and associates farm animals and pets with family life as he knew it before his own father died.

Martha and Lambie-Pie don't like each other at all. Martha bites Lambie-Pie's feet and Lambie-Pie butts and kicks at her and does everything he can to keep her out of his shed. One day when Martha is about six months old and already bigger than Shag, she goes to the shed alone and bites Lambie-Pie's tail completely off, leaving only an angry red sore where his tail had been. We think this is pretty amazing but expect Lambie-Pie to get well and live happily ever after without a tail. So does everybody else.

A few days later, Duke and I are walking in the yard. He says, "Let's go see how Lambie-Pie is getting along without his tail." We open the door to the shed and find the goat lying in the dirt on his back, kicking and twisting and making a strange high noise like a bird's. I don't need anybody to tell me that Lambie-Pie is dying.

My father, who a few minutes before had been walking with me in the sunshine toward the shed, now stands in front of me looking dark and bloated as if his whole body were being pumped full of some gaseous combination of hatred, horror, and grief, his mind leaping to the possibility that Martha has rabies and that our world is about to come tumbling down. What if she bites Jane or me or Hattie Jo or somebody else? What if she has already bitten someone and they just aren't sick yet?

Although I don't know it at the time, I am seeing the evidence of my father's extreme fear (made all but unbearable by being wedded to a deep-branded memory and the expectation that what happened once can—and probably will—happen again) of something terrible happening to someone he loves or is responsible for. And standing behind the fear is the guilt—that if somehow he had been a better person or more farseeing or more alert, whatever it is that has happened (this time) wouldn't have happened (this time or ever). And if only he can be more (and more and more) vigilant in the future, it will never (ever, ever) happen again. And behind the guilt is rage and fury at himself and everybody else who has any connection with the thing that has happened—and the belief that fear, error, sorrow, and the need for comfort are not allowed.

Standing in darkness in the middle of the shed, he sees everybody he loves suffering and dying like Lambie-Pie, and sees himself as condemned by his own helplessness. Just as automatically, and simultaneously, he associates every sorrow that lands on his doorstep with the terrible suffering of the father who had been soul mate as well as companion and guide to the wistful, temperamental child he had been until his father's death turned him into the sullen, rebellious adolescent he sometimes still is. For as long as he lives, I will see him transmute so instantly and so totally out of one demeanor into another that it begins to seem impossible that the two could belong to the same person—until, finally, I grow to fear the one and love the other as separately as if my father were, in fact, two different people. The mingling of love and terror and the division between nurturing and rejecting were, I believe, too extreme in him for the man himself—much less anybody else—to have any idea who he would be at any given moment.

At five-going-on-six, I am bound to him by his every move and absorb rage, fear, resentment, guilt, arrogance, love, joy, freedom, wisdom, and sorrow as mutually as if they were identical drops of rain falling from the sky. And with the raindrops comes the conviction that whatever he feels in my presence was caused by me. Better for a child, I suppose, to think that something she did (and therefore can stop doing) caused the trouble than to realize, admit, accept, understand that the father on whom she depends is as emotionally erratic and undependable as the mother who drifts in and out of her life like a cloud. Better all the guilt, premature accountability, and hypervigilance in the world than the fear-sorrow-loneliness of knowing that both her parents are unreliable and she is alone.

"Get out of here, Judy. Get *out* of here," Duke says, staring at Lambie-Pie twisting in the dirt. I feel the fear in his fury and think we are in danger; I feel the anger and think I have done something wrong. He strides toward the house like an infuriated giant. I follow behind him, squinting into the sun like the Lilliputian I am.

Though there doesn't seem to be anything wrong with Martha except that she doesn't like Lambie-Pie, she is taken away and either shot or put to sleep. I have no memory of how I know this. I must have seen my father go to the house and get her and take her to the car. If there was a shot, I may have heard it. I am sure I didn't see it. What I know is that the memory fills me with terror. And that the blackness in my father seems derived from the very heart of chaos itself.

Emily is sober now, waiting for a new baby to be born, sitting with a big stomach in the sunroom or on her bed, reading the bright-covered novels she gets from the lending library at Amy's Gift Shop. I spend as much time at Gram's and the Greenhouse (which now encompasses 250,000 square feet under glass and many acres planted outside) as I do in the country. I go with Duke in the mornings and eat breakfast with Gram, who pours sweet coffee and milk into a bowl for me and lets me thicken it with pieces of hard buttered toast she calls "fishes and frogs."

Gram's days start early and follow a pattern as rural as if she had never left Wilcox County. She cleans house, feeds chickens, churns butter, and harvests pecans, figs, and pears from the trees around her house. In the afternoon she collects eggs, makes supper, listens to the radio, and sews. If a chicken is to be cooked, she catches it in a burlap sack, takes it to a special place in the back yard, wrings its neck with a flick of her wrist, plucks it, scorches the last feathers with a torch made of newspaper, cuts it up, and either fries it or makes a dumpling stew.

Halfway through the morning, she sends me to get an RC Cola out of the drink box at the Greenhouse. "Be sure you get the RC," she says. "It's bigger than a Coke." Gram pronounces RC "ahh-see." The black people at the Greenhouse say "are-ro-see." An RC is big enough for her to divide three ways between me, herself, and Pearlie, the black woman who comes every day to help her with the housework and the chickens.

Pearlie is as black and gaunt as her ancestors must have been the day they got off the slave ships that brought them to America. Though she can't read, write, or tell time, she can count and make change and she knows all there is to know about raising chickens. On Mondays she washes Gram's clothes and boils them (which Gram says is the only way to get them really clean) in a black wrought-iron pot set on an open fire in the back yard.

Scary things hardly ever happen at Gram's. If I want to, I can walk to the Greenhouse by myself and see my father, whose work-days consist of walking through the Greenhouse all day, looking at things, giving instructions, pinching leaves and shoots, rubbing dirt between his fingers, seldom slowing his pace, gliding like a man being carried by the muddy, sun-speckled earth itself rather than his own two feet. His closet, his car, his clothes, everything he owns is permeated with the Greenhouse smell of earth, fertilizer, chemicalized water, and human sweat. "Fresh sweat never smells bad," Duke says, and I agree.

He shows me a full, golden-hued rose called Talisman that smells like honey and is so beautiful I think God must have made it for some princess or queen. After that, the Talisman roses belong to me. They bloom in two concrete beds at the back of the Greenhouse, remote and precious behind rows and rows of ordinary reds, whites, yellows, and pinks.

Black and white women sort roses in special "grading houses" lined with long tables. They stand there all morning, gossiping and singing, separating the flowers—still pebbled with water— into bunches they put in tin buckets and carry to the refrigerated storage room. Grainy with dirt, their hands dance to the songs they sing.

Unlike many of the flower-growing men who sometimes stay for a lifetime and pass their jobs on to their sons, the women rose graders come and go in nameless, itinerant shifts. A giant of a black woman named Gussie is the exception. The self-appointed boss of the "grading house," Gussie is there from my earliest memories until her death in the 1970s.

Gram doesn't enjoy the company of black people as much as either the Patersons or the Ware–Walkers. In Wilcox County (where three-fourths of the people were black as coal, where most of the white people looked as Scotch-Irish as their ancestors had looked in Ulster), people like the Watsons had struggled too long and pitted too much freelance sweat and pride against blacks (first as slaves, then as tenants) to have much sympathy for a people whose presence threatened (as they saw it) all they had gained by sacrifice, endurance, and a rock-hard solidarity of class and race.

As a rule, the Watsons of Wilcox County had little use for either the descendants of slaves or the planters who had owned them, thinking both classes frivolous and indolent compared to plain, hardworking people like themselves. Somehow, despite all that, Gram and Gussie nurture a friendship that lasts half a century. Gussie brings Gram flowers and plants that would otherwise be thrown away. In return, Gram gives Gussie clothes to take to poor people and sometimes makes Gussie lunch, which she eats either inside at the kitchen table or outside on the back steps. Neither of them would have dared break the taboo that forbade them to sit down together and eat at the same table, though Mary Willie and Emily do it all the time when Duke is away.

Sometimes Gussie eats on the steps in silence, washed in the sunlight that pours through the branches of the pecan, mulberry, and persimmon trees that shelter the house. Sometimes I sit with her and she talks.

"I love pot liquor; that's how I got so *big*. You want to be big as Gussie, eat your grammy's greens and pot liquor," she says, soaking the bread in the tart gray juice. "Your daddy always did lose his temper, and now he's gotten to drinking . . . No need to tell Miss Ila I said so."

The Greenhouse and the Highland Avenue Baptist Church are the two poles of Gram's life. For sixty years, she tends the small needs of many people in the maze of little streets that connect the two places, going about her work with the methodical devotion of a nun or an old-fashioned welfare worker, distributing whatever she can find or beg or spare herself to whoever needs it most.

Sometimes I go with her. We take people to the doctor, the grocery store, the nursing home, the cemetery. We take cooked food, plants, and magazines up tall, dark steps and into tiny apartments that smell like cabbage, mothballs, and dust. Climbing dark stairs, carrying whatever I am big enough to carry, holding her hand, I learn one of the meanings of love.

Sometimes we stop at Pop's concession stand, where Oak Park faces Highland Avenue, and buy hot, dry popcorn or roasted peanuts in paper bags. We don't do that often, because Gram doesn't like to spend the money. Sometimes Uncle Sonny gives me two nickels and Gram and I sit on a bench in the park and split a bag of peanuts and a Coke so cold ice floats in it.

One day Jane and I go with Pearlie and Gram to feed the chickens and we find the usually placid creatures squawking and flapping and huddling in the corner of their pen opposite the henhouse where they lay their eggs. The henhouse—which is nothing more than a big, windowless shed with straw-lined planks built along the sides where the hens roost—is usually as peaceful and dark as a tomb. Today something is so wrong inside the shed that the hens huddle at the other end of their pen and refuse to go near it.

We peek inside and don't see anything. Gram suspects rats and calls Aunt Burton to come over with her "rat terrier," Tiny. Aunt Burton and Uncle Will live a short walk from Gram's, on the other side of the Greenhouse. Because Aunt Burton has arthritis, she and Tiny come in the car. We turn Tiny loose in the henhouse and he goes crazy, running into the walls and yelping and scratching so ferociously that we all get scared and run out. Aunt Burton is afraid whatever Tiny has found will kill him. Gram scoffs at first, and then her brow starts to wrinkle.

Aunt Burton stands at the door of the henhouse and calls, "Tiny, Tiny, come here, Tiny." But Tiny doesn't come.

Jane and Gram and Aunt Burton and I stand outside and listen for a long time to the terrible, invisible battle being waged inside the shed. Aunt Burton is on the verge of tears, and Gram gets more nervous and upset than I have ever seen her before. Finally, Tiny exits, covered in blood and bearing the still-squirming body of a rat almost as big as he is.

Tiny's battle was just scary enough to be exciting. But the scariest thing that ever happened at Gram's was of a very different sort and also involved Aunt Burton.

I am visiting Gram's with my cousin Margaret, who is three

years older than I am. Gram takes us to Aunt Burton's in the car. Gram and Aunt Burton sit in chairs in the yard and talk. Margaret and I play in the forest of bamboo that grows between Aunt Burton's and the Greenhouse. Margaret wants to trick Gram by hiding from her in the bamboo when she gets ready to leave. I don't want to do it, but I let my cousin talk me into it. We do it. Gram and Aunt Burton can't find us. They look scared.

I don't like Gram to be scared. I don't like what we are doing. "Let's come out," I say.

"No," Margaret says. "It's working. This is fun."

Aunt Burton and Gram run into the house and around to the front yard and back toward the Greenhouse. Gram walks fast to her house and back, an old lady with gray hair wearing a gray dress, running and afraid. We get in the backseat of the car and lie down on the floor. Gram comes and takes the car home and parks it in the tin-roofed shed that serves as a garage. She still doesn't see us. We lie there a long time.

"Please, Margaret, let's go in and tell her we are all right."

"No."

Finally, I don't know how, Gram finds us. It is the only time I ever saw her really mad. Only she doesn't look mad. She looks sad, old, and afraid. She spanks Margaret and not me. Margaret hides under the bed until her mother comes to get her.

I think Gram is very smart to know it is not my fault and to spank Margaret and not me, but I can't stop feeling bad and wishing we hadn't done it. My grandmother is the bedrock of my life. I don't want anything bad to happen to her. I don't want anything bad to be my fault.

137

Pass the Ammunition

 I was six years old in the fall of 1942. General Dwight D. Eisenhower had been made commander of U.S. forces in Europe and was about to take some 400,000 U.S. servicemen to Morocco and Algeria in North Africa. The Germans had attacked Stalingrad. Close to one-third of Europe's 9 million Jews had already been exterminated. Gasoline, coffee, and other foods were being rationed at home, and all the men were going to war.

Emily says Duke's place is to do all he can at home for a family that has already sent most of its men to fight for no reason. He says what he has always said, that the war is about freedom and courage and everybody who can go, must. The women could run the business. With Gram and Mary Willie to help, Emily would be fine. And he would be home in no time, having done his duty (and seen the world and escaped their heartbreaking marriage for a while).

Gram takes Jane and me for our first day at Mrs. Helen Cottingham's kindergarten. The school is in a long, one-room, many-windowed building in the yard behind the house where Mrs. Cottingham lives with her banker-husband, not far from Gram's house and the Greenhouse. It is not the same place where I saw the puppets do *Cinderella* and *Little Red Ridinghood*, but it is near there and seems the same to me. There are trees, swing sets, and sandboxes outside; long tables, paint sets, and easels inside. I know some of the children already and like the place as soon as I see it.

My sister and I sit in a circle of children listening to Miss Helen (as everyone calls her) telling about the school. She is plump and middle-aged, but handsome and stylishly dressed, with the dramatic flair and husky voice of a woman who has done her share of smoking and drinking. The flair reminds me of my Aunt Kitty and my Grandmother Knoxie. She talks to children as if they were grownups, and I am immediately taken with her.

Jane and I are wearing hand-smocked, pastel, pima-cotton dresses. These dresses are de rigueur for girls at Miss Helen's. Some of the dresses are works of art, and most of the mothers make them themselves. Emily pays the best seamstress in town to make ours. My favorite is a pale bluish-gray with dark smocking, soft as swaddling and so light it feels like wearing nothing at all. Gram thinks it is unladylike that I like to sit with my feet in the chair, either cross-legged or with one knee propped under my chin, thereby exposing the white ruffled underpants that are as requisite as the smocked dresses for girls at Miss Helen's.

We sit at the tables and sing songs and drink apple juice and eat ice cream cut in flat squares and decorated red, white, and blue like the American flag. Gram sits across the room, gesturing to me and mouthing, *"Get . . . your . . . feet . . . down."* I pretend I don't understand what she is saying.

We sing "America the Beautiful," "The Caissons Go Rolling Along," and "Praise the Lord and Pass the Ammunition." Afterwards, Gram tells Emily and Duke she thinks "Praise the Lord and Pass the Ammunition" is sacrilegious—as if the Lord condoned all that killing.

We stand up and act out "I'm a little teapot short and stout, tip me over and pour me out." We get in a long line and chug around the room, singing, "Coming down the track, track, track, smoke upon my back, back, back . . . little red caboose upon the tr-aa-iinn." Kindergarten is just the way I thought it would be. One day a boy named Bert is swinging by himself on a swing at the far end of the playground. I'm playing with Jane and some others closer to the building. We call him to join us. He swings harder and harder, chanting louder and louder, "She's too pretty for me. She's too *pret*-tiii for meeee." Finally, I realize he is saying I'm too pretty for him to play with.

At six, I am an energetic, sturdy-looking child with sparse white-blond hair and the kind of round-featured face that people called cute. I don't like to be looked at the way people look at me when they take my picture and I'm almost always either scowling or looking glum in photographs taken at that time. The only other quality that stands out in my looks is a sort of blank-faced ability to focus my attention in a way that my father says makes me look like a bird dog pointing a quail. I am a child who had rather observe than be observed.

I don't like Bert saying what he is saying, because it makes the others look at me too hard. I feel my face going sullen and decide to pretend I don't hear him. I don't like children who say stupid things and make trouble when there isn't any.

Gram comes to get us. Jane tells her what Bert said. Gram says, "Well, *pretty* is as *pretty* does." I only vaguely understand the equation. I'm just embarrassed and irritated with my sister for telling about it.

"Well, he did *say* it," Jane says. "You know he did."

"That doesn't mean you have to *tell* it. Some things are too stupid to tell."

"They are not."

Jane and I are still arguing about what you should and shouldn't tell when Gram tells us we have another sister, born full-term but weighing less than four pounds and with an exposed thymus gland that has to be repaired before she is even given a name. Emily comes home but the baby doesn't. Finally, they decide the baby is going to live and name her Joan Elizabeth. The Elizabeth is for Aunt Bessie and goes back in Momma's family at least as far as Judith Anthony Ware's mother, who was born Elizabeth Clarke in 1720 and became a Quaker preacher and died at almost a hundred, leaving three hundred descendants split between slave-holding and abolition. The Joan is to keep the alliteration going with me and Jane and because Duke's real name, Julius, also begins with a "J" and they know that if they ever have another boy his name will be Jim, like our brother who died.

A few weeks later, Bessie takes Jane and me downtown to see Walt Disney's *Bambi*, and when we get home, our new sister is there, a tiny, brown-skinned morsel, hardly human to look at, too feeble to cry, and determined to live. Her chest sinks in the middle as if it had been crushed by a fist. Her breath goes in and out in harsh, wheezy gasps that can be heard all over the house. Jane sits on the floor beside her, deeply identified with her damaged sister, believing her presence is what keeps the baby alive. I don't want her to die. I wish she'd stop making that noise.

The very sight of the baby is a reproach to Emily, who can hardly bear to look at her. Not only was the new baby supposed to be healthy, she was supposed to be a boy, and she was supposed to keep Duke home from the war. My mother must have known, too, that everybody thought her drinking and poor health habits had harmed the child. Bessie loves Joan because she is named for her. Duke's heart goes out to her because she is so weak and helpless. Gram and Mamie take turns feeding her with a tiny bottle. As for me, I have come to think of her determination to survive and grow from such a start without a mother's love as one of the bravest things I ever saw in our family.

In a year strangely empty of memories of my mother, one incident stands out. I am running through the schoolroom at Miss Helen's. The child ahead of me slams a many-windowed door in my face. My hand goes through one of the glass panes. Though the cuts are tiny and hardly hurt at all, orange blood speckles the floor. Miss Helen wraps my hand in a big gauze bandage and makes me the wounded hero of the day, singling me out in all the games and telling everybody how brave I am.

When the time comes to go home, I find Emily waiting for me in the car with Duke. I know Miss Helen must have called them; otherwise, my mother wouldn't be there. Emily unwraps my hand, smiles at the little cuts, and slumps back in the seat where she is sitting next to my father. She looks like a doll propped up in a chair. I think Daddy went to get her and made her come and she is saying, "See, there is no need for me to be here." She doesn't seem angry with either him or me, just exhausted, sunk so deep inside herself that she seems hardly to be there at all.

Even though it is one of the big occasions of the Paterson year, Emily doesn't go with us on Thanksgiving to watch the black high-school and college bands parade down Dexter Avenue, heralding the annual football rivalry between Alabama State College and Tuskegee Institute. The event is both a reunion of family and old friends and a commemoration, with everybody gathered in the long, bare, second-story rooms where the first Rosemont Gardens store had been, above a hot-dog stand run by a Greek named Chris Katechis.

We eat hot dogs that cost five cents each and have a light, garlicky flavor all their own. Duke says they taste that way because Mr. Chris has been boiling them in the same water for thirty years. "That's right, son," Mr. Chris says, "and that's about how long you've been eatin' twice as many as you pay for." He marks on the bottom of a cigar box, with a pencil, how many hot dogs we eat. Once in a while, somebody comes from the new Rosemont Gardens store on Perry Street and pays up for everybody; then Chris erases the tally and starts over.

We hear how people used to gather at the old Rosemont and

Chris's to talk politics and do business and leave their belongings while they shopped. If someone forgot a package, the first Will Paterson would either send it to its owner by one of his sons or return it himself.

I see a sweet-faced old man in a worn suit, still running the school that had once been Alabama's first Normal School for Negroes, driving a horse and buggy (perhaps remembering the dairy wagon his father had driven to keep bread on the table in Tullibody) laden with fresh flowers, potted plants, and forgotten parcels. Although the business produced enough income to educate Will's sons and bring them all into the business, they lived out of the cash register day-to-day with a loaves-and-fishes kind of faith, harking back to the days when flowers were grown and sold to feed the family and meet whatever need happened to be most pressing.

Every Thanksgiving, somebody tells how Chris advanced the Rosemont payroll during the Depression. "When people were buying hot dogs but not flowers," somebody always says. They talk about my Grandfather Jim, "the one who made the roses grow" and "bootlegged all that whiskey back from Cuba in a motorboat and bought that Roamer touring car and would have gone again if Miss Ila hadn't stopped him."

We stand in the window above Chris's hot-dog stand and watch the Alabama State marchers strut by in yellow-and-black uniforms. Light bounces off their instruments and into our eyes. Flags blow in cool air. We clap and yell. Everybody agrees that State's band is better than Tuskegee's. We inherit the rivalry without knowing that it goes back five decades to Booker T. Washington's bitterness at having Will's established school put so close to the one he was just starting.

My mother's ancestors bought and sold slaves not far from where we stand. From here, they watched Jefferson Davis being inaugurated President of the Confederacy and four years later saw a parade of Federal cavalrymen march up to the Capitol, replant the Stars and Stripes, and declare the Confederacy dead. From here, we can see the Dexter Avenue Baptist Church, from which in less than fifteen years the college community my great-grandparents built will mastermind the bus boycott that will catapult the young Reverend Martin Luther King, Jr., to national prominence and make Montgomery the birthplace of a civil-rights movement powerful beyond what anybody standing there in 1942 would have been able to imagine.

After the parade, my sister and I go back to the Greenhouse with some of our cousins and watch Duke load white-and-yellow chrysanthemums into a truck to take to the playing field. We eat turkey at Gram's, and sometimes Duke and his brother and cousins go to the State–Tuskegee game with their uncles, who grew up at the college and by their own athletic prowess convinced their father of the importance of college sports.

Most of my memories of that year take place either at Gram's house or at Miss Helen's kindergarten. Though my grandmother's house is plain, it is fairly spacious, with two middle-sized bedrooms in addition to the large one Gram both sleeps in and uses for a sitting room. All are heated by open gas heaters and sometimes the sheets on the beds in the back bedrooms are almost unbearably cold. Jane and I share a double bed in one of those rooms (unless circumstances require us to double up with one of the grownups). The third room has two single beds and is almost always occupied by one or more of Gram's visitors.

Gram's retarded sister, Babe, often stays for long periods of time. When she isn't sitting alone in the living room making quilts from the scraps Gram collects for her, she plays with us like another child, teaching us riddles and folk facts that we like to hear but don't believe. She says if we stand on our heads too long, our livers will turn upside down and we will die. Though she imparts this information with a smile on her face, she really doesn't like for us to stand or lie with our heads beneath our feet for long. She thinks it is very unhealthy for people to eat too much, and when we do, she puffs her stomach up like a drum and pounds on it to a riddle that starts "Tom . . . Tom . . . greedy gut . . . greedy gut" and goes on to describe the calamities that befall poor greedy Tom.

Because our tubercular cousin, Cobbie, stays with Gram only when he is well enough and sober enough to work and go about his own affairs, we see him only at breakfast. Though we take little interest in Cobbie, we are very interested in his disease. Every morning after he leaves, Gram boils his dishes and utensils in a big pot on the stove and puts them in a special place, so nobody else will use them by mistake. Gram, Sonny, and Duke are very tolerant and solicitous of Cobbie, who they think is dying, which he does in 1948, a few months after his thirty-ninth birthday, having spent the last few years of his life in a sanatorium in Colorado.

Aunt Kate, Aunt Babe, and Cobbie are regulars at Gram's house in the years before the war, and there are others as well, mostly kinfolks from Wilcox County coming to shop or see a doctor or visit someone in the hospital. Occasionally, there is someone extraordinary.

Some time in 1943, just as Duke is getting ready to leave for the war, we have the excitement of a visit from a friend Gram and Aunt Kate call Sparrow, who, as a young working woman, had boarded with Aunt Kate and lived there like a member of the family for almost twenty years, helping her rear her children and brightening a household darkened by the death of the older woman's husband. Because Sparrow is a tiny, spirited person who sings all the time, I naturally attribute her name to her bird-like qualities. In fact, she had garnered the nickname (though surely it would not have stuck if it hadn't been so suitable) from a brief, youthful marriage to a Mr. Sparrenberger, whose name she kept.

Sparrow was the first (and for a long time the only) woman I knew who looked and lived and acted like what has come to be known as a "professional woman." She must have been in her middle fifties in 1943 (not much younger than Gram and Aunt Kate, though she seemed much younger to me), and had already lived a decade (and would live another) beyond the cancer that was supposed to kill her, and become a successful life-insurance saleswoman, first in Montgomery and then in Chattanooga.

She comes from Chattanooga on the train and arrives at Gram's in a taxi, wearing high-heeled shoes, a blouse with a bow at the neck, and a bright blue suit perfectly tailored to her tiny frame. She breathes freedom, opportunity, and travel, unlike anything I have ever seen in a woman before.

Gram and Aunt Kate stay up almost all night talking and listening to Sparrow and laughing in a way I never heard them laugh before, as if all the constraints of their hard-lived lives had fallen away and left them young again. And I am left with the image of the three of them sitting in flannel nightgowns around an open gas heater, laughing and joking and growing young before my incredulous eyes. My grandmother's enthusiasm plus the re-membered excitement of wartime travel link Sparrow's visit with one of the rare appearances of our exotic cousin, Edgar Flack.

Cousin Edgar was a nephew of my Great-grandmother Maggie Flack Paterson, and the only one of our Northern cousins we ever saw. He was fifty years old in 1943 and had traveled the world many times over in the Merchant Marine. He kept no permanent address except "Rosemont Gardens, Montgomery, Alabama," and had few family connections other than his Paterson kin—so few, in fact, that when he died in New Orleans in 1956 his body was brought to Montgomery and placed beside his missionary aunt and uncle in the Negro section of Oakwood Cemetery.

Though Edgar Flack's visits were always cause for celebration (what strange gifts had he brought this time, and from what far-off place had he come?), his cosmopolitan ways were sometimes more than his small-town kin could take. Like the time Aunt

Burton had to call Uncle Will home from the store to deal with his cousin, who was sunbathing naked in the back yard in plain view of the road, the Greenhouse, and my grandmother's front porch.

I don't know whether that happened during the same visit I remember or on another one like it. What I remember is a strong-bodied, red-faced, big-headed man in a white uniform and cap walking up to Gram's seldom-used front door and being greeted "like somebody come." It is the only time I ever remember my grandmother behaving in a way that implied the superiority of the other person. Perhaps what I see is simply her pleasure at having the family celebrity call on her at home. Perhaps it is my plainspoken grandmother going timid in the face of the question she finally asks.

What does Edgar know about the Seabees, the construction battalions of the Navy? Duke wants to join before he is drafted into some branch of the service that doesn't suit him, though everybody knows he could get out of going if he wanted to.

"Grand, grand," Edgar blusters. "Couldn't do better . . . go some places . . . do some good . . . might not get shot."

Gram is reassured, and I am aware for the first time that my father might be leaving, though it is impossible for me to imagine his absence. Nor can I imagine his death, though I have long imagined my mother's.

It was in the same newly enclosed back porch facing the Green-house, where Edgar sat in his white uniform with his cap in his lap and told Gram about the Seabees, that I heard the only theo-logical discussion I ever heard in my family. Gram and Aunt Kate sit in the glassed-in back porch with their separate Singer sewing machines set up to take advantage of the afternoon light coming in the windows. Jane and I sit at their feet, sewing something for our dolls and debating whether you thread a needle toward you or away from you. Gram and Aunt Kate think we are very astute to ask such a thing and settle the argument by saying it can be done either way. They keep talking. Something in Gram's tone catches my ear.

"You know, Carol," she says, calling her friend by her first name and emphasizing the last syllable as she does only in moments of relaxation and closeness, "sometimes I wonder what Jesus really *is*. I mean, what *are* we supposed to think it all means . . . somebody rising from the dead like that?"

Drawing herself up stiff as a pole and making a stern face at the suggestion of doubt, Aunt Kate says, "*Miiz-izz Pat*erson!" in a horrified tone that ends the discussion forever.

Gram stomps the Singer foot pedal, pulls a stream of cloth out from under the needle, cocks her head to one side, puckers her mouth, raises an eyebrow, stares out the window, and smiles one of the ironic little smiles she directs at Aunt Kate when she thinks her friend is being too stuffy. Though Gram's Christianity was without question serious and important to her, it was, as far as I could tell, almost altogether a religion of service and common sense rather than of either dogma or mystery. Daily life taken simply as it was seems to have sufficed, leaving little need for either miracles or explanations. Her sons, on the other hand, took a different view of the human condition, one that left them longing for some mystery, some transcendence, some romance from her that they never got. Sitting in a pink puddle of afternoon sunlight, threading a needle and listening to them talk—that is all I know of Jesus and all I need to know. We are loved. We are safe. The sun is pink.

Deepened by their mutual need to make lives for themselves after the death of their husbands, the friendship between Gram and Aunt Kate seems to have been enlivened rather than limited by the substantial differences in temperament between them. In contrast to her circumspect and stern-appearing friend, Gram (who could be outrageous, willful, and even ribald) loved games, public events, and shows of all kinds—and always needed someone to go with her. Though, as I came to know later, Aunt Kate was more openhearted and open-minded than she seemed, she struck me when I first knew her as so staid and serious that I doubted she would have had any fun at all without my grandmother. As it was, they had lots of fun together, and I was often part of it.

It was sitting on the floor at their feet that I started learning to write by tracing words they printed on the backs of used envelopes with the big flat-sided pencils Gram got from the Greenhouse and sharpened with a kitchen knife. Sometimes someone else—Duke, Sonny, Kitty, Cobbie—would see me there and write down something new. I had no idea how lucky I was that—despite our troubles—there were so many people who took me places and read to me and talked to me and taught me things I wanted to know.

I learned a few things at kindergarten, too, and some things happened there that I didn't forget. I was six years old and the others were five, which was probably a good thing, since I was much better at some things than at others. Although I could read and write a little, I couldn't carry a tune and was not good at remembering the words of songs and playing rhythm games. I never learned how to draw or paint pictures like the others, and it took me half the year to learn how to skip properly. I liked having so many children to play with and I liked the games we played.

One day, Duke brings seeds and fertilizer to the kindergarten and helps us plant a Victory Garden. In no time at all, we dig up radishes and tiny carrots and wash them off and make them into a salad that we eat at our tables with cookies and juice. The radishes are purple and hot on my tongue. The carrots are tiny and taste like sweet potatoes.

Another day, I am sitting at a table coloring pictures with a new friend named Alis, who likes to be bad. She scribbles all over the picture she is coloring and then takes dark crayons and scribbles some more.

"You do that to yours, too," she says, "and then we'll show them to Miss Helen like we think they are good."

"Why?" I ask.

"To play a trick on her," she says, "because she thinks we're smart."

"I like for her to think I'm smart."

"That's why it's a trick."

We color our pictures, then ruin them with a tornado of black and green scribbles and take them to the front of the room to show the teacher, who seems genuinely shocked at what we have done and sends us back to our seats to do better. Alis thinks it is funny. I wish we hadn't done it. I like Miss Helen and she likes me. I don't like to be bad.

Later in the year, a child named Conrad joins us in kindergarten. Nobody knows him. He is pale and timid and cries every day to go home. Miss Helen tells us to be nice to him. We try, but he refuses to play and cries more and more. His mother brings him every day; some days he stays and some days he cries so much she takes him back home. One day he stays but keeps on crying, until Miss Helen makes everybody get in a circle around him and shout, "Cry baby, cry, stick your finger in your eye . . . Conrad is a sii-iisy . . . Conrad is a sii-iisy," at him to make him stop crying and go outside and play.

I go off to another corner of the room with two other children who don't want to do it. Miss Helen says, "Come here and help me get Conrad to come to his senses." We don't go. Conrad is afraid. This is not a game.

The others clamor around him, yelling and jeering. He cries and cries and crawls up on the window ledge like a trapped animal and tries to jump out and looks like he is going to go crazy or die of grief. The brokenhearted Conrad crouching on the ledge of the window, the children and Miss Helen taunting him and jeering stick in my mind as an image of pure torture—and pure evil and the pure abuse of the power to make someone who is suffering suffer more.

Conrad never came back to kindergarten and, after that, Miss Helen with her hoarse voice, jittery ways, and black-dyed hair looked mean and scary to me, like the stepmother in *Snow White*. The image of the terrified Conrad clinging to the window ledge has been with me ever since, associated in some way with my mother's suffering and, I have come to believe, with the extent to which I had begun to identify with that suffering and all suffering that resembled it.

Two Moves and a Departure

 It must have been during my kindergarten year that my twelve-year-old cousin Jimmy Hillman fell and broke his arm at the Sophronia, standing on a packing trunk, trying to replace a light bulb for Knoxie, who called a taxi to take him down the street to the Fitts Hill Infirmary, where they set his arm and called another cab to take him home. The next day, Duke and I went downtown to Mr. Poulos's newsstand near the Tavern and bought a bagful of comic books to take to my injured cousin, whom we found sitting in the middle of his bed like a king, drinking a Coca-Cola over ice and making a model airplane.

Jimmy loves and admires my father, who is one of the few men in his life and the only one who pays any attention to him. He is very happy to have such an array of comics—"Only Uncle Duke would have thought of it"—and spreads them out on the bed like an exhibit, to admire and choose from at his leisure.

Daddy makes a point of bringing Jimmy to our house when important things are happening, so I suppose he was there the spring day the sheep were sheared. Strange men arrive with big trucks loaded with electrical hand shears powered by heavy engines. The men seem foreign and rough to me. The engines smell like grease and make a terrible noise and some of the sheep struggle and run and don't want to be clipped. Duke has hired these people because he wants the shearing done right, and he wants to make some money off the wool before he sells the sheep, which he is going to do as soon as the shearing is done.

One sheep is especially uncooperative and struggles so long and hard that the professional shearers decide to let him go unsheared. Duke says, "No." He is a strong man, with a torso like a bull, and the sheep is not all that big. He grabs the creature and a tussle ensues that to my childish eyes seems sure to end in the death of either the sheep or my father.

Duke is straining and grasping to keep his arms around the flailing animal. His face is so red it looks purple. I don't want my father to get hurt (I don't even want him to be unhappy), but I don't want anything to happen to the sheep either. Finally, Duke gets the creature firm enough in his grip for one of the men to take most of the fleece off its terrified hide.

Though it is a victory of sorts, my father is not happy. He hates suffering and fear, especially in animals, especially if he caused it; and yet it is plain for me to see that he could have left the now humiliated, naked, pink-skinned creature alone.

I remember the shearing because of the violence with which the animals had to be subdued and because of the ferocity of my father's wrestling match with that one sheep. I remember it, too, because I associate the shearing and selling of the sheep with my growing awareness that our lives are changing and that both my father and Jimmy Hillman are leaving.

The next thing I know, kindergarten has ended, summer has begun, and Jimmy Hillman is with us in the country. It seems like any other summer day. We are outside. Jimmy is teasing Jane and me by taking everything we hand him and pretending to make it disappear. We give him a toy car and . . . *whooosh* . . . it is gone.

"Give me something else," he says, "and I'll send it to get the car and bring it back." *Whooosh* . . . it's gone. *Whoosh* . . . *whoosh* . . . *whoosh* . . . everything we give him disappears. We know it is a joke and that he will soon give everything back, but we think our big cousin is very clever to make things disappear into thin air like that.

Duke comes out the back door and calls Jimmy to help him mow the front yard. My father standing framed by the back door of our house in the country is my last memory of him before he leaves to start training with the Seabees at Camp Peary in Williamsburg, Virginia. I don't remember his going and seem only gradually to have realized he was gone.

He is gone. Emily is sitting on her bed in a light blue peignoir, her hair still damp from the shower. Early-morning sun shines on the rose trellises that climb the wallpaper behind her. The grass is green outside her window. I am standing at the foot of her bed. Mary Willie is near the door.

Momma says she is going to call Daddy, even though she knows she is supposed to call only in an emergency. Her hands shake so much that Mamie has to help her dial the number. Mamie leaves the room. I stay. Emily waits a long time, cradling the black telephone in her arms like a puppy.

Finally, she says, "Yes, yes, operator, it *is* an emergency. I have to talk to him. His wife has had a heart attack."

I know my mother hasn't had a heart attack. I also know she is very upset. She hangs up the phone and sits there for a long time, waiting and wringing her hands in a frenzied way that I associate with the death of my brother.

The phone rings. It's Duke.

"I'm all right," she says in an exhilarated voice, laughing and crying at the same time. "I just said that so I could talk to you. I thought you were dead or had left me for good. I thought I was going to die." She wants to go where he is and bring us.

He's in boot camp. We can't come. Anyway, it would cost too much. They had agreed. He had rented the house in the country to a Colonel Biggs at Maxwell Field and made plans for us to move to a furnished house in town to save gas and to be closer to Gram and Bessie and the school where Jane and I are supposed to go to the first grade. It was all arranged.

"I can't stay here without you," she says. "I'm going to bring the children and come anyway. I'll die if I can't come. I'll get the money from Pro," she says finally, using her childhood name for Aunt Bessie.

She hangs up and sits on the bed shaking and crying loud noises like a child. "I can't *staaaand* it," she wails, pacing up and down the room and wringing her hands. "He's left me . . . He doesn't *want* me . . . He's going to leeeeave me . . . I can't *staaaand* it."

The picture freezes a still-shot in my mind. My mother in an exultation first of joy and then despair, crying as if her heart had exploded and poured itself out in her weeping. Roses, bright sunshine, and green grass behind her. Something exploding inside her. Something congealing in me.

I remember when the baby died and Emily got sick and left on the train with Duke. I remember Connie leaving and Emily hurling herself up and down on the bed and afterwards being gone for a long time. I watch her cry and wring her hands and remember what everybody thinks I have forgotten. My mother is sick. Mamie can do nothing, and neither can I. Daddy is gone and we're moving to town.

Before we leave, Mamie takes us downtown to the colored movie theater to see Lena Horne and Fats Waller in *Stormy Weather*. Mamie falls in love with Lena and for a while sings only . . . Ain't no sun up in the sky da da da da . . . By then, Ethel Waters had already been singing it for ten years. "I was singing the story of my misery and confusion," she said, "the story of the wrongs and outrages done to me by people I loved and trusted." Keeps rainin' aaaall the tiiiime.

Jane and I put our dolls in the closets in the room where Mamie sleeps with Joan, and tell them not to be sad while we are gone; we'll call them on the telephone when we get to town and tell them about our new house. "Goodbye, Suzie. Goodbye, babies. We are moving to town."

The house we move into is small and made of red brick, with a wide front porch and a long back yard for us to play in. A little girl whose name I have forgotten lives next door. She is fat, has freckles, is fun to play with, and eats the snot out of her nose. I don't remember much else about either the house or the neighborhood, except that it was from there that Mary Willie and Emily took Jane and me to our first day in Miss Simpson's first grade at Cloverdale School.

The school is big, with long halls and rooms on every side. Jane is afraid and doesn't want Emily to leave. Finally, Miss Simpson makes her go. Jane gets sick and throws up, and then I throw up, too, and we are ever afterwards remembered by those who were there as the children who threw up on the first day of school in Miss Simpson's first grade.

We come back the next day and sit together at a little round table with five or six other children. One day a boy named Bill says, "Do-do," and Jane says, "I'm going to tell Miss Simpson that Bill said do-do," and gets up to do it.

"No, Jane," I say. "Don't you dare do that."

"I am, too," she says. "He said a bad word."

I can't stop her and she walks up to Miss Simpson in front of everybody and says real loud, "That boy who sits at our table said do-do." I'm embarrassed, but Miss Simpson doesn't pay much attention to it and sends Jane back to her seat. After a while she comes over and whispers something to Bill. That is all there is to it. Jane is disappointed. I am relieved.

Our teacher pulls her graying hair into a knot on the back of her head in a way that makes her look like the stereotype of the old-fashioned schoolteacher I suppose she is. She keeps promising to teach us to read, but she never does.

Meanwhile, Duke—who is ten years older than most of the men he joined up with—has gone into the Seabees with the non-commissioned officer's rank of boatswain, first class. He likes the authority and responsibility the position gives him and applies to go to officers' candidate school. But by the time the opportunity comes, Emily has talked him into letting us come to be with him, which made it impossible for him to take the training required to become an officer.

And so, in late October, within a few weeks of Duke's arriving at the naval receiving station at Lido Beach on Long Island, New York, Emily, Gram, Mary Willie, my sisters, and I close up the house we have lived in for only a few weeks and get on a train headed for Long Island. Aunt Bessie and Duke's cousin Haygood see us off on the train. Emily is so happy. She is going to be with Duke; nothing else matters.

At first, Mary Willie rides in a separate car with just colored people. Emily says when we get far enough north, Mamie can come sit with us, but after a few hours she tells the conductor that she's sick and needs her nurse to look after Joan, and the conductor brings Mamie to sit with us. She and Emily act like schoolgirls who have gotten away with something. Gram ignores their antics but admits she didn't like the idea of Mamie in that other car by herself with all those "colored soldiers."

We eat the fried chicken Gram packed and get in our berths to go to sleep. The rocking of the train makes me sick. Gram gives me olives and sliced lemons to eat. They don't make me feel any better, but I don't throw up. We are on the train a long time, rocking and swaying.

We get off at Pennsylvania Station in Manhattan and start looking for the train to take us to Long Island. I stand there with Gram and Mamie and look up, up, up into a dome so high it looks like the sky—like a church, like a palace, like nothing I have ever seen before. Gram takes me to the bathroom, and when we come out, Mamie and Joan are there, but Emily and Jane are gone. Mamie says, "I thought they went in there with you." Gram says, "I thought they were out here."

I didn't know Gram and Mamie could be afraid, but they are. We walk faster and faster, asking people if they have seen a lady in a red coat with a little girl. Everybody says no. Gram keeps saying, "Look for the red coat. Look for the red coat."

Finally, she and I leave Mamie sitting in a chair with Joan and go off by ourselves. We look everywhere on that floor and start taking the escalators up and down between floors. Gram yells, "Be careful. Be careful. Don't let anything get caught in the steps." I have never seen an escalator before, and I doubt she has either. We are lost inside a maze of stone columns, stairwells, and balconies, and I think I will never see my mother and sister again.

Finally, Emily appears, floating eerily up on the escalator opposite the one we are going down on. First we see her tobacco-colored hair and then her fire-engine-red coat and then my towheaded sister holding her hand. I can tell from the slack grin on her face that my mother has been drinking. At first, the relief is so great I think I will faint. And then I am angry. And then sad, as if the bottom is falling out of my heart.

I want somebody to hold me close and say, "We are not lost. We are safe. We are all safe." Instead, Momma and Gram stand there staring at each other like two statues, Emily in a coat so bright I can hardly stand to look at it, and Gram in the navy-blue suit she bought for the trip. Gram says unless Emily stops drinking, she's going home on the next train. Emily says, "Okay. I'm sorry. I won't do it again."

We find Mamie and Joan sitting where we left them, and suddenly we are all so happy we don't know what to do. Mamie starts singing and snapping her fingers, "I been in some big towns and heard me some big talk . . ."

We buy sugar-coated doughnuts that taste like licorice and get on the train for Long Island, where Duke has rented us a two-story house backed up to a canal on a narrow street within walking distance of the Lido Beach Hotel, which sits at the center of the naval complex where he is stationed. Gram takes Jane and me to see the Atlantic Ocean and the boardwalk. Everywhere we go, we see sailors in uniform. Emily finds an Episcopal church for us to go to on Sundays and Mamie goes with us. The church has stained-glass windows but is much smaller and plainer than St. John's. Emily says the people who go there aren't very friendly. Mamie says the only thing she doesn't like about Northerners is that even the colored people say "Jesus" as if it were a cuss word.

I walk to the drugstore in the village with Gram. The pharmacist calls her Dixie because of her accent but has to admit he has never heard of White Wonder, a silver-colored, mint-smelling salve made in Alabama and famous for its healing powers. Gram goes along with the teasing but can't imagine how people get along without the world's best treatment for stuffy noses, fever blisters, burns, cuts, and anything else that needs soothing.

My grandmother's ongoing astonishment about the absence of White Wonder on Long Island becomes a joke. Emily mocks her mother-in-law's simplicity behind her back. Duke and Mamie smile.

Gram is fascinated with the white "oleo" that people are using in place of butter and teaches us how to work the little orange tablets of oily color into it to make it look more like what it is supposed to be. Yellow oleomargarine is still in the future, and Gram will use the cheaper self-mixed stuff for years, to save a few pennies and enable her to conserve the sweet, fluffy butter she churns at home. Such a view of life alone was enough to separate her from Emily, raised as she had been in what Gram would always see as profligate luxury. That they might be saved from ruin by the tiny difference between the cost of white margarine, yellow margarine, and home-churned butter was a thought Bessie and Knoxie would simply not have been able to think.

Christmas comes. We decorate a tree and sit around the radio listening to President Roosevelt put General Eisenhower in charge of Allied troops in Europe. Gram teaches me to write IKE in big letters. Duke teaches me SEABEE.

After Christmas, Aunt Kitty and Margaret come in their car from Indiana, where Uncle Sonny has been in training with the Army. Jane and I help Gram and Emily and Mamie cook and clean all day and pull all the tables we have into the living room and push them together to make a long banquet table for the reunion we are planning so far from home.

We hear something and run to the front of the house. Aunt Kitty and Margaret stand there in the living room just like at home. Emily and Mamie and Gram run in. They chatter and hug and laugh like little girls. Buttery sunlight fills the room in a moment that never leaves me—Aunt Kitty wearing pink and my tall cousin finding us in a place so distant and strange we can hardly believe we are there.

We wait and wait for Sonny, who is driving from somewhere else in New York. We talk and laugh and wait. He said he would come no matter what, so we know he is coming.

At last he arrives. Flushed with cold and exuberance, he stands in our midst in his Army captain's uniform and tells how he had a flat tire and no tools to change it, in the dark of night on a desolate road in a borrowed car. Finally, a black private comes along with tools and a flashlight and insists on changing it for him; after all, he is an officer going to see his family.

Sonny doesn't know whether to offer to pay the soldier or not.

In Alabama, you wouldn't offer to pay if the man was white (unless you knew for sure that he was very, very poor); but if he was black, you would offer him money and he would take it. Things are different in the North (though Sonny doesn't know quite how), where even white people expect you to offer to pay when they do you a favor.

Sonny offers. The man is offended and refuses the money. "We are both soldiers," he says. "We are both Americans. What would *you* think if I offered to pay *you* for something you did for me out of the goodness of *your* heart?"

Sonny is disturbed by what happened and talks about it off and on for the rest of the night. He hadn't known what to do. He wouldn't have offended that man for anything.

Jane and Margaret and I sit at the long jerry-rigged table and listen and talk as if we were grownups. In the middle of it all, Margaret says, "What I want to know is why Duke and Sonny don't act more like brothers . . . I mean, why don't they hug or pat each other on the head or something." Hilarity erupts. Because Gram is there, nobody is drinking, and we are all so happy.

The next night we have an air raid and pull down the shades, and Jane and I have to be quiet. Duke goes out with some men with flashlights to be sure everyone has turned out the lights and drawn the shades, so enemy airplanes can't see to bomb us. I understand what they are saying, but the danger doesn't seem real and I am not afraid. We must have done this many times, but I only remember the time when Gram and Sonny and Kitty and Margaret were there, and Daddy came home to go out on patrol and it seemed like a game.

Before they leave, we go down to the beach and walk on the boardwalk and watch the ocean lie gray and cold in its bed. The wind blows hard and the shore looks endless. Gram says, "It's hard to think that Dookie and Sonny are going way out there farther than we can see."

Sonny leaves for Europe and Gram drives back to Montgomery with my aunt and my cousin. We stand on the steps and wave. "Bye, Aunt Kitty and Margaret. Bye, Uncle Sonny. Bye, Gram."

New York

 As soon as we get settled on Long Island, Mamie and Emily take Jane and me for our first day at the private school Duke found for us. Emily tells Mamie she wouldn't mind our going to school with colored children; but since we will go to all-white schools in Montgomery, she thinks it would be best for us to do the same here. Mamie seems to agree with her, and so we go to a progressive private school run by a Mrs. McGitchum in a framed, three-story Victorian house.

After that, we go to school in a little bus driven by one of the teachers. At first we like riding in the bus better than we like going to the school. A big pile of black coal stands in white snow in the middle of the playground. Some of the children throw pieces of coal at us and make fun of the way we talk and the little white Mary Jane shoes we wear under our rubber boots. I tell Emily I want some brown oxfords with thick soles like the ones the other children wear.

"I wouldn't dream of letting you put those ugly things on your feet," she says. "People at home would think I was crazy."

I keep asking.

She keeps saying no.

Soon, despite our shoes, a girl named Joy and a boy named Steve start playing with us on the playground and sitting with us in class. One day, we are sitting with our new friends and some other children at a long table in a long room, looking out on the snow from an upstairs room. The sky is very blue above the snow, which also looks blue. I say, "The snow looks blue." Somebody else says, "Don't you know snow is always white." I say, "It looks blue to me."

Steve asks where we lived before we came here. I say, "Montgomery."

"Never heard of it," he says. "Does everybody there talk funny?"

"I think y'all talk funny," I say. "And I never heard of New York before I came here."

A tall teacher stands behind us holding yellow cookies and paper cups full of apple juice on a tray. "Did you ever see snow before you came here, Judy?" she asks, smiling as if she likes me. I tell her about the time it snowed in Montgomery when I was little. The juice tastes autumn-sharp and sweet like at Miss Helen's. We eat lunch at school every day and stay until four o'clock in the afternoon, which Emily thinks is too long for us to be gone.

The school has a science room with plants and rocks in bowls and maps on the wall. Everybody goes to the science room and to the playground and to lunch together. Because Jane likes to draw and I don't, she goes to a special room for that. The teacher wants me to go into a class of children who are sitting in a circle reading. Jane wants to go with me. The teacher wants to take Jane somewhere else.

We stand with the teacher outside the room and listen to the children reading. I already know some of the words they are saying.

The teacher squats down beside me and tries to make me go in. I want to go, but I want Jane to go with me. The teacher says no and makes me go by myself. And then I am sitting in a chair in the circle with a flimsy little paperback book in my hand. I like this school.

Jane tells Emily she doesn't want to go to school anymore. I'm scared my mother will make me stay home with my sister. Instead, she makes Jane go to school.

One Saturday, Jane and I are playing alone at home and decide to pile snow up at the back door of a grumpy neighbor whose German shepherd had bitten Jane. The lady didn't even act sorry and had tried to blame Jane. We pile handfuls of snow up at the door all morning until we have a small blockade as solid as a wall of bricks. And when the woman can't get out, we are amazed—it worked!—and delighted with our success.

Because the woman doesn't have a telephone, she has to yell out the window. A neighbor we like named Mrs. Foster hears her screaming and comes with a shovel to dig her out. We can tell she thinks what we did is funny, though she makes a straight face and tells us to say we are sorry. We keep saying it was a mistake; we didn't really think it would work; we were just playing. Emily and Duke think it is funny, too. Everybody tells us not to do it again, and we don't.

On another snowy day, we are playing with neighborhood children in the front yard, yelling and running and inventing games to play. I head toward the house to get something. My body is warm and happy inside my clothes. I make smoke with my breath and feel my feet crunching in the snow. I see Emily and Mamie at the window watching us and hear my mother say, "Don't they just get along with everybody? And listen to them; they are beginning to have regular Yankee brogues." My mother is there. She loves me. She is watching.

Duke is very resourceful about getting away from the base to be with us. Sometimes he comes for just a few hours and sometimes he spends the night. Because he is so close, we never know when he will show up, how long he will stay—or what he will bring. Sometimes he brings a few extra ration coupons so we can have a little more sugar and coffee than we otherwise would. Sometimes chewing gum, including the first bubble gum I ever saw.

One night he appears at the door in his navy-blue uniform and cap, pridefully bearing two boxes of Peter Paul candy bars—dark, coconuty treats which he hides in the top of his closet. There they stay for him to dispense on special occasions with a ceremonial flourish that never fails to impress us with the value of such booty and our father's prowess in securing it for us. Who knows how he came by such wartime valuables or what he paid or traded to get them.

It is my father who finally talks Emily into letting me exchange the white Mary Janes for a pair of brown oxfords, little leather treasures, perfectly fulfilling my deepest desires. I don't remember the day we bought them. What I never forget is the night Daddy comes home and puts newspaper down on the floor beside the chair where he reads and teaches me to polish my shoes the way he polishes his, with thick, sharp-smelling brown paste and two soft rags, until all the scuffs are gone and my oxfords shine brighter than the day we bought them.

My father sits in his chair in a red flannel shirt. I sit on the floor with my shoes and my rags on the newspaper. The lamp he reads by shines on us both. The shoes glow like jewels in my hands.

Jane and I go to school every day on the bus. Emily and Mary Willie take care of the house and cook shad roe, chicken à la king, Polish sausage, and other things we have never eaten before. Though Joan is still very small and can't walk yet, she is learning to talk. My father and mother act like a couple in love on a holiday, and our family seems as secure (to my childish eyes) as can be in this snow-frosted place we have come to.

And then one morning, without any warning that I can remember, I find Emily in the kitchen, staring out the window, before anybody else is up. She stands a long time, then gets a sweaty green bottle of beer out of the refrigerator and starts to drink it. A strip of morning sunlight silhouettes her body under the long shirt of Duke's she sometimes sleeps in. Her flanks look wasted and her large breasts hang heavy in front of her.

I stand beside her at the sink and ask for a swallow of the second beer she opens, hoping, I suppose, either to reduce the amount she is drinking by that little bit or to draw her gaze back into the room where I stand. She hurls me a look of utter malice, throws her head back, and gulps the rest of the beer in a single swig.

Soon she is drinking in a tavern in the village on the days Duke doesn't come home. Sometimes on Saturday she takes Jane and me with her—the place is dark and everybody knows her—but mostly she goes alone while we are at school. If she isn't home when we get there, I can think of nothing else until I see the dark outline of her body advancing unsteadily in the twilight toward the house.

On such a day as that, Jane and I are playing in the hall near the kitchen so we can talk to Mary Willie and Joan while we play. It is getting dark. I'm worried because Emily is still gone. I don't want to say anything to Mamie, because she likes to act like nothing is wrong and always tells me not to worry.

Finally, I can stand the fear/tension no longer and ask Jane where she thinks Momma is. She says, "Drinking beer, I guess," and looks away. I interpret my sister's response as indifference and feel it as betrayal, though she was, I now believe, even more frightened than I was and even less able to tolerate our mother's absence. Terror goes all over my body and I realize (either on that night or on another one like it) that too many nights have gone by since we last saw Duke.

"When's Daddy coming home?" I ask.

"Soon as he can, baby," Mamie says, but I can tell from her voice and the way she twists her neck that something is wrong.

And so I begin to watch and wait for my father as well as for my mother. My father who had always been there in a way that my mother never was.·

That was how I learned to pray, sitting in an alcove before a dark window in a house on a canal on Long Island, looking into the street and saying to myself, "God, bring my father back. Bring him back, and I will always be good and never wish for another thing."

Stop my heart from pounding in my chest. Stop my fear. Stop my loneliness. Stop Momma's drinking. Stop my father from leaving. Stop our family from being the way it is.

I don't know how long Duke stays away, but it is long enough for me to know that Emily and Mary Willie are worried, too. Long enough for me to become almost as afraid of their noticing my fear as I am of the fear itself. Long enough for me to become adept at both hiding my anxiety and keeping a secret vigil.

Supper is over. I go to the window. The pink light of the sun is almost gone and there are so many stars in the sky that I think I might as well give up and enjoy the hour or two of relief I get between when I leave my post for that day and when I go to bed. I wait a few more minutes, push my face against the cold pane, and see my father coming down the street in a cluster of sailors in white bell-bottoms and caps. Relief comes in a rush as intense and glorious as a shot of morphine in my veins. My body settles. My mind goes free. I feel my worries justified and assume my vigil brought him home.

The last time I had seen him, he had been wearing navy-blue. Now he is in white. He struts and his face is red and changed in a way that tells me he has been drinking. Though my father has been drinking to escape his problems since before I was born, this is my first memory of knowing that his drinking had something to do with our troubles.

I sit in the darkness and watch until he is almost at the door and then jump up, yelling, *"He's home. He's home. Daddy is home."*

He is there, but he doesn't stay long; and after that, he doesn't come as often as before; and when he comes, he and Emily usually argue. Once he is there long enough for Mary Willie to take the day off. Jane and I are playing by the street. Emily is sitting with Joan on a blanket in the yard. Daddy comes out and tells Momma to come inside and talk to him and tells Jane and me to watch Joan so she doesn't crawl into the street. I can tell he is both afraid for us to do that and desperate to talk to Emily alone. I know we can look after Joan, but I don't want them to go inside and argue.

They go inside. Jane keeps going off with other children and leaving me to watch Joan by myself. I start to scream, "Daddy, Jane's not helping. *Daaaddy.*"

He comes running out of the house and down the steps to the street. As soon as I see his terrified face, I know he thinks something has happened to Joan, and I know I have made a mistake. He towers over me, shaking me by the shoulders and yelling so loud I can't tell what he is saying. Young as I am, I know that his inability to make my mother do what he wants her to do and his fear of leaving us alone with Joan has more to do with his anger than with anything I have done. I hear the rage in his voice and think he is going to hit me, though he never has and doesn't now. I also hear frustration beyond what he believes he can bear and think I would rather he hit me than go on feeling so stymied and helpless.

Emily appears. "It's not fair," I say. "Jane was supposed to stay with me and help."

Jane is back by then, saying she had just gone to get something and was coming back. I call her a liar and then Momma starts yelling, "Don't you dare, *ever, ever* call your sister a *liar.*"

I didn't know it was so bad to call somebody who tells lies a liar, but I don't say anything. I hate for my parents to be upset and angry. I hate myself when I make it worse. And still I am less afraid when they yell at me than when they yell at each other, and I liked the way it felt standing there in the yard watching my sister run away and bellowing to the skies, *"Daaaddy . . . Jane's not doing her paaart."*

I want things to be the way they were when we first came to New York. I want my parents to be happy and look after me. I want my sister to help me when she is supposed to.

Jane and I get bad colds and stay home from school for a long time. We get well, but Momma decides not to send us back to school until the next Monday. She likes to look after us when we are sick and she likes to have us home with her.

We are all still asleep on Monday morning when the bus comes. The teacher honks. She comes to the door and knocks. I hear her and start getting dressed in a hurry. Emily is running around the house in a green nightgown, pretending nobody is home and acting like a child playing hooky. Mamie joins in the silliness. I don't like it, two grown women acting like children, mocking me and my teacher. Finally, Mary Willie goes to the door and says we are still sick, even though we aren't sick and had planned to go to school.

The school keeps calling, and Emily keeps saying we are sick. A truant officer comes, and she tells him we are going back to Alabama soon and acts as if she has gotten away with something. The bus stops coming. Momma tells me to stop pestering her about going to school, and finally I do. She says not to pester Daddy either. She wants us home with her. She doesn't think school is all that important. She thinks we aren't as smart as the other children.

Jane and I are cutting out paper dolls and planning to make a make-believe long-distance call to the dolls we left in the closet in the country. We have paper dolls with cut-out wigs as well as cut-out clothes, so we can make them look like different people. I put plain Buster Brown hair on my doll and pretend she is me. Mamie takes off the Buster Brown wig and puts long, yellow curls in its place.

"That's the prettiest," she says.

"I hate it," I say, because I'm still mad with her and Emily for stopping us from going to school and for acting silly in front of the teacher who believed snow could look blue.

"Good girls don't hate things," Mamie says. "Now, poke your mouth back in and let's call Suzie on the phone." I say, "Okay," but sometimes everything makes me feel sad and all I want is to go back home.

Silenced

 Some time in the spring, after we stop going to school, Aunt Bessie comes to stay with us in New York. Emily is happy she is there and together they plan all sorts of things for us to do. We go to church again and ride the train to Manhattan and go to Best's on Fifth Avenue, where Bessie buys spring clothes for Jane and me and buys Emily two jumpsuits that look like dresses but are really trousers. They are silky and printed with big tropical flowers, one in all colors of blue and green and the other in reds and yellows. I think they are beautiful.

Jane and I go on the train with Emily and Mamie to the Bronx Zoo and leave Joan at home with Bessie. We see giraffes eating from the trees and alligators sleeping in the sun. Mamie says she's seen alligators with jaws strong enough to bite people's arms and legs off. We buy popcorn to eat and peanuts to throw to the elephants. It is getting late. I want to see the hippopotamus.

"Okay," they say. "One last thing."

We walk and walk and finally we find him, an astonishing creature lying huge and slothful in a pool of black water as if he were dead. Suddenly I realize Momma is so drunk she can hardly stand up. She is wearing a brown dress, staggering around. Her period has started. Mamie goes to find her a sanitary napkin and tells us, "Sit down here by the hippopotamus and stay with your mother. Don't dare move." We wait until the sky is as dark as the plum-colored pool in which the hippo soaks his oblivious hide, and I understand for the first time that there is no pleasure that cannot be destroyed by my mother's behavior.

Mamie comes back with a sanitary napkin and some safety pins. Emily stands up and falls to her knees. Mamie looks utterly help-less, standing slack-armed with a brown bag in one hand and two safety pins in the other; and yet, somehow (I can't imagine how), she gets us home.

After that, Mamie leaves for a while to be with LeRoy, which was one of the reasons Bessie came to New York. She came, too, I'm sure, to try to help Emily "get a hold of herself" and to make things better for us. Only, things don't get better; they get worse.

It is early evening. I stand at the door of Emily's room and watch Bessie trying to stop my mother from putting two little white pills in her mouth. I watch them push and pull and say mean things to each other, and think one of them will surely be hurt. In the end, my stout sixty-year-old aunt is no match for my frail, determined mother—who finally crams the pills into her mouth and lies down on the bed in the blue-and-green jumpsuit we bought in the city.

Bessie reads to me every night from *The Snow Queen*, about a boy and girl who play together every day until a sliver of bewitched glass turns the boy's heart to ice and causes him to run away with the coldhearted Snow Queen. We do everything exactly the way we did at 410. We bathe and get ready for bed. Bessie smells of lavender and Listerine. Her glasses sit low on her nose. Words roll out of her mouth, time stops, and we float in pure pleasure.

Because the girl in the story, whose name is Gerda, goes looking for her friend Kay and has many adventures along the way, the story is very long—and the words are too hard and the print too small for me to figure any of it out for myself. I like the stark, icy pictures that go with the story, but I like the words better. I want Bessie to skip some of the adventures and go to the end, but she refuses to skip a line. Finally, Gerda stands at the gates of the Snow Palace "in a cold, biting wind," and I know her journey will soon be over.

Duke comes home. He can only stay a little while because the Seabees are training night and day to go to Europe when the time comes. All the men are tired. Every time he comes home, somebody else has to pick up the slack. He and Bessie stand in the kitchen and whisper about Momma and then he and Emily go out.

I am ready for bed. Bessie promises to finish *The Snow Queen* after her bath. Her baths are long and ceremonial and this one lasts longer than usual. I start getting sleepy and beg her to hurry so we can read. I beg at the door and finally go into the bathroom.

"Please hurry. You promised."

"This is how I keep my skin looking so young," she says, soaking in the green water and sponging her face and neck with the liquid from the melting ice that sits in a bowl on the edge of the tub. "You must always take care of your skin . . . and your elbows. Nothing looks worse on a woman than rusty elbows. Your mother never did any of those things . . . And now look at her." As if dry skin and rusty elbows were the cause of all our troubles.

Please, Bessie, please. Gerda stands at the gates of the palace in a cold, biting wind. And there's a frozen boy waiting inside to be freed.

All I do is wait. Wait for Emily and Duke—who seem more and more to be either gone or on the brink of leaving and not coming back. Wait to go to school; wait to hear the end of a story; wait to feel happy and safe again. Waiting and waiting for something not coming, something not happening. Waiting and waiting until the simple act of waiting becomes a torment of frustration and fear.

I stand in the door of the steamy bathroom watching Bessie's balloon-like breasts float in the water and feel a mound of crystallized terror break loose inside me. I have become, in my way, as habituated to my diversions as my parents are to theirs and think only finding out what happened to Gerda and her playmate will stop the blasts of fear going off inside me.

Suddenly I am stomping my feet and yelling, "You're mean. I'm sleepy. You promised. It isn't fair," with all the air in my seven-year-old lungs. "I want to go *hooooooome.*"

Storming in and out of the bathroom and up and down the hall, I see myself acting just like my father, expanding to the size and force of his will, swelling up with the belief that I can stop any outrage and make people do anything I want by screaming and yelling and saying mean things. Though I will be a long time learning the cost of it, I have already learned that it sometimes works. I already know that though anger and "badness" are sometimes tolerated in our family, fear, sadness, loneliness, and the need for consolation are not.

Bessie finally gets out of the tub but refuses to read to me no matter how many times I say I am sorry. And—to my further amazement—when Duke and Emily get home, she tells on me. Duke listens, then kneels down in front of me and says he is disappointed in me; he counts on me to be good and help because I am the oldest.

I don't remember being particularly hurt by his words. They are home; the fear is gone; my heart is back in my chest. What I remember is that I pitied my father kneeling there before me and saw with a sudden precocity how hard he was trying in that moment to put right all the things that were wrong in our lives.

He had given up the opportunity to become an officer like Sonny and brought us here because Emily had promised everything would be wonderful if he did. And though he had known we would be better off in Montgomery in the house he had rented near the school, in the end he had done what she wanted.

When Duke says I am to have no more stories for a week in

punishment for talking to Bessie the way I did, I am stunned and stop the objection rising inside, only because I know I must. Though I remember counting the days until we could read again, I don't remember finishing *The Snow Queen* and didn't know for years that Gerda made her way into the Snow Palace, found Kay, and melted his heart with her tears.

One morning I am standing in the kitchen with Bessie in early-morning sunlight. Mary Willie is back and Emily is better. Bessie is ironing, humming . . . I'll be lovinnnnnnng youuuuuuooooooouuuuuu . . . and spelling words for the letter I am writing to the dolls we left in the closet at home. I want to tell Suzie we are going to call her long-distance again soon. Bessie says "telephone" and "long-distance" are too long to spell, so I don't write that. Instead, I write, "DEAR SUZIE. I LIVE BY A CANAL. IT SNOWS HERE. I MISS YOU. LOVE, JUDY."

We mail the letter to Gram's house, where it stays in a drawer for thirty years, along with some letters from Duke, including the one he wrote that March, thanking his mother for the ten dollars she had sent him for his thirty-first birthday and adding, "Seeing the things one has to do to raise kids, I want to thank you very much for all you have done. I see some few whose mothers didn't do as good a job as mine."

I am leaning on the end of the ironing board, printing words, when an idea hits me. "How do you spell 'help'?" I ask. It's a short word, so she tells me. I write it on a scrap of lined paper, H-E-L-P, and sign my name, J-U-D-Y.

Later Jane and I go outside and leave the scrap of paper at Mrs. Foster's back door. The wind blows it away. We find it, put a rock on top of it, and leave it again. "It's a secret," I say to my sister. "Don't tell anybody we did it."

I don't know why I wrote the note (if it was a note) or what I meant by it. I seem to have thought of it as a "joke," like the time Jane and I piled snow at the grumpy lady's door and everybody said, "Don't do it again," and thought it was funny. The day passes. Nothing happens. We think the note has blown away.

Duke comes home. Mrs. Foster appears at the back door, looking upset, holding the scrap of paper in one hand and the rock in the other, as if the little brown stone were part of the message and not just a weight to hold it down. I am curious and excited but not really afraid. At least, that is the way I remember it. In any case, Mrs. Foster takes the note seriously, which is what, at some level, I must have intended.

She must have asked, "Is anything wrong?" and must already have known there was. Knowing what I know now, I have to assume that my father used the stressful occasion as an excuse to drink more than one drink.

All I hear of the conversation is Bessie saying, "She was playing in the kitchen and I was ironing. She asked me how to spell 'help' and I told her, but . . . but . . ."

We eat supper. Nothing happens. I think they have forgotten it. Then we are in the living room. Emily sits slumped in a chair. Mamie and Aunt Bessie watch from the kitchen. I see myself and my father standing in front of them, looking stunted and strange, like people on a stage photographed from above. He starts off slow, using words I don't understand. I think it is going to be like the night I yelled at Bessie about *The Snow Queen.*

"I wanted Mrs. Foster to see I can write," I say, jumping up and down. "I know lots of short words." Jump. Jump. I can write short words. I wrote Suzie a letter. Bessie helped me. Jump. Jump.

My father towers over me, puffing and pawing like a bull. Sounds hit my face like stones. His face looks black. I think he is going to kill me. I think I may already be dead.

"*Why?* Why? Don't you ever, ever, ever . . . Are you crazy? Are you *craaazy?*" I can't hear the words. I can't think. I don't understand. I can't believe it. I won't believe it. I want my mother. This man is not my father. He is shaking me and shaking me.

My chest and shoulders hurt so bad I think something must be broken. God help me. God help me. I was playing and writing and "help" just came into my head.

"*I can write,*" I yell back at him, thinking, I suppose, that the man who taught me to plant radishes in black dirt and polish my own shoes will have some appreciation of what I am learning, though I suppose I must have known by then that the problem was not that I wrote but what I wrote. "*I can wriiiiii-te,*" one more time, before my teeth go together so hard on my tongue that I taste the blood in my mouth.

He keeps shaking me. And one powerful slap that feels as if it has broken my neck. Everything goes black and I think I am blind. Bessie says, "Lord God, Duke, stop it." Emily just sits there. Mary Willie stands in the door. Nobody can do anything.

My father's rage seems to open a hole in my body into which all the discord and anguish in the family is poured. My life seems to depend on my being able to stand it. They think I am the cause of all the trouble. I think so, too. My parents are insane, and I am alone. The hole is made.

Something snapped in my father that day. Young as I was, I understood it that way: "something snapped." And though he would demonstrate his love for me many times after that and the old tenderness of my early childhood would sometimes return (and the memory of it never left me), after that there was no pretending the violent, vindictive, out-of-control side wasn't there. No pretending the "snap" wasn't there to be triggered by the right amount of stress, outrage, and booze. No pretending that I was exempt from it.

My crime in writing the help note wasn't so much that I let Mrs. Foster know we needed help as that I let my father know that I knew it and forced him to look (and resort to drink and violence rather than look for long) at the problems in our family and his obvious inability to solve them. All the desperation, futility, and helplessness of his situation must have been implied in that one childishly scrawled, capitalized word.

I am sick in bed for a long time after that. My skin feels like fire. Sounds roar in my ears. I neither cry nor speak. My body aches, but inside I feel nothing. One day the sheets of the bed are wet with sweat. Mamie says, "People stink when they're sick." Finally, I cry, sobbing like a grown person. "It's all right," she says. "Everybody smells bad when they're sick. I smell bad when I'm sick."

Mamie smells like cotton and starch. She takes me in her arms and rocks me and sings, the way she used to in the country . . . Rock-a my soul da da da da da da da da ooooh rock-a my soul. Trying to make me smile, she plays a game she used to play with us when we were little.

"When a little white baby is born, the doctor says, 'Oh, what a pretty little baby,' and does this," she says, pinching my stubby nose between two strong fingers and pulling it straight. "When a little colored baby is born, he says, 'Oh, what a pretty little baby,' and does this," she says, pushing my nose into a flat pug. She rocks me and jokes. My legs hang off her lap. I'm too big for silly games and baby jokes. Nothing interests me. Nothing is funny.

All I can think about is getting to be big enough to do what I please. I hate Mamie and Momma and my sister, and for a while do mean things to Jane, like sticking pins in the carpet for her to step on and pulling dresser drawers out for her to fall over. To my surprise, the mean things I do work and then she is really hurt and really cries, and I don't like that.

My sister is a creative and resourceful playmate, but she is not the source of strength and support that, more and more, I want her to be. What I longed for, I believe, was an older sibling, a wise companion and guide who would help me and look after me without being one of the grownups. In the beginning, there had been something of that in our love for Mamie and hers for us.

Now, most of the time, she is one of the grownups, and Jane and I are too young and too sunk in our own fears to be much help to each other.

Just before Easter, Mamie leaves for a vacation and Bessie goes back to Montgomery. Duke stays at the base and we are alone with Emily for a few days.

I know there is no Easter Bunny, but I don't want Emily to forget to put out the baskets and hide eggs in the yard. I like for things to be the way they are supposed to be, so I can pretend things are all right even though I know they aren't. I want Emily to wake up. I'm scared to shake her the way Aunt Bessie does, so I put wet washrags on her face and shout in her ear, "Momma. Momma. Wake up. Look at me. Look at me." She says, "Go on back to bed, *Judy*," spitting out my name like a dirty word. I don't want Jane and Joan to know she forgot. I don't want to know it myself.

I lie down beside her, squirming and pestering her and wondering what we are going to do when Daddy leaves and how we will ever get back home. Finally, she gets up and puts on a long striped shirt of Duke's and starts cavorting around a mound of dirty clothes piled up on the floor, picking up one pair of underpants after another, sniffing until she finds a pair clean enough to put on. "Momma," I say in prissy determination, "the eggs. . . . the baskets."

The others get up. Emily gets colored eggs out of the refrigerator and puts them on the table in the plainest little straw baskets I ever saw. "War baskets," she says on her way back to bed. "Yankee baskets."

That Mother's Day, Emily starts drinking in the morning. Duke comes home with presents for us to give her. He makes her bathe and put on a clean gown, frilly and flowing like the ones she used to wear when she went to the hospital. He props her up in a chair in the living room, too inebriated and miserable to smile or focus on our faces. We stand before her with the presents. Duke unwraps them, leaning over her from behind, tender, defeated. Jane's present is a gown almost exactly like the one Momma has on; mine is a bed jacket—two pale, cold-smelling garments emblematic to me of the invalid life my mother lives.

Emily finds out she is pregnant. The doctor tells her that unless she stops drinking, the baby will either die or be sick like Joan. She stops drinking.

June 6. D-day. One hundred and seventy-six thousand troops land on the beaches of Normandy between Cherbourg and Le Havre and take the coast of France for the Allies. I sit on the floor of our house on Long Island and read IKE and SEA and FRANCE in the newspaper.

"I'm going there," Duke says and shows me the map of France and a bombed church and says that people in France eat horse meat. He teaches me *chevaux* and how to count to ten in French and tells me he wants me to remember it until he gets back. I don't know what it means that he is leaving, but I know I can remember the words.

A few days later, Emily reads about a soldier who survived in battle when the bullet that should have killed him bounced off the silver-covered New Testament he carried in his pocket. For two days, she and Mamie run around town in different directions looking for one like it for Duke. Finally Mamie finds one, only it isn't real silver. Emily goes out and comes back with a fat little book covered with a thin sheet of metal. She wraps it like a present and gives it to Duke the night he leaves, but I can tell he doesn't like the way she is acting. He doesn't intend to get killed. He doesn't think he is a hero. The Seabees aren't going to fight; they are going to repair the bridges and roads destroyed by the invasion. He's going to do a job, that's all. He wants to go, but he's worried about us. He wants to be left alone.

Gram comes to see Duke off and go home with us on the train. We stand at the window waving. "Goodbye, Daddy. Goodbye, Dookie. Be careful. Come back safe." I watch his white shirt disappear into the night. My mind goes blank. The only parent I have really had is leaving.

Wilmington Road

 The next thing I know, I am waking up inside sensations as soft and warm as swaddling, awakened so it seems by a certain texture to the air coming in the window smelling of dew, dust, grass, and bacon frying in somebody else's kitchen, awakened by a rush of pleasure so intense that it jolts me upright and sends me squealing into the yard . . . EEEEEEEEEeeeeeeeeeeeeEEEEEEEEEE

"Hush, girl. We in town. Folks sleeping."

We are home. Home not in the country but in another brick house in town on another little street of plain houses, some owned and cared for, others rented and shabby with overgrown yards like ours, all full of children whose fathers are at war.

The house is on a short street called Wilmington Road, in a self-contained neighborhood where screen doors swing on their hinges and all the children have the freedom of the whole street and all the houses on it. Because Emily wants the baby she is carrying to be healthy, she doesn't drink while she is pregnant and for what seems to me like a long time afterwards. For me, the first year of our time on Wilmington Road will become an oasis of pleasure and growth in a long-stunted time—a period during which I will learn what it means to be my mother's daughter and be closer to her than I have ever been before. I credit that year, at least in part, for building the fortitude and independence of mind that would enable me to survive what was to come. Looking back, I sometimes wonder if some unconscious maternal inkling didn't guide my mother to prepare me for the life that lay before me.

Emily gets letters from Duke almost every day and writes him every night, sitting in the lamplight, propped up on pillows in her bed, with her writing paper spread on a book on her knees like a schoolgirl. Though none of the hundreds of letters my parents wrote each other has survived, Duke also wrote Gram regularly, and she saved the correspondence.

"Lots of rain and work," he wrote from Cherbourg shortly after the Seabees arrived there in August. "I can get along with the work but this rain and muck will run me crazy before long. The people are right pitiful trying to keep out of the mud. The streets are real narrow and the trucks passing splash it all over the people walking on the sidewalks. I always try to slow down when passing them but sometimes you can't and there they are just dripping, with the blackest mud you ever saw."

Where we are, it is dry and dusty and the heat rises with the sun. Black peddler women float down the street in sandaled feet and long flowered skirts, hawking vegetables carried on their heads in baskets, or they ride in rickety wagons pulled by mules, crying a long lament that combines the advertisement of their wares with fragments of spirituals and African sounds of work and sorrow. Freeeesssshh veg-taaaaaables . . . oooookra . . . peeeeees . . . aauuuuuuuaa . . . sweet charioooohhhuuuuaaa . . . fresh-picked be-ee-erries . . . Mamie beckons them to the back door and buys vegetables to cook and strawberries to eat with cream and sugar or put on cereal. When the wagon comes, she buys a watermelon and cracks its red belly open in the driveway and lets us tear the juicy heart out with our hands.

A skinny white ice-cream man comes with a black boy pedaling

Wedding portrait of the missionary educators Margaret Flack and William Burns Paterson. Portrait made in 1879, Selma, Alabama

Paterson house and gardens on the campus of Alabama State College for Negroes, circa 1895

Knoxie Polk Walker, Montgomery, Alabama, circa 1900

Bessie Ware Walker, Montgomery, circa 1905

Jim Hillman, Birmingham, Alabama, circa 1910

Ila Watson Paterson, Montgomery, circa 1935

Emily, age ten, Birmingham, circa 1924

Duke, age eighteen, Sidney Lanier High School, Montgomery, circa 1931

Emily, age twenty, Montgomery, 1934

Duke, age twenty-three, Montgomery, 1936

Emily and Judy, Montgomery, 1937

(left) Emily and Judy on Narrow Lane Road, Montgomery, 1937
(right) Judy, Montgomery, 1938

Emily and Duke with friends on Long Island during World War II, 1944

(left) Emily and children on Wilmington Road, Montgomery, 1945
(right) Clockwise from left: Monnie Bagwell (in pool), June Compton, Bill Compton,
Louise Paterson, Jane, Duke, Emily, Judy, and Haygood Paterson, Montgomery, summer 1946

Jane, Joan, and Judy, Montgomery, 1947

Duke, one year after Emily's death,
Montgomery, 1947

a hot-ice cart full of ice-cream sandwiches and chocolate bars and little cups with wooden spoons. Sometimes the boy comes alone and gives us pieces of hot ice to make smoke with. Hot ice is so cold it burns. The freezer box is white, with red letters written in script. I-c-e/C-r-e-a-m/H-o-t/I-c-e.

In September, Emily takes Jane and me to Cloverdale School to see what they will do with a seven-year-old and an eight-year-old who have had almost no schooling. They put Jane back in Miss Simpson's first grade and me in Miss Lamb's mixed class of first- and second-graders.

The second-graders sit at a special table. Lucile and Virginia (whose parents know mine and who will be my friends for life) are there, and twins named Bob and Bill, whose father is at the air base, and three or four others whose names and faces have left me. The rest sit at desks and are starting school for the first time. They look like babies to me, and I don't remember a single face or name among them.

That I am being placed in a class of slow learners and am two years older than most of my classmates never crosses my mind. We are home. A little table of second-graders floats in sunshine and dust. I am going to school at last.

Miss Edith Lamb is one of those old-fashioned women for whom teaching was a life's work and a calling. She is plain and matronly-looking to my childish eyes (though probably still in her thirties), with a terrible scar on the lower part of her right arm. Lucile's mother says the scar was caused by a burn, but it looks to me like somebody just took a knife and cut the muscle right out of the arm below the elbow in front. The scar is just there, part of her arm, which she doesn't bother to conceal. She teaches me to add and subtract on paper in a matter of days, so it seems. After years of piecing words together, I find the Dick and Jane books hardly a challenge, but I love them anyway. Sometimes Miss Lamb lets me take one home, though she isn't supposed to. She tells me I have to be very careful with the ones I take home and bring them back to school the next day, which I always do.

Emily takes Jane and me to school in the car every day and picks us up every afternoon at the same time. One day she is late and we wait for a long time. I look down Fairview Avenue past the Cloverdale Pharmacy and watch and strain and stare and see only brightness and dust and one strange car after another. I stand frozen at my post on the steps of the school. Jane plays in the dirt at my feet. Everybody else is gone. The sun is in my eyes, my head starts to hurt and I remember the time Emily cried and asked the pharmacist for pills and the time we lost her in Penn Station and all the times we didn't know where she was in New York. I want my mother. I want everything to be all right. I want to be safe all the time like other children. No matter how hard I try, I can't stop the tears from running down my cheeks.

I see our car coming down the street in the sun at last and start swallowing my tears and wiping my face. Emily is driving, but Mary Willie is with her. I think something must be wrong.

Emily is acting gay and silly and doesn't say why she is late. I think she is mocking us, the way she does when she drinks. Relief that she is there battles inside me with anger at the way she is acting.

"I thought I saw somebody up there on those steps crying," Mamie says, trying to save my pride and josh me into a good mood. I pretend I don't know what she is talking about.

"Well," she says, "I know it couldn't have been my big girl. It must have been some little boy."

"It must have been," I agree.

After Thanksgiving, the second-graders start learning *Goldilocks and the Three Bears* to perform on the stage for the whole elementary school. We practice different parts every day, sitting at our round table and working on the script as solemnly as if we were preparing for Broadway. In the interest of preventing stage fright (not to mention sloth and pride of place), we aren't to be told which part we will have in the "real play" until the day of the performance itself.

One of the twins is big and lumbering and the other is tiny, so we know they will be Papa Bear and Baby Bear. All the girls learn Mama Bear and Goldilocks, but because Goldilocks' part is so long, nobody knows it very well.

Emily and I sit at the kitchen table every night and practice the Goldilocks part. She takes turns reading the other parts and teaching me the lines. Sometimes Mary Willie takes a part. "This porridge is too cold. This porridge is too hot. This porridge is *juuuuust* right."

Mamie stands above me, pointing at something in the script. Emily sits cross-legged and sideways at the little wooden table, a carbon copy of the script at one elbow, a cigarette-filled ashtray at the other. "Rest a minute," she says, lighting a cigarette and swinging one foot back and forth. "I want you to know the whole thing perfectly."

I don't know why Emily is spending so much time on this assignment. All I know is that I am center-stage in a narrow, linoleum-floored, light-bulb-lighted kitchen and my mother is teaching me something.

Of course she knows I am to be Goldilocks, and on the day of the play she takes me to school with my costume hidden in the trunk of the car so I will be surprised with the rest of the class. I don't seem to have given any of it much thought and am surprised that I am chosen.

Onstage, I am as calm and confident as a professional. My mother taught me the part. There she is in the audience in a rust-colored dress that matches her hair. Gram must have come, too, and maybe Bessie. All I remember is that Emily is there in the audience just for me.

By Christmas, Emily's stomach is big with my brother. She and I go to Aunt Bessie's in the car. Bessie's house is cluttered with wrapped presents. She and Emily sit at an oilcloth table in the kitchen and drink coffee and tell stories about Knoxie, who is sick in her apartment downstairs. Emily holds a white crockery cup in both hands. Her hands are well shaped but large for her body, with fingers that square off at the end like a man's. "Truck driver's hands," she says.

Bessie hands me a cup of coffee that is half condensed milk. Her kitchen smells like coffee, condensed milk, and gas leaking from the stove. Bessie says she and Knoxie are going to have to send Jimmy Hillman—who is thirteen years old and "running wild" on the Cushman motorcycle Duke had talked Knoxie into letting him have—to New York City to live with his mother. Jimmy hasn't seen his mother in ten years. She writes him and sends him books and recordings of classical music. He says his mother is famous and sings in the chorus of the Metropolitan Opera and has her own radio show. Jimmy has agreed to go to New York if he can take the Cushman. Emily says Duke will pack it up and send it when he gets home.

Emily and I leave Bessie's to walk the few blocks down Court Street to the doctor's office so I can get a tetanus shot because of something I stepped on at Gram's. Buttery sunshine warms the sides of the tall old houses that line the street. Only the soft sound of doors and windows opening and closing on the casual privacy of people who have always known each other and always will and the dull thump of our shoes on the brick-paved street breaks the morning silence.

The ritualized insularity of the old neighborhood was hell for Emily in 1935. Today it is heaven. The stillness. The sunlight. The certainty. Bessie waves from her upstairs porch. The sun is too bright in my eyes for me to see her when I look up, but I hear her "Yoohooo . . . bye . . . be a big girl . . . Aunt-ee loves you."

I get the tetanus shot in a dark room a few blocks away. The shot hurts. We head back up the street toward Bessie's. Cold sunlight strikes my face, I start to sweat, and everything goes black. I am falling and falling . . . Emily's arms go around me. Her stomach presses big against my chest and I am in her arms in a way that never leaves my body but doesn't come back as memory until twenty years later when my own daughter gets the flu and faints in my arms—and the lost moment flickers back. I had a mother. She loved me. I remember.

She takes me home and makes tea for me and sits on the bare wooden floor in our bedroom and teaches Jane and me how to wrap presents with Christmas-decorated tape. I feel her eyes go happy and proud watching us wrestle with the tape and the flimsy tissue we bought at the store. I feel loved by my mother and grownup wrapping the presents.

We sit on the floor in a Christmas-tree glow, listening to carols on the radio. I think the moment will never end and that this is the way my life will always be. Our Christmas tree is the biggest one on the street, though it is nothing like as big as the ones we had in the country. On Christmas morning we have lots of presents under the tree, including bicycles to learn to ride in the city.

"No matter what, we will always have a big tree with lots of wrapped presents under it," Emily says—because when she was little and lived in the antique-crammed house on Mountain Avenue in Birmingham with her mother and her two brothers, Knoxie didn't bother with a tree and left their presents unwrapped at the foot of their beds in brown paper bags tied at the top with red ribbon.

I see the lonely child my mother must have been, emptying the brown bag on her bed. Finding what? Toys, fruit, clothes, books? I have a few books inscribed "To Emily from Mother": *The Camp Fire Girls in Old Kentucky* and *The Camp Fire Girls at Lookout*

Pass by Margaret Love Sanderson, *The Little Lady of the Fort* by Annie M. Barnes, a book called *The Young Folks' Treasury of Heroes and Patriots*, and the three-volume *New Practical Reference Library*.

A few weeks after Christmas, my brother Jim is born. Like our brother who died, he is named James for our two grandfathers, but instead of Porter for his Paterson grandfather and the Yankee soldier killed at Resaca, he is named Duke for Daddy. James Duke Paterson, the healthy boy we prayed for, has come into the world a plump cherub with yellow straw for hair and one ear bigger than the other from his habit (from the womb, apparently) of folding it beneath his head when he slept.

Duke, who has just returned from France, gets a few days' emergency leave to be home when Jim is born. He has been gone five months. Things are so changed in my life that it seems like five years. And though I remember the French numbers, it seems like eons since I learned them. He brings Jane and me little French dolls with peasant's dresses and metallic-feeling hair. He knows they are ugly, he says, but he wanted to bring us something authentically French.

A month after the Liberation, he had met Sonny and some of their cousins in Paris and bought a dress for Joan and the dolls for us. He tells us about his cousin Bill eating what he thinks is beefsteak with a French family. Bill compliments the beefsteak and they tell him it is not beefsteak but horse meat. "No bifsteck. Chevaux," Duke tells us in GI French.

"I told you before I left, they ate horse meat," he reminds us, as if it were the funniest thing in the world that he had known something his cousin didn't. "Well, anyway," he says, "it must have tasted pretty good after the K rations he'd been eating."

Jane and I go with Duke to crate up Jimmy Hillman's Cushman and put it on the train to Manhattan. Duke goes back to the training base at Davisville, Rhode Island, not knowing where he will go from there—or when he will be back. Gram and Mamie bring Emily and Jim home from the hospital in Gram's car. My heart is shocked by waves of feeling the likes of which I won't know again until my own children are born. I am madly in love with this boy and immediately stake my claim out against my sisters (after all, I'm the oldest, the biggest, and the most determined to make him my own) and brook no competition from the first time Emily sits me in a chair and puts his fat little form in my arms.

By the end of March, Sonny has crossed the Rhine and been made commanding officer of General Patton's 773rd tank destroyer battalion in Germany, and the Navy is preparing to send Duke to the Aleutian island of Attu with the Seabees to build a landing strip for troops preparing to invade Japan. Gram and Emily want Duke to find an excuse not to go into danger again.

He wants no part of that idea. "You mentioned my ulcer," he writes Gram. "I haven't got a thing in the world wrong with me, Gram, and if I did I wouldn't use it to keep from going out— even tho' I don't want to go, I couldn't very well be happy with myself if I hid behind some minor ailment to keep from going. I expect to live a long time after this war and I don't want to feel guilty every time anyone mentions it in the next thirty years. See, Mama?" I never once heard him call her "Mama" in person, only "Mother" or "Gram," and sometimes "Miss Ila" in jest.

Our lives stay the same. Emily reads Duke's letters and writes to him. Sometimes Jane and I write notes to go along with the letters, mostly annotated cartoons—little stick figures with labels like "Gram feeds the chickens" and "Judy and Jane play with their friends."

Most of my friends on the street are girls about my own age. Lucy McKinney is my best friend, and Caroline Cooper the next, mostly because her mother's friendliness and afternoon snacks make her house the hub of our activities. For a while, I strike up a friendship with a child much younger than I am whose first name I've forgotten. Her last name was Upchurch and her grand-mother was a friend of Gram's.

One day we are in our back yard and I am showing her how to pull the skin off a ripe peach without using a knife. I feel Emily's eyes on me from inside the house and hear her say to Mamie, "Look at that. Isn't Judy something?" Though I don't know exactly what she is praising, the warmth and implied praise in the overheard words make me suddenly, enormously happy.

The love in her voice, the intensity of my pleasure, and the smell of the ripe peach in my hand linger with such force in my memory that I have often attributed a satisfying teaching career to that one moment, in which a talent that may or may not have been inborn was made precious by my mother's approval. Our first year on Wilmington Road was full of such moments.

I learn to ride a bicycle, skate, and play with children in groups for the first time that year. The girls in the neighborhood use colored chalk when they have it, and the white edges of broken rocks when they don't, to draw a monumental hopscotch temple and instigate a tournament that lasts all summer and is played to a set of mystifying rules and gestures they seem to have been born knowing.

I am awkward at it at first, and never acquire the skill (or commitment) some of the others have—although if we hadn't gone back to the country perhaps I would have. One foot . . . two feet . . . one foot . . . two feet . . . Hop . . . Plop . . . Hop . . . Plop . . . HOME.

My feet go in the wrong place half the time and I can't seem to remember the rules—which adhere to a logic that doesn't come naturally to me. Still, I want to get good at what the others are good at so badly that I talk Emily into letting me practice when everybody else is inside taking naps. This is against the rules of all the mothers on the street, but she lets me do it. Hop . . . Plop . . . Hop . . . Plop . . . Hop . . . Plop . . . Hop . . . Plop . . . HOME.

I get tired and go inside. "You smell like pennies," she says, sniffing the sun and sweat in my hair. She twists an ocean-blue stone out of a cheap earring and gives it to me to mark my place in the squares. The others use little rocks and pieces of glass and think my blue stone is too beautiful to play hopscotch with.

One day we are playing late in Caroline's yard and in the street in front of her house. It is almost dark and the spring air is growing warm. A new boy has moved into the neighborhood. He is twelve or thirteen years old. He is throwing a softball for us to catch. He is light-haired. His chest and arms are muscular under a white T-shirt. The grace of his hand on the ball and of his arm throwing it attract me and scare me at the same time. I am suddenly unexpectedly shy and afraid to go near him. I am glad he is there and yet wish he would go away and let us play the way we always do.

Something in my reaction to this boy, standing as if alone in the middle of a crowd of younger children, makes me remember my father and the feel of his body close to mine—which I thought I had forgotten and didn't know I missed. The moment was, as far as I know, my first conscious sense of what it might mean to be sexually attracted to a person of the opposite sex—a lovely being with a body and a manner like my father's.

Mrs. Cooper comes into the yard and says, "Go home, all of you, right now. The President is dead."

It is Thursday, April 12, 1945. President Roosevelt has died at Warm Springs, Georgia, from a massive cerebral hemorrhage and the stress of a war that seems endless.

I walk home in the twilight, thinking, "The President is dead. The President is dead," and knowing for the first time that I belong to a world larger than the world of my family and friends, that the war is real, that America is real, that some things are more important than others and that the things that happen to all of us together are the most important of all. The insight comes with a jolt of ecstasy. I am me. I am here. I am part of something big.

Gram and Emily and Mamie sit at the kitchen table listening to the news on the radio. The room is dark. They seem frightened. They don't know what it means that the President is dead. They were expecting the war to end soon and for Duke and Sonny and LeRoy to come home. Now what?

Duke leaves for the Arctic island of Attu by way of Seattle the day after the President dies, and writes to Gram about the trip by train across America. "The ride out here—particularly from Chicago on—was beautiful. In Wisconsin the trees were beginning to bud and plowing was going on. When we got into Minnesota it began to change a bit and in South and North Dakota there was snow. In Montana and Idaho everything was covered with snow. I saw ducks by the thousands, pheasant too numerous to count and forty-eight deer. The Cascade Mountains just before we got to Seattle were the prettiest. It snowed day before yesterday and there were millions of 'Christmas trees' on the mountains."

He found wartime Seattle booming, "almost like a picture show of a gold-rush town. Everybody is running all over everyone else and making more dough than they know what to do with. It's a city of half a million people—lots of country people from the farms and most everybody seems to be from somewhere else. I don't know *who* was in Seattle before the war."

My father's life will be very different on the frozen desert island of Attu than it was in coastal France. To begin with, there is the Arctic weather, which he calls "beyond description"—and the loneliness and isolation and worry about Emily and us and the seeming futility of what the Seabees are doing there. They work; they watch movies; they eat cold cuts; they play cards—and whenever there is something to drink, they drink it. Afterwards he says, "I never want to see another picture show or eat another cold cut as long as I live," and I don't think he ever did. He didn't mind the work and the company of the men whose labor, as chief petty officer, he was now in charge of, but the futility, the isolation, and the distance from home came close to driving him crazy.

The Germans surrendered in May and the war in Europe was finally over—thanks to Sonny, we all said, though Gram didn't like the idea of her oldest boy being decorated for killing people and she thought General Patton was a little crazy, though her son idolized him and would carry something of the General's strut in his own posture for the rest of his life.

Some time that spring Knoxie gets sicker. She is not herself. She is having little strokes, they say, but won't go to the hospital—or can't afford to.

I go with Emily to see her. The living room is littered with full ashtrays and unwashed cups and glasses. The kitchen is stacked with dirty dishes and smells of decaying fruit. The dogs are ravenous.

Knoxie looks sick and pitiful and a little frightening. Emily seems very happy caring for her mother and getting her house in order. I put water and food in bowls for the dogs and stack the dishes in the kitchen for us to wash. I love being alone with my mother when she is happy and working like this.

I stand at the door of the bedroom watching Emily struggling to keep Knoxie in the bed. "The bed's clean now, Mother," she says. "I want you to get in there and stay there. You're sick. I've got someone coming to look after you." Though her words are stern, her tone is jocular, as if she is teasing and playing with this ravaged remnant of her beautiful mother, this woman who has never been anything but trouble for the people who love her.

To me, my grandmother looks like a huge terrified frog, all head and arms and legs, scrambling to get out of the bed. Her hair is wispy and thin. Her skin is yellow. I see the brown aura of death all around her and feel sick with the smell of dogs, cigarettes, and rotting food.

My mother is not afraid and does not feel sick. We take the beer out of the refrigerator and put it under the sink and go to the store and buy cigarettes, tomato soup, and tea bags and call an old colored woman named Elizabeth to come stay with my grandmother. While we wait, Emily tells me about the time Knoxie got so tired of her children calling "Moooooother . . . Moooooother" from all over the house in Birmingham that she made them call her "Mrs. Hillman" for a whole day. "Miss Knoxie," she says, "was not a motherly woman."

Elizabeth comes. Her hair is yellow-white, her eyes are gray, and her skin is as light as mine. She pays a lot of attention to me and tells me how sweet and clever Emily was when she was little. "And everybody loved Miss Knoxie in spite of herself."

Though I don't know the nature of the wound in Knoxie's heart, I know it was deep and dark and everlasting. Her love for her children and her husband—and for Charlie Gunter, too, for all I know—mingled intense affection with ruthless criticism and joined sentiment to cruelty in a way that was sure to do harm. She never loved Emily in the way her fatherless daughter needed to be loved and, as far as I could tell, didn't love us at all.

I remember mainly her self-involvement and her inexplicable inability to tell Jane and me apart. Although I know she must have visited us in the country at least a few times, I have no recollection of it and only a handful of memories of being in her apartment. She died at seventy-four on June 21, 1945, the day the Japanese surrendered at Okinawa after some 12,000 Americans and 160,000 Japanese had lost their lives.

I don't remember much about Knoxie's last illness and death, except that Emily was gone a lot, and then Knoxie was dead. After the funeral, Gram said, "They dressed Miss Knoxie in lavender lace and she looked almost like her old self. Her face was lovely and all filled out again." I couldn't imagine Knoxie looking lovely and didn't understand how her face could fill out after death.

Lots of people I don't know come to our house. Nobody seems sad. Everybody says, "It's for the best." Gram says, "Miss Knoxie was just so impractical," forgiving in death the very thing that in life she had found nearly unbearable.

I go with Emily to clean out Knoxie's apartment. I want to dress up in her dresses and shoes, but Emily won't let me. We put some silk dresses and feathered hats and a few pairs of fancy shoes and some shawls and pictures and books in a big leather trunk.

"This stuff is just so much like her, I have to keep it," Emily says, with tears in her voice, though she doesn't cry.

We give Knoxie's two Pekingese dogs to a little girl who lives in the Sophronia with just her mother, who for some reason is not supposed to be quite nice enough for us to play with, though Bessie lets us play with her anyway and sometimes invites her into her apartment and gives her some of our clothes. A few days later, Emily and Jane and I go back to Knoxie's and get Polly the parrot and take her to the little zoo at Oak Park to be put in a cage near the monkeys. We leave her screaming, "Emily . . . Emily . . . wanna cracker," and walk backward and wave. "Bye, Polly . . . Bye, Polly . . . We'll come see you."

We took some of Knoxie's furniture to Bessie's and some to Wilmington Road and put the trunk in the barn in the country, where it remained untouched until Emily's granddaughters found it and dressed up in the shawls and the boots that made me think for the first time in a very long time of the day we packed them. Years after that, the scrapbooks, photographs, and letters Emily and I had tossed into the trunk along with the clothes became the basis of much that I now know about the strange, damaged woman who was my grandmother—a woman bereft, it seems to me, of all hope that life might have meaning beyond the desperate gratification of her own need to be approved of and desired.

I think Emily must have wanted the love of her charming, frivolous mother more than anything else in the world. She buried her, I believe, still wanting it, not having gotten it even in those last months of devoted attention to an old woman's childish needs. Except for the day we packed the trunk and I wanted to put on her dresses and shoes and Momma wouldn't let me, I saw no tears for Knoxie and no sadness. And I am left in the end with memories of the summer of 1945 that link the childish happiness of being alone with my mother to a haunting sense of the never-assuaged longing of my mother for her mother and me for mine.

The Old Trouble

Some old and new friends of Emily's start coming to our house at night. They come at first, I believe, to cheer Momma up because Knoxie has died. They come in the afternoon and bring supper and stay late and sit on the beds and the chairs in Emily's bedroom and talk and laugh and tell jokes. My Aunt Kitty is there one night with a beautiful dark-haired woman I never saw before or after that and whose name I don't remember. She is sitting Buddha-like on the top bunk of the double-decker bed Jane and I sleep in. She is laughing. Her face is radiant and a wild shock of dark curls tumbles around her head. Emily is happy and I am overjoyed to be included in the fun.

Summer lasts forever and most of the time we play outside. Sometimes, some of my friends come to my house and we shut all the doors to the living room and push the two velvet-covered Victorian settees Emily brought from Knoxie's together to make ourselves a private little "doctor's office" to play in. One lies down on one settee while another sits across from her on the other settee and caresses her "naughty place," as we call it, slow and sexy, outside her shorts. We take turns. We all like being the patient better than being the doctor, such a soft feeling, such a delicious new thing to do. We seem to have been born wanting to do what we are doing and knowing to keep it a secret. Don't tell the grownups. Don't tell the boys.

One day Emily and Mamie come flying into the room, making a lot of noise at the door and acting like they don't know what we are doing. At first I am scared. I know we aren't supposed to be doing this. I know they know. Something about the way they are acting reminds me of the day they threw me in the shower for telling Jane that Shag would bite her if she didn't come down the sliding board.

They say, "Let's put these chairs and things back where they belong," and take us to the kitchen to drink Kool-Aid. They scare us, though, and we don't do it again—at least not in the house where they can catch us.

If we get messy enough in the yard, Mamie puts us all in the shower together. We laugh and giggle and touch each other's bodies and splash water all over the floor. Mamie says, "Y'all cut out the commotion and stop all that splashing."

The country and New York seem so long ago and so far away that the things that happened in those places seem hardly to have happened at all—or at least not to have happened to the child I now seem to be. Though Emily often says "When Daddy comes home," and "When we go back to the country," I think our magical new life will last forever and that—even if those unlikely things do happen—nothing will really change. Only now and then, a strangeness in Emily's voice, a fleeting blankness on her face, or something someone reads to me out of a book brings back the fears that once governed my life.

Jane and I have been sick in bed for two days. Emily sits between us on the bed reading *The Little Match Girl* from a fairy-tale book with pictures. A frail child huddles shoeless and starving in the snow. Emily's voice sounds funny. I start crying and can't stop. I don't know whether I am crying for myself or for Emily or for the cold and abandoned Match Girl or because I don't feel good. Emily stops reading.

"Please, Momma," I beg. "Read the rest."

"It's just a story somebody made up," she says. "The little girl goes to heaven because she loved other people more than herself." As Hans Christian Andersen tells it, the child (loved only by her grandmother, who has died) freezes to death amid holiday plenty and soars toward God "in a halo of light and joy, far, far above the earth, where there was no more cold, no hunger, and no pain." Perhaps Emily (whose instincts leaned toward protection) feared what it would do to me to learn that life could be so harsh and bereft of love that even a child would welcome death. And how and where (and why), she might have wondered, should such a truth be told? And why must children suffer? I'll never know what my mother—a woman who could look into a suicidal abyss one minute and deny the existence of all suffering the next—thought of such questions, but I think she thought of them.

Some time that year, Bessie takes Jane and me to see the movie *Jane Eyre*, starring Margaret O'Brien and Joan Fontaine. The image of the child Jane (who would let herself be kicked by a horse or have her arm broken just to be loved) and her ailing friend Helen walking cruel punishment tours in a downpour of rain in payment for their affection for each other sticks in my mind as the image of childhood suffering. Two orphaned girls with nothing to cling to but each other, walking and walking in a black-and-white circle until one is dead of exposure and the other bereft of her only protection.

I had by then, I suppose, begun to understand what suffering means and that terrible things happened to people (and children) and that other people endured the same sorrow and loneliness I felt in myself. Although the intensity of the identification could come close to unbearable (as in *The Snow Queen*, *The Little Match*

Girl, and *Jane Eyre*), fictional anguish attracted me and may have helped me put my own fears at a distance and see that emotional suffering was not exclusive to my family and could (if you didn't freeze to death in the snow and the fairy godmothers helped you) be endured, survived, and risen above.

I didn't care how many terrible things happened in a story so long as I could anticipate a comprehensible outcome—a believable escape, an earned victory, a satisfying revenge, or a merited exposure of human folly. Jane and I loved the exposure of human folly, and so did Bessie, especially when it was acted out by animals and made-up creatures like dwarves and witches. Certain truisms stuck with me: to love is to risk bereavement; survival requires courage and is not guaranteed; one way or another, people usually get what is coming to them.

Bessie takes us to see Elizabeth Taylor in *National Velvet* that year, too. All that lingers is an image of an adorable, adolescent Liz galloping a make-believe horse in her bed and my aunt enraptured by the star being born before her eyes. Although Bessie seems not to have had an artistic bone in her own body, she knew good fiction and star quality as if by instinct and partook of the best that was available to her and shared it with us.

Seated in her favorite wooden booth in a dark corner of the Tavern, her short torso pulled erect, her hands on the back of her hips, and her eyes flashing, she delivered adjective-laden movie and book reviews that often took longer than the works themselves. "Splendid . . . gorgeous . . . atrocious . . . appalling," she'd say, giving away every turn in the plot as she went. The others stood and sat around her, nodding or shaking their heads, agreeing or arguing and consoling one another about the state of art and the world. Everything was changing. What was to become of America now that the fighting was almost over?

Montgomery had two bookstores in those days, Neeley's and the Little Book Store for Children, both owned by the same family, a few blocks apart, a few blocks from the Pickwick, the Tavern, and the movie theaters, a few blocks from the artesian basin where slaves had been sold, a few blocks from the First White House of the Confederacy, a few blocks from where the Yankee missionaries started the Swayne School for the freed children during Reconstruction. I can't imagine that there were any better bookstores anywhere in America at that time. They had everything—all the classics and everything new—or so it seemed to me. They were small and dark and quiet, with books lining the walls and spread out on wide tables between long, narrow aisles in two or three rooms smelling of dust, new paper, and bookbinder's glue, stuck back on the ground floor of two of the tall old buildings that made up the center of town. Though they were sometimes busy with two or three people demanding attention at the same time, they were never crowded.

Mrs. Neeley would get Bessie a chair and there she'd sit, for hours, it seemed to me, with her fat legs spread comfortably apart, talking about everything and everybody to anybody who would listen, all the while glancing at the books the proprietor recommended and nodding like an expert buyer at an auction when something caught her eye. And when we left, we'd leave with a bag almost too heavy to carry.

Looking back, I am struck at the perfection of her taste and the range of what she bought. Everything by Louisa May Alcott, Mark Twain, and P. L. Travers; all the Uncle Wiggily, Bobbsey Twins, and Miss Minerva and William Green Hill books; Honey Bunch and Five Little Pepper books; many collections of fairy tales and legends (including King Arthur); *The Wind in the Willows*, *The Secret Garden*, *Bambi*, *Heidi*, and later Nancy Drew (girl detective) and Cherry Ames (nurse), along with precocious, less predictable choices like Mary Webb's *Precious Bane*, W. H. Hudson's *Green Mansions*, and Marjorie Kinnan Rawlings's *The Yearling*, stocking an ideal little library for me, advancing my taste as my abilities grew, and reading aloud to me for as long as I would let her.

The Ware–Walker women as I knew them were, as a rule, more inclined to give material things and behavioral directives than to give of themselves. In these gifts of my childhood, Bessie (whose hyper-energies and abrupt affections might not ordinarily have appealed to me) gave all that she had and opened vistas far beyond the tiny world in which we lived, and gave me the thing I most needed—a mental and imaginative escape from family troubles that might otherwise have swamped me.

Oddly, given his influence on the time and place in which we lived, Bessie couldn't stand Sir Walter Scott—an author so devoutly read in the antebellum South that some people (Mark Twain included) charged him with creating the Southern character that caused the Civil War. At the heart of the romantic paternalism brought to the planter South from England and Virginia, and propounded by Scott, stood the image of the white woman on a pedestal—exalted by a male aristocracy that was honor-bound to guard, protect, and provide for her.

In truth, by the time Knoxie (who, unlike her sister, adored Sir Walter) and Bessie were born, there hadn't been a man in the family capable of doing those things for three generations. Yet Knoxie—whose whole view of her life seemed to depend on her ability to believe that her existence had meant something because men had admired her—lived both controlled by the myth and in seeming rebellion against it, elevating romantic love, chivalry, and female dependency to almost religious heights, while flouting the prescribed behavior women were expected to adhere to. She was still clipping poems of yearning out of the newspaper in old age; and when the sweetheart she never married died in 1932 when he was sixty-seven and she sixty-one, she wore black for a year and claimed his casket had tipped in her direction when it passed by her at the funeral. And still—what with her thirteen-year debut and her ambitions to be either a poet or a businesswoman or a nun and the troubled husband she never loved and the lover she never married and her drinking and smoking and gallivanting about and irresponsible spending and the inattention to her children and what other people thought—Knoxie lived further from the ordained roles for Southern women than anyone else I knew in those days.

Bessie, though she loved a certain kind of romance in fiction, always seemed to me to be too interested in doing what she pleased on a daily basis to be bothered by sexual drama in real life. I believe she disliked the overwrought romanticism of Scott (and protected us from it) because she thought it a bad example for living in the real world, a fact plainly witnessed (as she liked to point out) in the all-too-apparent decline of the "celebrated Miss Knoxie."

Although many of the books Bessie bought favored a sentimental and paternalistic Southern view of things, some had decidedly feminist leanings. Even the post-Confederate *Little Colonel* stories by Annie Fellows Johnston, which Bessie liked better than we did, featured a stubborn, independent-minded female nonconformist. And it was the enterprising, boyish, literary-minded Jo March of *Little Women* who was, I suspect, her highest standard of what a girl ought to want to become.

By the time we got back from New York, *Gone with the Wind* had been out several years and Bessie had seen it more than once, but wouldn't take us to see it and made no bones about not really approving of it even for adults. Since she loved sexual drama (no mean thing, certainly, between Nelson Eddy and Jeanette MacDonald) in fiction (if not in her own life), that can't have been what bothered her. Nor would she have minded the romantic image of the antebellum South and the caricatured Yankees, Southerners, and Negroes—all of which jibed with her own view of things. What caused her upper lip to lift in disdain was, I believe, the gory depiction of the fall of Atlanta (where her own father had been among the vanquished) and the unspeakable comedown of the planters after the war.

As a rule, Southerners don't talk much about what happened to their families during Reconstruction, and Bessie was no exception—though the hardships of the times would have been well known to her from the destitution of some of her relatives and the narrowness with which her immediate family escaped the same fate. Bessie's version of that story always played up the success of the escape and her grandmother's sagacity rather than the humbled circumstances of the Wares and the wolf at the door—two facts she never admitted. That she herself lived erratically on a modest inheritance (mostly in land she sold "on time" for income) she stretched to last a lifetime was something I only knew later.

So some weekends we spent with Bessie going to the Tavern, buying books, and seeing movies, and some we spent with Gram helping her with the chickens and the rabbits she raised to sell and cut down on the wartime meat shortage. We liked to look at the twitchy-nosed, red-eyed bunnies, but didn't find them as interesting as the hens we fed in the morning and gathered eggs from in the afternoon. Every few weeks a butcher would come and take a penful of rabbits off to kill and sell for food. Sometimes he'd also take a chicken or two and some eggs.

In memory, Gram still stands in her back yard in a gray print dress with her hands on her hips, bartering with the grocer, leaving me with an image of the kind of entrepreneur she might have been had her life and the times been different. Although she loved a bargain and never bought anything she didn't need or paid more for anything than she had to, she was not much of a negotiator. She simply enjoyed doing business, I think, and making a little profit from an enterprise everybody said was sure to fail.

During the war, Gram began renting her spare bedroom to a woman named Lillie Bealle for three dollars a week—just for the duration of the wartime housing shortage, she said. Miss Lillie, as we always called her, was a big, aging ox of a woman with cropped reddish hair, pink skin that mottled in the heat, and a dour sense of humor that attracted children and offended adults. Her room was bare of all decoration except for the little desert cacti she bought at H. L. Kress' five-and-dime store across the street from the Lerner Shop, where she worked as a salesclerk. The sharp cheese she liked (so sharp we didn't like to sit beside her when she ate it) and the cacti were the perfect symbols of Miss Lillie's prickly, off-putting personality (so the grownups thought), but children's standards are different and Jane and I liked her because she treated us like equals, was always herself, and for our benefit turned the little happenings of her workdays into wild, exaggerated tales, of human corruption and degradation.

Her "lady boss" cheats the salesladies (villains all, except for herself) out of their commissions; the traveling "big boss" is a half-crazy Yankee who understands nothing about the business of selling clothes to women in a place like Montgomery; customers try on all the clothes and leave the dressing rooms a mess, don't bathe as often as they should, and seldom buy anything anyway.

Miss Lillie doesn't think a nice white lady from the country like herself ought to have to wait on colored people. But—she has to admit—some of them are as nice as they can be and often smell much sweeter than her white customers.

When the narration is over—and we drag it out and stoke it with amazement and horror as long as we can—we eat supper and play dominoes or Chinese checkers while Gram and Miss Lillie, and sometimes Aunt Kate, listen to programs like *Stella Dallas*, *Amos 'n' Andy*, *Pepper Young's Family*, *The Hit Parade*, and *The Grand Ole Opry* on the radio and wait for the nightly news to tell us it is time to go to bed.

Miss Lillie seemed born for spinsterhood, until her sister died some time in the late 1950s and she married her brother-in-law, who, I suppose, must have found her enthusiasm for human foibles and petty drama as entertaining as we did—egged on, no doubt, by his children, who were, I believe, the only people on earth besides ourselves who already loved her as much as she deserved to be loved. By the time she married, Miss Lillie had been at Gram's house ten years, still pitching in on groceries and paying three dollars a week for her room.

At home, Jane and I get up from our naps and join the other children on the street collecting nickels and dimes from our mothers so we can go to Heacock's Drugstore and buy candy. One day, everybody is going, but I don't have any money because Emily is in her room with the door shut. I ask Mamie for some money. She says, "Your momma's not feeling good and I don't have any money for candy."

She is sweeping dirt too forcefully out the back door. The door slams. She is not in a good humor. "You just walk with them," she says. "I'll give you something to eat when you get back."

I go out and tell the others. I'm not even hungry. I don't want any candy. I'll just go with them and not buy anything, like Mamie said.

"No," they say. "Ask your mother for some money." They say that because sometimes Emily gives Jane and me more than a nickel apiece and we buy things for them. I don't know what to do. I'd rather stay home than open that shut door, and Mamie is in no mood to be asked again. They insist. I open the door.

Emily is lying on the bed, lying there flat on her back in her clothes, with one arm dangling off the side of the bed, drunk for the first time in so long that I thought I had forgotten all about it—as if everything that happened before Wilmington Road had happened to somebody else.

I ask for the money, pretending to my mother (and trying perhaps to convince myself) that I don't know what is wrong. Maybe she's just tired or in a bad humor. She doesn't move. My friends stand outside the door. I don't want them to see her. I ask again. She doesn't say anything. I say, "They're waiting, Momma. We're in a hurry."

Finally, she says in a mean voice, "Get whatever you want out of my pocketbook." I don't do it. I hand her the purse. She takes it and flings a shiny half-dollar at me. I don't know what to do with that much money.

"Now, for God's sake, get out of here and leave me alone," she says, turning her face to the wall.

Emily looks like a flat brown paper doll lying on the bed. I smell the beer in a glass on the table and see the despair in her body. Despair, sorrow, and who knows what else in the face of a deficiency so fundamental in her that it seems to have been impossible for her to imagine herself without it. And where did it begin? And how could it end other than badly?

Did it begin with the troubled, failed, incongruously romanticized father she never saw even though he lived several months beyond her third birthday? Did it all go back to the powerfully driven, powerfully torn man who had been her grandfather on that side, already old and half mad, with half his fortune gone five years before the last child in his last set of children was born? Did Mary Ann Gentry Hillman—the young woman he married in old age and saddled with a lifetime of responsibilities impossible to fulfill—have something to do with it? What about all those gambler-pioneers driving south, following slavery and iron ore on the one side and slavery and cotton on the other? And kinsmen on all sides betting their souls and their fortunes on the Confederacy and never admitting the part their own errors played in the disaster that befell the country their ancestors fought to create? And grandparents on the cotton side who by the time Emily was born seemed to have lost their emotional moorings altogether, along with whatever inkling they once had that life might have meaning beyond the preservation of the little that was left?

And now Knoxie was dead—whose love Emily had needed and wanted so much and who (as far as I can tell) had never loved anybody at all, including (and least of all perhaps) herself. And Bessie's frenetic, often wrongheaded attentions hadn't, in the end, been enough to make up for all that was lacking—or to stop new sorrows from climbing on the backs of the old ones. The cruel betrayal of the love who left her when she was still so young that she thought all she had to do to be loved and happy was to be kind to people (unlike her mother) and refrain from drinking alcohol (unlike her mother). And now—despite the sweet letters between them—there was all that trouble with Duke, whom she ached for and loved and who when they were together hurt her at every turn (and suddenly the realization that the happiness of the past year had been predicated on his absence) and whose suffering hurt her as much as her own. And the dead son nobody mentioned anymore and four children to worry about and try to make happy every minute of the day, for of course she had pledged that, too—that her children would never be as unhappy in childhood as she had been. And the money not going as far as it used to, and nobody knowing when the men would be home.

I stand in a brown fog watching Emily on the bed, knowing that the pain that has erupted in her is more than she can stand. My mother is licked (by booze and life and her own frailty and a dead-end heritage), and I know she is going to die, as viscerally as if a finger had traced the words on the air between us.

Buried in the past I try to forget is the memory of separations as stark and real as death. Drink turns my parents into frightening monsters, and the ones who loved me might as well be dead. They are there. Not there. I am loved. Not loved. The fluctuation is unbearable and I learn not to feel it. And every time the drinking and hurting stops, I tell myself it is over for good and believe it for as long as I can.

Something starts to break inside me and then goes hard. If she loved me, she wouldn't do this. If I can't stop her from doing it, I will have to stop loving her. I won't love her anymore. I will stop loving her. I will have to stop . . . unless . . . unless I can find some way to stop her from drinking.

Since I can't stop loving her and I can't stop her from doing what she is doing and I can't die, I walk down the street with my friends and juggle my worries like stones in my head and vow not to love or trust or need anybody this much again for as long as I live.

I go to Caroline's house and show the half-dollar to her mother. Mrs. Cooper is horrified. "Ohh, why in the world would she give you that much money?" she asks. I hear criticism as well as astonishment in her voice. It's wartime. Nobody has money to throw away. I don't know which would be worse—for her to think I took the money (which I think she thinks) or for her to know about Momma (which I am afraid one of the other children will tell her).

"I don't know," I say. "I think it was all she had."

I know Emily is drunk and I also think she acted the way she did to get back at me for bothering her. Finally, Mrs. Cooper tells me to spend a dime on Jane and me together and get forty cents back.

"Four dimes," she says, "or eight nickels, or some combination like that."

"I can't remember all that," I say.

"Then show me the change when you get back," she says.

"Okay."

It is very hot. We take our time walking the three blocks to Heacock's and play as we go. I buy the cheapest candy, which is also my favorite, a tricolored bar of pressed coconut stuck together with sugar. I ask the lady who sells it to me how they make it three different colors. She says, "I guess they put food dye in it." I didn't know you could put dye in food.

We go back to Caroline's house and eat our treats sitting in the grass in front of waxy-leafed gardenia bushes that smell strong in the sun.

Mrs. Cooper gives us lemonade and asks me about the forty cents. I show it to her.

She says, "Go on home now and give it back to your mother."

I say, "Not yet."

She says, "Go ahead, before you lose it."

I go home and try to give the money to Mamie. She acts mad with me, but I think she is really mad with Momma. "I told you to leave her alone," she says. "I don't want anything to do with that money."

I go in Emily's room and tell her I brought forty cents back—I now thoroughly understand the relationship between a half-dollar and forty cents. "I meant for you to *spend* it," she says in a mean voice, not taking the money, not looking at me. Still drunk. Still mean. Still acting crazy.

Duke is gone, Knoxie is dead, and all that she owned and might have left to her children (even—somehow—Aunt Emily's bequest that was supposed to have been held in trust for them) has been squandered—squandered on hats and shoes and careless management and gifts to people she hardly knew, as if she were determined to go to the next life unfettered by a burden of wealth and leisure she had done nothing to deserve and had never known what to do with.

Emily had counted on some kind of inheritance from her mother to make things easier when Duke came back and—perhaps, perhaps—to give herself a greater claim to independence if things got as bad between them again as they had been before the war. But Knoxie has left nothing but debts and some cotton fields nobody knew what to do with.

The day Emily gave me the half-dollar is the only time like it that I remember on Wilmington Road, but I can tell from the way she looks in photographs that there were others and that some of them must have been terrible and that she must have been mixing the alcohol with pills again. Late in the summer, Gram brings a professional photographer to the house to take pictures to send to Duke. Emily sits in a lawn chair in a yard that needs mowing. Her body is so frail that I know she must be drinking more than eating. Her hair is lank and thin and her nose seems disproportionately large amid her otherwise delicate features. Her attempts to smile do nothing to mitigate the strange effect of the unfocused look on her face.

Jane and I hang over her, looking anxious, frightened, and full of concern. Jim is a fat cherub in her lap. Joan—who has finally learned to walk, pushing her brother's stroller—stands beside her, a tiny, wispy-haired reproach to our mother and a living emblem of how troubled a family we are. No matter how hard we pretend. No matter how much we don't think of it most of the time.

In a little snapshot taken earlier that same summer, my friend Lucy and I stand beside Emily, who again is seated in a lawn chair, this time with Joan in her lap. Her face looks plump and pretty, her hair is permed and held back on one side with a comb.

My mother is becoming two women again.

The healthy one is the one I usually remember when I think of Wilmington Road. She gives me all she has to give, staying sober much of the time and grooming me for independence as if from some premonition of separation. She gives all she has to give and I take it—as greedy and unthinking as if all the fine moments would last forever.

213

Mrs. O'Gwynn's Room

 A few days after the photographer comes to take our pictures because Gram thinks Duke is going to be gone so long he will forget what we look like, the United States Air Force drops an atomic bomb on Hiroshima. The city is leveled. One hundred thousand people die. Three days later, Nagasaki is hit. A third of the city is destroyed. Seventy-five thousand people are killed or wounded. We hear it on the radio.

Gram is the only person I know who objects. "It's just not right," she says, "killing all those women and children, even if they *are* Japs, even if it *does* end the war."

It does end the war. People run out of their houses and yell in the streets. Victory over Japan. The fighting is over. Everybody is happy. Everything is going to be fine. Emily only drinks sometimes. Duke is coming home. I have a brother. School starts soon.

I go to the third grade. My friends from Miss Lamb's room are there and lots of children I never saw before. Our new teacher is a plump, round-faced woman named Mrs. O'Gwynn who twists her prematurely salt-and-pepper hair back in a tight bun that makes her look "old-maidish" to us. In truth, she is probably not much older than Miss Lamb and has a husband she adores, a dark, well-built, romantically handsome police detective who occasionally visits our class in uniform and tells us about his work, emphasizing his role as protector and friend to children in trouble. And she beams at him and he beams at her, and it seems to me that the dashing Mr. O'Gwynn is as in love with his plain, dumpy wife as she is with him.

Except for special occasions, like a visit from Mr. O'Gwynn or a trip to the police station to see where he works, Mrs. O'Gwynn sits most of the day calm as a Buddha behind her desk, her arms crossed in front of her, picking at a little sore on the top of her right arm and controlling the class with the smallest of gestures. I wince every time she touches the little red spot and watch all year for it to improve or get worse, which it never does.

The sight of true laziness in one of her pupils, especially in arithmetic, occasionally heaves her from her chair and down one of the narrow aisles between our desks to whack the offender (almost always a boy) on the knuckles with a thick wooden ruler. Since such an expenditure of energy is rare on her part, most of us experience her reprimands only by the example of someone else's suffering. But the example is enough and the sound of a . . . *thuuwhackkkkk* . . . on a neighbor's knuckles sticks in our minds for life, inspiring mathematical ambition in some and numbing it in others.

What I like most about the third grade is the hour after lunch when we act out fairy tales. My favorite role is Gretel in *Hansel and Gretel.* A tall, smart, messy-haired girl named Eve Harwood specializes in female villains and plays the wicked stepmother as the true psychopath we know her to be. Every day we ad-lib a different story from beginning to end, knowing the plot (and required to get it right) but free to make up the words to suit ourselves. It is the most carefree, high-spirited, creative time of our day and the only time my new teacher seems more interested in fun than in performance.

One day Mrs. O'Gwynn calls me to the front of the room and tells me to write her name (I have long since forgotten why) on the blackboard. I do it, but I make the "O" much too big. My classmates gasp in derision and I adjust by making the rest of the letters tiny, so that the word looks like an odd diagram of a mother duck trailing her ducklings.

Somebody says, "Quack . . . Quack." The rest of them howl. And that moment becomes my first memory of awkwardness in school and my first realization that my self-schooling has left me with a spindly scribble that bears little resemblance to the neat circular figures my friends make when they write.

Mrs. O'Gwynn naturally inaugurates a campaign to improve my handwriting. Despite the embarrassment of the moment at the blackboard (which may have been part of her strategy), I have little interest in this endeavor and suspect her efforts to be futile from the beginning, which doesn't stop her from making me (along with a few of the slower boys in the class) spend part of every recess trying (or pretending to try) to make a certain number of fat vowels and symmetrical consonants to her specifications.

Mostly we talk and giggle and draw pictures. One of the boys draws pictures of animals and naked people doing bad things with each other. One day he brings whiskey to school in a medicine bottle and lets everybody taste it, and after that he has to go to another school. Before that, he had tried to kiss Mary Alice Till on the mouth and she hit him in the head with a Webster's dictionary, but that hadn't stopped him either. As far as I know, nothing ever did.

Every school day begins with one of the smartest, best-behaved students leading the devotional, which consists of the Pledge of Allegiance to the Flag, a reading from the Bible, and the Lord's Prayer. The leader is assigned the honor well in advance in order to be prepared to sit at the front of the class in a throne-like green chair and lead with distinction. Mrs. O'Gwynn is full of praise for those who handle their duties well. We applaud the readers who read stories we like—Noah and the Flood, Jonah and the Whale,

Daniel in the Lion's Den, the Shepherd and the Sheep, Moses in the Bulrushes—and read them well. Nobody wonders how (or if) the strange things we hear could have happened. Anything can happen in a story.

What I wonder is if I am smart enough and important enough to be chosen to lead the devotional. Some children read so poorly they are never chosen. Nobody mentions it, but everybody notices it. Finally, I am chosen. Gram helps me pick the story of the Loaves and Fishes (after I finally get it across to her that I want to read an interesting miracle) and I sit in a big rocking chair at her house and read it over and over until I know it almost by heart. When the day comes, I sit down in the green chair with my heart thudding and rise feeling for the first time like one of the smart children in a regular classroom.

There are three or four Jewish children in our class. As soon as I figure out that Joe Klein and Ed Steinberg are considered the smartest boys in the class, I make it my goal to be as smart as they are. I don't know where I eventually learned that girls weren't supposed to be, or to seem, as smart as boys. I certainly didn't learn it from my elementary-school teachers, who pushed us all unmercifully, often to the detriment of those who couldn't keep up.

Even though everybody knows Joe and Ed are the smartest boys in the class, they aren't among the first devotional leaders. Before Joe reads, Mrs. O'Gwynn talks to us about the Pilgrims and religious freedom and tells us Jews have different beliefs from the rest of us and always read from the Old Testament and don't have to say the Lord's Prayer if they don't want to. After Ed reads, we want him to read all the time because he reads very dramatically, which most of us don't have the nerve to do. One time, though, he was reading and pronounced the "w" in "sword" and the teacher kept trying to correct him and he kept repeating it wrong until everybody laughed. It was the only time I ever saw him squirm.

Having recently made the mortifying mistake of pronouncing the title of the book *Hugh and Nancy* as if it were *Huff and Nancy*, I vow to stay on guard against silent and deceptive letters.

It was on a day such as that one that Mrs. O'Gwynn took the class down the hall for the first time to the converted classroom that served as the elementary-school library. In memory, the room is huge. All four walls are lined with books guarded not by a dragon but by a frail, gray-haired, part-time librarian demanding absolute silence from behind a heavy wooden desk at the front of the room. Long school tables occupy all the space in the middle. We are allowed to look at as many books as we like for as long as we like and then choose one to take home for a week. And the next week another. And the next week another, even in the summer.

Sunlight falls across the room so bright you can see a million specks of dust floating in it. The musty, ripe-apple smell of small children in a schoolroom before air-conditioning comes simultaneously with the memory of light and my life as a bookworm begins.

I turn nine years old three weeks after school starts. Emily says I can take all the girls in the neighborhood to Oak Park for my birthday. Knowing how my mother felt about Knoxie's neglect of such matters, I think there must have been some kind of birthday celebration for Jane and me every year, but this is the only one I remember. And this time I don't have to share it with my sister. She will be there—and Mamie and Emily and Gram and Bessie, too, I suppose—but the occasion and the invitation list are to be mine alone. I don't know any particular reason for this, except that my mother now treats me more and more like a person separate from my sister.

The invitation list consists of the six or seven girls I like most in the neighborhood. Emily says we don't have to dress up. It is not a fancy birthday party. We are just going to Oak Park to play and eat ice cream and cake in the pavilion. They can wear shorts if they want to. The important thing to me is that my mother thought it up and she is doing it just for me.

Mrs. McKinney doesn't like the idea of Lucy wearing shorts to a birthday party. She and Lucy keep asking me about it. Yes, I'm sure. That's what Momma said. We don't have to wear dresses.

Lucy keeps on asking. I start to worry but am afraid to say anything about it to Emily, who doesn't like to be pestered. I think being pestered is one of the things that makes her drink, and I especially don't want her to drink before the party.

The day of the party arrives. Jane and I stand in our bedroom with Emily. Mamie gets dresses out of the closet for us to wear. School dresses, but dresses just the same.

I say, "I want to wear shorts. You said we didn't have to dress up."

Emily says, "I didn't mean shorts. I meant school dresses." I know she said shorts, but I don't say that. I say, "I told the others they could wear shorts."

She says, "I'm sure their mothers will make them wear dresses. Girls don't wear shorts to birthday parties."

I hear her voice go sharp and feel the tears coming in my throat. I don't want her to be angry. Or mean. Or drunk. I don't want to go to Oak Park. Maybe I never did. Maybe it was just something Emily thought up without asking me at all.

The others gather in our yard to go with us in Gram's and Emily's cars. Everybody is wearing a dress except Lucy, who is wearing light blue shorts and a frilly white blouse her mother made her put on so she would look dressed up. I think it is an interesting outfit and tell her she looks pretty, but I know she's mad.

"You lied to me," she says between her teeth. "You said you were going to wear shorts. I think you told all the others to wear dresses and told me to wear shorts to be mean." I don't know how to tell her what really happened.

We go to Oak Park. Lucy pouts the whole time and I worry the whole time and try both to make her feel better and to keep my mother and Mamie (who would surely tell Emily) from noticing that something is wrong.

Except for that, it is a wonderful party. We play all over the park and use all the power of our growing bodies to set the flat-platform merry-go-round going as fast as it will go before we jump on. Mamie and Gram push with us and keep pushing when we jump on and we take turns pushing and riding and pushing and riding until the wind blows our eyes dry and we seem to be moving at the speed of sound.

We throw peanuts to the monkeys on their little island and visit Polly in her cage and even Lucy laughs at the talking parrot which knows my mother's name, "Emily . . . Emily . . . Polly wanna cracker . . . Cracker . . . Cracker . . . Bye now . . . Bye now." We don't have any crackers and Polly doesn't like the peanuts we throw, but she talks and yells for as long as we stand there.

We go back to the pavilion and sit outside, around a square table, and eat cake and ice cream with flat wooden spoons. When we get home, Lucy says, "I just wish I'd known to wear a dress like the others."

The next big event in my life was Halloween, which had never been important before, because in the country there had been no one to dress up for. Until we moved to Wilmington Road, I had never heard of children roaming the streets in costumes, scaring people and begging for treats.

At school we decorate the room with orange pumpkins and black witches riding broomsticks. Mr. and Mrs. O'Gwynn decorate their house the same way and invite the whole class to eat hot dogs in their back yard the day before the holiday. They live in a big cottage in Montgomery's first suburb, the old part of town near the school. The house is dark-looking and has a big porch across the front that reminds me of the Holt cottage we moved down the hill in the country. Emily takes me in the car and lets me out to walk up the steps and across the porch and into the dark house alone. I hear the other children inside and feel my mother's eyes watching me going to a party by myself.

At home the next day, Emily and Mamie talk about whether or not it is safe for Jane and me to go out with the older children at night. Finally, they decide we can go with some children they trust and stay until 8:30, which is an hour after dark and very late for us. Emily gets out some old Mardi Gras costumes of Knoxie's. They are very elaborate and different from the homemade cat and witch costumes the other children have. Jane chooses a pink fairy godmother's dress with a crown and a wand. I pick an orange lion's costume that comes complete with a bushy mane, a swinging tail, and padded paws. Everybody says I look like the Cowardly Lion in the *Wizard of Oz*. The costume is much too big, but I hold it around me and set out in the twilight with my friends. Emily watches from the porch, satisfied with our efforts and wearing that Judy-is-getting-to-be-such-a-big-girl look I associate with my growing awareness of her love for me on Wilmington Road.

Emily takes me to the beauty parlor for us both to get permanents. Jane doesn't have to go because her hair is long, thick, and caramel-colored and only needs brushing to be beautiful. Mine is thin, white, and wispy and people are always doing things to it to make it look better. Gram says, "Mary Willie is the only one who can do a thing with it."

In the summer, Mamie puts my hair in French braids on both sides of my head and it stays out of my eyes and I like it that way, but that is not what Gram means. What she means is that sometimes Mamie curls it on the curling irons she heats on the stove and uses for her own hair. I have to sit perfectly still, so she won't burn me while she makes ringlets all over my head. After that, she brushes my hair out hard (I like that part) and it looks soft and curly for a few hours. Mamie says white women have to get permanents because they don't know anything about curling irons and don't like to put grease on their hair. Sometimes she puts a little on mine to make it go around the curling iron better, she says, and to protect it from the heat.

I go to the beauty parlor with Emily and sit under the dryer and look at books and draw on a school pad and watch ladies sitting around in pink and green aprons with their legs crossed and their hair in curlers, talking, smoking, and drinking Coca-Colas from bottles with straws in them.

Two ladies with gray hair are talking about Zelda Fitzgerald (only to them she is Zelda Sayre, Judge Sayre's daughter, and always will be), Montgomery's bad girl gone mad and come home at forty to roam the streets, muttering and kicking stones and tossing sticks like a child.

"Ahh, what *could* have happened to that girl . . . and Lord! her poor mother."

Emily is light-spirited today, and these women act as if they know nothing of her troubles. But something in their description of the ravaged Zelda (the blank eyes and lost look on her face, the horror-story transmutation from beauty to madwoman) makes me look to be sure Momma is still "hunky-dory," a phrase she uses so specifically that I have come to interpret "Everything is hunky-dory" to mean either that she is not drinking or that she is drinking and doesn't want me to know it. Today everything really is hunky-dory.

I draw a picture of a woman with the bearing and body of a crone and the face of a startled child. I ask Emily how to spell Zelda. She tells me, nods toward the others, and says, "Don't let them see the picture; they'll think you're being mean."

I got my first permanent that day, but I don't remember what my hair—or Emily's—looked like when we left. I remember that my mother and I enjoyed ourselves. I remember the indelibly imprinted half-hospital, half-chemistry-lab smell of the place. And I remember the picture I drew. It was a likeness, I believe, of my idea of my mother when she was ill. Though I didn't see them until many years later, it also looked eerily like the images Zelda drew of herself.

We go to the depot to get Duke. He has all his clothes in a blue duffel bag. He looks bigger and more red-faced than I remember. Emily is driving. He sits on the passenger's side. Jane and I sit in the back with Mamie, who holds Joan in her lap. My father seems like a stranger to me and also like he never went away. I feel awkward in his presence and a little afraid of him. Emily is as excited as a schoolgirl on her first date and primed to "get Duke's goat" by telling him that his roly-poly son has gotten frail and sickly. As soon as she starts it—her demeanor straight and serious—I start jumping up and down in the backseat, wanting to stop her but not daring to do something she has told me not to do.

"Judy, be still," she says, shooting a "keep quiet" look at me.

No, Momma. Please. Don't do it. Don't start anything.

Duke puffs up like a toad. His face goes crimson. Nobody says anything. Nobody smiles. Horror fills the air. I want to scream, "It's not true, it's not true!" but nothing comes out of my mouth. I sit frozen with fear, watching the nightmare that had stopped start to run again.

We ride all the way to Wilmington Road like that. We get out of the car like that. I walk behind my father and see the gnome of too much loss and too much fear sitting on his shoulders. The whole family follows him in silence up the back steps and into the house, where Jim plays in the sun, fat as a pig on the floor at Gram's feet. The joke's on Duke.

The laughter is the out-of-control laughter of relief mixed with meanness and terror. My father is back and so is anxiety and unforgiveness and the ghost of my dead brother.

"Duke's different since Attu," Emily tells her friends by way of explaining why she is not as happy as she promised to be as soon as her husband returned. I don't know what happened to my father in Attu—or how his sorrows shifted in the year of isolation he endured there.

He liked the work—building, fixing, making do, putting something of use where there had been nothing. He enjoyed the position of authority he had there and the respect the younger men accorded him for his abilities and his extraordinary willingness to help and sympathize with anybody in trouble. But it was lonely and cold, the sun never set, and there was nothing to do but read and think and talk until he was sick to death of his own thoughts and his own words.

Applying the ingenuity that came naturally to him, he found ways to supplement the terrible food and the meager supply of beer and whiskey allotted him and his friends—and drank heavily on occasion, too heavily—and then the remorse and the shame and the suspicion that he couldn't, after all, control it and the awful dawning dread that maybe some of the problems at home were as much his fault as Emily's.

He grew heartsick, worn out, bored to death with the grueling sameness of every day. He talked long hours to the chaplain, a Methodist named Welsh from Texas, whom he liked. But if those talks produced anything resembling a theology, I never knew of it. He enrolled in a college English course by correspondence but never completed it. He missed his wife and worried about his children. He had a son he had seen only once. He wanted to go home, and yet . . . and yet . . . the longing for home must have been riddled with despair over problems that were, though he never fully admitted it, unsolvable.

In two years my father—who had seldom been out of the South for any length of time—had lived in big cities, seen the antiquity of Europe, the vastness of America, and the strangeness of the arctic north. He had seen other lives he might have lived and other work he might have done. Though he came back to us, because it was not in him to do otherwise, I believe the decision was made in sorrow and placed atop a vast reservoir of unrealized ambition and tormenting disappointment in himself. I don't think he ever forgot the roads he now knew existed and might have been taken—if it hadn't been for Emily, if it hadn't been for us. I don't think the despair embedded in the circumstances to which he returned ever altogether left him. No matter what he did to forget it, it was there, always there, the very bedrock of the rest of his life.

By the time Duke gets back, I think of myself as very grown up and hardly remember the baby I was when he left. In his absence, I have learned to read and write and go into the world on my own. I have come to love and need the mother I had hardly known before. Until we went to New York, my father had been my favorite playmate and teacher and for all intents and purposes my only parent. He returns an unreachable stranger, an interloper in a maternal present that has all but erased the memory of a past in which he and I had loved each other almost exclusively, or so it had seemed to me.

The house on Wilmington Road that had, in his absence, belonged mainly to the children now belongs to him and feels suddenly cramped and terribly small. Duke is edgy and nothing about my glorious brother seems to suit him.

At first, Jim walks on his bent-over toes like a ballerina. He should walk on the bottoms of his feet, Daddy says. He's *too* fat. We baby him too much. I should stop carrying him around like a doll. He'll grow up to be a sissy. It doesn't take long to see that

Jim's being Jim isn't going to make everything wonderful the way Emily said it would be when Duke got home.

Daddy wants to go back to the country. Momma wants to move to a bigger house in town. I want to stay on Wilmington Road.

"You can have a horse in the country," he says.

"I don't want a horse," I say, although I do want one.

"She doesn't want a horse," Emily says, although she and I have already talked to Uncle Dan about getting me one. "She wants to stay in town. We all do but you."

They stand in the dining room shouting. Duke is threatening to leave and not come back. I hang on to him, yelling, "Don't go. Don't go." Emily says, "Oh, let him go. Who in hell cares. I'm the one who loves you."

She sounds so much like Aunt Bessie that she starts to laugh and mock Bessie's Old South way of talking, "Who in *heh-yul* cares. *III'yahum* the one who luuvs yuh."

Duke hates it when Emily jokes in the middle of something serious. Jane thinks it is funny. I think it is funny when my mother is sober but frightening when she drinks and terrifying when she argues with my father.

"I am sick to death of women," Duke shouts.

"Women!" he shouts again, this time at me, pawing the ground like a bull. "For God's sake, don't *you* start acting like a woman."

His hand is on the doorknob. My heart is racing. I think he is leaving and not coming back because of something I did. Because I said I wanted to stay on Wilmington Road. Because I was glad when he was gone. Because I wish he hadn't come back.

Blamm! Out the door.

Jane appears and we start giggling and chanting . . . Don't grow up . . . don't grow up . . . don't grow up to be a wooooooman.

"Y'all hush," Mamie yells from somewhere else in the house and then starts up a childish parody of a Bessie Smith song she likes: "Please check your chewing gum and raisins at the door."

Lifting her head from the kitchen table where she is slumped, Emily chimes in: ". . . and tell us Bible stories like we never heard before."

And then all of us from all over the house: ". . . Old folks, young folks, everybody come . . ." And suddenly we are back like we were when Duke was gone. Only he isn't gone.

Emily mounts every argument she can think of to keep us in town. She likes it better; we like it better; Mary Willie likes it better. The people who are renting the house in the country want to stay. Gas is still expensive. It's easier for her to look after us in town. Nothing works.

The country is home, Duke says. We are going back.

Back to the Country

Men from the Greenhouse move our things back to the country. The sky is bright and dry. The ground is cold under my feet. In school I am still big, but in the country I feel as small as I did before we left. My body relearns pine straw and dry leaves and the sound of insects at dusk.

Soon it seems as if we were never gone and I forget I didn't want to come back. We inherit a big white cat from the Biggs family, who had rented the house while we were gone. We call the cat Mrs. Biggs because she is squat and flat-faced like her owner. The next morning after we sleep in our own beds for the first time in two years, we find Mrs. Biggs dead in the downstairs bathtub.

At first we don't notice it, since she is white like the tub. Daddy thinks she licked insect poisoning off the top of a can he left by the tub. He puts her in a sack and gags taking her outside to bury behind the pool.

The Biggs have moved our dolls from the closets in the room where Joan and Mamie used to sleep and put them in the Holts' old smokehouse, a square cured-ham-smelling shack where we have an old-fashioned washing machine with a wringer that mashes the clothes flat and squeezes out the water. Mamie tells us she read in the paper about a boy who got his hand caught in a wringer like that and had his arm jerked off. We don't altogether believe her, but we keep our distance.

I find Suzie in the corner of the smokehouse, still wearing the frilly dress I left her in but with one of her soft, flesh-like arms gnawed off at the elbow by rats. I am very sad looking at her arm, remembering how we used to call her from New York, thinking she was safe in her room upstairs. Mamie wraps the doll's arm in gauze like a wounded soldier's and I sleep with her until she oozes stuffing from every limb. Finally Mamie says, "I think we might as well give her a funeral," and we do.

We have been back in the country only a month when Christmas morning dawns blue and icy. Uncle Dan arrives in a truck and unloads my Christmas present, a chestnut-and-white-dappled pony called Dimples, already saddled and bridled for me to ride. Dimples is high-spirited and ornery, he says, too much horse for me now, but I'll grow to her.

"Be careful around her head, Turkey Buzzard," he adds. "She bites." I hope he's joking, but I don't think he is.

He puts me up and tells me what to do with my hands and my knees. My heart thuds, part joy, part terror. "So what do you think of your little girl now, Tutta?" he asks Emily, using the baby-talk word for "sister" that he has always called her.

I feel my mother's eyes on the back of my head. Women riding horses for pleasure belongs to her family, not Duke's. She wants this for me even more than I want it for myself. She wants some part of me to be more hers than his. I feel her desire and her approval go into me.

After Christmas, Emily starts taking flying lessons with Duke, who had come home from the war determined to buy an airplane and learn to fly. To justify another luxury paid for with her money, he insists Emily learn, too. She loves the idea.

They buy first a Piper Cub and then a four-seat Cessna that they keep at a private field called Allenport on the Narrow Lane

Road in the country not far from our house. One of the images that lingers from that spring is of my mother striding through the house in trousers on her way to her lesson, her face glowing and her spirits high.

Amid the old troubles, something new flickered in my mother that year, an inkling of the woman she was trying to become and might have been had she lived long enough and conquered her addictions, a woman drawing for the first time in a long time on the old confidence, energy, and tomboyishness of her youth. And some of it was shared with me.

On Saturdays and Sundays, I sit with her, watching Duke shooting for practice in the front yard, throwing clay "birds" up with a metal contraption he has made, shouting and bragging and showing off for anybody who will stand at a safe distance and watch. He is a good shot and proud of it, taught by his own father when he was little.

He and Emily buy a croquet game and set up the wire wickets on the lawn and play with us and with friends who show up in the afternoon. Though I don't find the game very interesting and never do figure out how to score it, I like to watch the colored balls rolling in the grass and to hear the *ka-thu* . . . *ka-thu* . . . of wood hitting wood. I like it that all of us are there together and that there is never any trouble between my parents when we are doing it.

On such a Sunday, Duke saddles Dimples and he and Emily sit in chairs and watch me ride in the front yard. The scent of horseflesh rises from under me. I grow warm in the cool air. I am riding and they are watching, so relaxed and happy together that Emily's hands hang loose off the arms of her chair as if they had never been nervous and jittery and never would be again.

Dimples starts galloping and I let her go . . . up . . . up and up toward the sky . . . and over a little pile of stones put there by Duke to make an outdoor cooking grill. I tumble off and land on my right shoulder. Duke puts me back on and I ride a little longer. "You always have to get back on when you fall off," he says. My arm hurts. They say it will be all right in the morning.

I cry all night. Emily drinks and rocks me in the bed. Pain and the smell of whiskey mix with the warmth of her body and I remember the time when I was little and cut my foot and she wouldn't let the doctor put stitches in it because I was afraid. I remember the unspeakable loneliness of my love for her in the years before we went to New York and came back.

She takes me to the doctor the next day. The upper arm is fractured. The doctor says, "When did this happen? Why didn't you come sooner?"

Emily has on a dark, short-sleeve dress and no coat. Her arms have goose bumps. Her face goes blank and her mouth quivers when she tries to speak. I say, "It didn't hurt all that much."

I get a cast from shoulder to elbow. We come out into the cold sunshine together, like the time I got the tetanus shot and fainted. I know my mother loves me. I don't want anything to happen to her. I don't want her to be upset and afraid. I don't want her to drink.

She tells Duke the doctor was rude to her and implied the accident happened because they were drinking and negligent. Gram says it happened because I stayed home to ride instead of going to Sunday School with her. I say it happened because Dimples jumped a pile of bricks I didn't know was there.

I am a hero at school for a few days and get the best parts in all the plays. Although I can write perfectly well with my right hand despite the cast, I use the occasion to learn how to write with my left. The other children think I am very clever. Despite all the recesses I have already spent (and more to come) filling long rows of double-lined paper with the fat vowels and tall consonants Mrs. O'Gwynn likes, my handwriting even with the right hand is still scrawly, like a boy's.

Mrs. O'Gwynn requires that all our test papers be signed by our parents and returned to her the day after we get them back. I get back a spelling test with a good grade on it, due to be returned on one of those mornings after Emily has stayed up all night drinking and crying. She is drunker when I get up than she was when I went to bed.

Duke has sent someone from the Greenhouse to take us to school. The horn is honking. Emily is sitting in half light in her nightgown in a chair in the sunroom, a cigarette in one hand, a glass of ice water in the other. Damn it, Momma.

I don't know which I dread most, doing something that might make her feel worse than she already does or being late with the paper like the kids with bad grades. Honk. Honk. I hand her the paper with a pencil.

"N'uh-uhh," she says.

I stand in front of her in a room that in memory seems practically dark, nothing shining but her satiny gown.

"I need it today," I finally say.

She signs it on her knee, shaking. As soon as I see the tiny, illegible scribble, I know I have made a mistake.

Mrs. O'Gwynn takes our papers from us one by one at the beginning of class. I hand mine to her, braced against the thudding in my chest.

"Did *you* sign this, Judy?" she asks, picking at the little sore on her freckled arm and not looking up.

My mind locks. My fear is so great that I think it may have caused her to say the very thing I feared she would say. Sounds stick in my throat. Finally I whisper, "Momma signed it."

I don't know what Mrs. O'Gwynn sees in my face when she finally looks up, but she looks a long time. I see myself standing before her, sick with shame at what I have told.

"It's all right," she says at last, folding the paper and looking away.

I know with all the instincts in my nine-year-old body that she knows about Emily and knows what the scribbled signature means. In my first memory of something resembling adult conflict, I am torn between wanting to succeed in school and wanting to hurl my very existence between my mother and the insults I see rushing her way.

Soon after that (I know it is soon, because my arm is still in a cast), I experience my first anxiety attack when faced with a task in school. The task is to copy something from a book as many times as it takes to get it right. Erasures are not permitted.

I hate to do things slowly when I have other things on my mind that I want to do—like practice writing with my left hand. I do the exercise in a hurry. It has a mistake in it. I do it over. Another mistake. I do it again. Still not perfect. The others are done.

I go back to my desk. My heart pounds. The sun hurts my eyes. Lines and words go blurry on the page. My head hurts. I can't see, can't make the words look right on the page.

Fear and shame rise together inside me . . . I can't do it right . . . I can't *do* it at all . . . I want to go home . . . I want my mother . . . A howl sticks in my throat.

I grab my first failed attempt out of the trash can, erase the mistake carefully (though attention to details of this kind does not come naturally to me), and hand it to the teacher, my heart pounding with the fear of getting caught. Though she had said "no erasures" and I don't like to do bad things, there was nothing I wouldn't have done at that moment to stop the panic and (miles below it and a thousand times worse) the bottomless ache for the mother I know somewhere beneath logic that I am losing.

Such moments were rare and mild in the beginning, more frequent and more intense later, and always concealed. I go suddenly mute and stupid when faced with the possibility of failure. Absolute terror mingles with outrage and shame and my wits fly apart. Error equals mental dissolution equals utter annihilation.

Temperamental explosions often spring from the chaos, understood by no one, least of all myself. And always under it somewhere, a whispered longing trying to turn into a shout, "I can't do it. Somebody help me. I want my mother." And then, finally, amid the storm and the disintegration of my senses, the strength comes to do whatever it is I think I can't do. Somewhere in the chaos, I always find it, connected, I believe, to that part of my mother that says to me, "You *can* do it; try it another way," but which in the moment I think I have lost.

After my arm heals, Emily starts taking me to a stable near Allenport to take riding lessons from a stocky, cowboyish woman called Ty, whose last name may have been Tyson. Ty was not, as I recall, the sort of woman who could possibly have gone by whatever ordinary female name she may have been given at birth.

She runs a business; she trades horses and trains riders; she wears boots and jeans; she is not like any woman I have ever seen before. Sometimes Emily leaves me there on the way to her flying lessons. Sometimes she brings me after school and sits in the car and helps Jane with her homework or walks out to the ring and leans on the fence and talks to Ty.

I see the two of them walking in front of me toward the riding ring. Ty, dressed like a man in an all-weather jacket and boots; my mother matching her stride in a loose skirt and flat shoes.

One day, Emily takes Jane and me to Allenport. The little Cessna sits with a few other small planes in a makeshift hangar in the middle of a dry field, a few miles from where Orville and Wilbur Wright gave flying lessons the spring Sonny was born, and conducted the first night flights in the history of aviation.

I go up in the plane with Duke. Jane and Emily look like dolls standing on the ground waving. I sit in the seat beside my father and steer while he tells me all the scary things he would be doing if I weren't with him. We fly over the tops of trees and see houses and dark-looking rivers and roads and red and black fields so far beneath us that they look like pictures on a map. Suddenly the old oneness with my father returns and momentarily washes away my growing fear of his drinking and his temper. We are together. He is teaching me something. The light around us is so beautiful I don't care whether I live or die.

That spring, everybody at school gets the measles. I don't like to miss school and don't plan to get sick. One day, we go outside for recess and the sun is so bright I can hardly stand to look around me. I have a headache more severe than any pain I have ever endured.

Headaches are for grownups. Emily has headaches. This is real pain, worse than a cut foot that won't heal. Worse than a broken arm. More riveting than fear or sympathy. Mrs. O'Gwynn says I look funny and calls Emily. I wait on the playground, balancing myself on the wooden rim of a sandbox, unable to believe the brightness of the light or the pain in my head.

Jane and I both have the measles and stay upstairs in our single beds side by side for two weeks. Emily brings us Coca-Cola and crackers and tomato soup and tea steaming in Knoxie's gold-initial white bone-china cups (another sign of how grownup we have become) and for two weeks our room is a private hospital and Emily our nurse. By the time we go back to school, spring is in full flower.

Back then, Confederate Memorial Day was the biggest day at school in the spring. The other children brought arrangements made from the camellias, azaleas, magnolias, and daffodils that bloomed in their yards. Jane and I and our Paterson cousins brought big, glossy-leafed magnolia wreaths professionally made by our relatives at Rosemont Gardens. Every year, the teachers pridefully praise our contributions and scorn the punier offerings. Every year, my classmates seem amazed and shocked at the in-appropriate majesty of our wreaths. Every year, I feel foolish to make such a spectacle of myself and try to get Jane to carry my wreath for me. Every year, she refuses. We have pretty things in our yard. I wish we could bring those.

Uncle Will says the same thing every year when we pick up the wreaths. The Confederacy had been "pure foolishness" and everybody knew how his parents felt about slavery, but it was Old Will and Maggie themselves who had started the Rosemont tradition of commemorating the Confederate as well as the Union dead.

"Anybody who dies for what he believes, deserves respect," they had said. Not that they had much choice, since to refuse to honor the Confederate dead would have been symbol enough (all by itself) to destroy all they had worked for in the town—which may have had something to do with why our wreaths were so showy. In any case, the family tradition of making special wreaths to honor the Confederate dead was established long before I had anything to do with it. My job was simply to deliver one of them to the school every year and endure the unwelcome praise I received.

After the flowers are picked up, we are loaded into cars and taken to pay our respects to the First White House of the Confederacy, the modest, columned house which President and Mrs. Davis had occupied for a while and which, like so much of Confederate Montgomery, had a connection to my mother's family. From there we go to the state capitol, which had also served as the first capitol of the Confederacy, to see the gold star that marks the spot where Jefferson Davis had taken the oath of office.

The day is so rich in hushed tones and commemorative form and so poor in content as to be almost totally lacking in interest for children. The girls like the china-faced dolls that sit on the beds in the Confederate White House. The boys scramble to stand on Jefferson Davis's star. We have no idea what it means. Something about cotton and a Lost Cause.

We know what cotton is and see it grown and picked outside

Montgomery in much the same way it had been in 1860. But "Lost Cause" is euphemistic beyond any image we can possibly conjure until we are finally old enough to be allowed to see *Gone with the Wind*, which makes it all perfectly clear.

We sing "Old Folks at Home," "Dixie," and "Old Black Joe." Nobody says anything about slavery (an institution I rarely heard mentioned in all my years of schooling in Montgomery), or a million people dead during four years of fighting, or the city's nearly burning itself down to keep the invading Federals from seizing the cotton stored by the river, or livestock and freedmen starving in the streets when it was finally over and the Yankees occupying the city for seven years after that (and living in Bessie's grandmother's house, which even Bessie doesn't like to remember). No doubt, we would have found the truth more intriguing than what we were given—which was in the end hardly more than an attitude, and a very imprecise one at that.

Almost all of what I knew as a child of slavery, the Civil War, and Reconstruction came from Bessie's strange, disembodied, out-of-context stories. But the spirit of the tension between families like my father's (though, in fact, there were no others like it) and families like my mother's (whose ways and beliefs still set the tone of the place) went deep into my bones as part of the class warfare between my parents.

I remember them arguing heatedly once because Duke said "Reconstruction"—like ordinary people, like Yankees, like people who don't know what they are talking about—rather than "the Reconstruction," the way Emily said it was supposed to be said, the way it was said by people like Bessie and Knoxie . . . *thu* Reekun*struuk*shun.

Emily walks out the back door into the yard where Duke is planting bushes and says something about how her Ware ancestors came to Alabama on the Old Federal Road in whose very tracks our house now stands. Duke says something about "Reconstruction," minus the article, perhaps insinuating the moral and economic slippage that had set in among those Revolutionary backwoodsmen since they made the pioneering trek from one Southern wilderness to another. Her reply—whatever it is—starts off logical, but in a voice overly emphatic and full of metal, the way people sound when a little thing suddenly becomes more important than it has any natural right to be.

"You *have* to say *thu* Reconstruction; that's the way it's *always* said because, you know, there was only *one*. You don't say just 'war.' You say '*thu* war.'" Loud now, defending something crucial. She doesn't say, "We get to name it because we suffered it, and it was *ours*. Your people lost nothing because they *had* nothing." Nothing but scrub farmland on Gram's side, down there in the wilds of Wilcox County, where people had either gotten filthy rich off slaves and cotton as soon as the seeds hit the ground or they had been black and owned by somebody else or they had been next to nothing.

She doesn't say, wouldn't dare, "Carpetbaggers, foreigners, Yankees, abolitionists on your father's side, living with black people as if they were white, and by some outlandish subterfuge turning it into something to be proud of and admired for even by people who would ordinarily have despised them [and for a long time did and never stopped condescending to in secret], that had no right to be here anyway; and everybody would have been better off if they had stayed where they were and minded their own business."

Who was she to talk, he might have replied, born to folks half mad on one side, as inept as they were arrogant on the other, believing nothing, contributing nothing, as if being itself were of no consequence.

For as long as my mother lived, battles flared between them over subjects too trivial to be remembered. Some things were said and some weren't, and some of the things not said were louder than those that were. And some of the things I never heard said between them, I heard plainly and often from Bessie and Gram.

In truth, Emily and Duke fought over race and class and their immense vulnerability to each other. Fought over things that were happening then and things that happened before they were born and either couldn't be remembered or couldn't be told. And though I couldn't say exactly where family history ended and personal destiny began, I believe some of the troubles between my parents and the terrible outcome of their love sprang at least in part from the extreme way in which Southern reality played itself out in our family.

Death

 In the first of the rapidly moving memories that mark June and July of 1946, Duke commemorates the beginning of summer by taking us to ride in the beige Chevrolet convertible we have had since before we went to New York. We are flying down the highway into the wind to see the new Rosemont Gardens farm, which is near the Ware plantation. Jane and I sit in the backseat with our seventeen-year-old cousin Cissy. Duke and Emily sit in front. The wind blows Emily's hair forward so that it looks like a wreath around her head and makes a pink, bald-looking spot in the back. The three of us laugh uncontrollably in the backseat. Momma's hair looks so funny blowing backward like that in the wind.

Jane and I had planned to go for two weeks to the YWCA's Camp Grandview, which our Aunt Kitty Paterson directed that summer. We both go when the time comes, but Jane gets homesick the first night and, instead of staying in the cabins with the other children, stays in the house with Aunt Kitty and sometimes goes home with Uncle Sonny in the morning and comes back with him at night.

Emily and Duke come to visit after the first week. I'm disappointed because I haven't gotten any letters. My friend Lucy from Wilmington Road is there, and she hasn't gotten any, either.

I tell Emily that Lucy and I are the only ones who didn't get letters. She says she asked me and I said I didn't want any letters. It's the first time I've ever been away from home. I don't know anything about letters and homesickness. Lucy is so mad about the letters that she goes home after the first week. Jane goes, too, but I stay and get a letter from Momma every day.

After I start getting letters, I like camp almost as much as school. We swim in the coldest water we can imagine and play games and hear ghost stories and visit a haunted house. We sleep in bunks and use an outhouse for a toilet and have only kerosene lamps for light at night. There are children there from an orphanage who wear old-fashioned-looking clothes and don't talk much. Emily says she wants us to know all kinds of people. Duke comes to pick us up at the end of the week. I get carsick on the way home and throw up in the backseat. He gags when he tries to clean up the vomit, then throws a towel over it and opens the windows and puts me in the front seat beside him and tells me how he got carsick, too, when he was little.

"When my father came home with our first car, I was just a little boy," he tells me. "He got it on a Sunday and drove it to the house. Gram and Sonny and I got all dressed up to go for a ride. We drove way out into the country, and I got sick and threw up in the backseat and got all the newness out of that car right from the start. After I was older, he would take me and my friends to football games at Auburn and I would try so hard not to get sick, but sometimes he still had to stop for me."

Sometimes Duke and Emily go to a place called the Narrow Lane Inn near the airport and the stable to eat and drink and dance late at night. The place has a swimming pool and a long room full of slot machines. Once that summer, they took Jane and me with them and let us play the slot machines.

Duke holds us up to put our money in and watch lemons, limes, and apples spin until we know whether we have won or not. We lose all our money, but a bald-headed man standing next to us hits the jackpot and catches the coins in his hat. People crowd around him.

"Ten bucks," somebody says. "That's gotta be at *least* ten bucks." Duke explains "hit the jackpot" to us. We stay up late and eat biscuits and peppery fried chicken and watch Emily and Duke dance alone to a jukebox on a wide, wooden dance floor. Emily is so small she looks like a child in her father's arms.

August 1946. Emily is driving Jane and me downtown with Bessie to see *Song of the South*. We are wearing dresses and white Mary Janes for the first time since school let out in June.

I know from photographs that by now Emily is jaundiced and emaciated-looking, with thinning hair. I don't remember that. I remember that her hair is damp and curly in the heat, that she is wearing a blue-and-white-flowered dress and going to the hospital to see Uncle Dan's second wife, Mary Lou, who has a new baby, a boy.

Something is wrong with the baby. They talk about it in the car. Bessie's lip curls because she doesn't like Mary Lou, who isn't as beautiful and socially prominent as Big Helen was, though now that she is gone, Bessie doesn't like Big Helen either. I think about all the babies that have died in our family and start swinging my foot against the back of the front seat. "For God's sake, Judy, sit still," Momma says. "We're almost there."

We get out at the Paramount Theater. I want to go with Momma to the hospital. "No," she says and drives off.

A few days later we are packing to go to Fort Walton Beach, Florida, before school starts. Mamie's cinnamon breasts rise smooth and round out of the top of the new bathing suit she models for us. Jane and I have new suits, too. Ours are red, white, and blue. Mamie's is black and brown with swirls, dark swirling tornadoes that make her skin look lighter than it is. She paints her toenails and ours bright orange for the occasion, singing about a lady who had to pack her suitcase because her house fell down.

"Whose house fell down?"

"The lady in the song."

"You're not going anywhere, are you?"

"All of us are going to the beach, baby, you know that."

That night Duke and Emily set out for a party. Emily has on a shiny red dress and high-heeled shoes and stands close to Duke in the twilight by the car, which is black and also shiny. Their arms touch. Emily is humming and pretending to dance in the twilight. Tomorrow they will go to the beach with friends who drink and because they are together they won't drink. They have decided to stay sober together forever.

Jane and I clown in a puddle of light from the kitchen. Emily laughs and kisses us, saying goodbye. Mamie waits at the back door.

The rest of the night must have been like any other. Mamie reads to us, plays records, gives us supper. Maybe Hattie Jo comes and plays upstairs and goes home early so we can go to bed and get up early for our trip in the morning. We have done it all so many times before, and Emily has been sick so long and bedridden so many times that even what happens next doesn't seem unusual at first.

I wake up. Momma lies collapsed at the foot of my sister's bed. Duke and Mamie are picking her up. Crickets hum. Frogs croak. The yard is still gray. I love it like this before day in the morning, but something has happened.

They take Momma downstairs to her bed. Her body droops; her face is the color of dust. I remember her drooping like that on the bed another time, holding a little gray, red-lettered box of white pills loose in her hand, saying, "I only took one or two more than I was supposed to." I remember Bessie struggling to take the pills from her in New York.

White sheets. Gray light. Duke dials the phone. Mamie stands by the bed. Emily whispers, "I don't want to die," and then repeats it slow and loud as if she is reading from a script.

Duke says, "Good God A'mighty," half swear and half prayer.

I stand still in the doorway, my heart going wild in my chest.

Mamie says, "Go upstairs, Judy."

Emily turns her head a little toward me on the pillow and says, "Go on now, baby. Ya momma loves you."

Duke's cousin Haygood comes and they go in an ambulance with Momma. Sun blanches the grass. Morning glories make a purple-and-white stair at the end of the arbor by the pool. I go back to bed and watch the sky get lighter.

My heart beats so hard I think it will jump out of my body. I lie on top of the covers and try to remember my mother's face and press my chest on the bed to stop the pain from breaking my ribs. Red dress, black car. A kiss, a smile, goodbye. No face. I want my mother. I want to die. I am not to blame.

This time she will die . . . This time she is going to die . . . The refrain thuds in my head as plain as if someone were saying it out loud. Without knowing the words, I understand the meaning of self-destruction and suicide, knowing, as I had known for as long as I could know, that my mother would die and that something in herself would be partly to blame and something in me would think I had caused it.

I know she is going to die. But I don't yet know just how much I love her and need her. I don't know I will never get over her death. I don't know what it is going to be to hold the gates shut on the tidal wave of sorrow already rising inside me.

After a while, Duke comes back with Sonny. They get out of the car, just the two of them, standing solemn and close in the dirt driveway where Emily had hummed and danced by the car.

Without looking at me, Duke comes inside and tells Mamie, "She died in the ambulance . . . Coronary embolism." Booze. Pills. Hunger. Failure. Outrage. Blues in the night.

Sonny squats in front of me, saying, "Your momma died this morning."

I shut my eyes and think I see her, shadowy and frail, like a statue carved from wood, wearing red. Momma is dead. The words mean everything and nothing to me. How can my mother be dead? How can anybody be dead? Like Lambie-Pie, like the sheepdog Martha, like our brother James Porter. I know it is supposed to mean that I will never see her again, but "never" means nothing to me. Never. Not ever. How can somebody be nothing forever?

Sonny hugs me. "You're the oldest," he says. "You'll have to act big now," which must be what they told him when his father died. Anger hits my chest like lightning and turns my heart to water. Never. Not anything forever. Impossible. I can't stop hoping. All I feel is fear.

Jane and I go inside and sit on Daddy's lap in a chair by the fireplace. He is crying hard, sobbing for a long time like a child. "Emily . . . Emily . . . baby." I don't know how to balance his sorrow with all the trouble and meanness I have seen between them. I didn't know he loved her like that.

Aunt Bessie comes and she and Mamie cry in each other's arms upstairs in our room, where Mamie and Duke had found her. I sit on a bench by the window and watch. Mamie has taken off her blue Indian-princess pajamas and put on a white uniform. In her arms, Bessie looks like a fat little girl who has fallen down at a birthday party and come running to her nurse to be comforted. The great love of her life has suffered terribly and is gone.

The ceiling fan above them thumps and buzzes, cooling the air against my face. Duke comes upstairs. Bessie stands in front of him and cries with her head in her hands. They stand there a long time, survivors of the same war, silent, not touching.

"Ah, Miss Priss," Duke says finally, using a childhood endearment of Emily's, touching her arm. Bessie cries harder. I watch his broad back go down the stairs. His left shoulder hikes higher than the other and twists toward the front. His head bends to that side as if he were cradling a puppy in his neck.

Emily's death threw my father's emotional life into chaos and all but demolished Bessie's. "She was my heart," Bessie always said, and though I never saw her cry again, I could always hear the tears in her voice when she said it. The emotional havoc of that day linked my father and my mother's aunt together for life.

I had seen Gram cry only once, when things were bad with Emily after we came back from New York and Duke and Sonny were both overseas. Now she stays in the kitchen with Sonny and Kitty and the others. Her glasses are thick and her left eye loses focus like Jane's when she is tired, but she doesn't cry. She says, "When I first knew Emily she was just the sweetest girl. She never touched a drop of whiskey before she met Duke." I don't think she ever altogether forgave him, either for his drinking or for Emily's death.

Grownups come and go all day, some we know and some we don't. When Jane and I enter a room, they act cheerful, as if we don't know what has happened. They go to the funeral without us.

A friend of Gram's stays with Jane and me and teaches us to crochet with a hooked ivory needle and silky blue thread. I pretend to be interested. It's Sunday. Joan and Jim are upstairs. The house aches with the silence of a place recently emptied of a crowd. We sit for a long time in the sunroom. I look out the window and suffer the *click-slish* of the needles and the woman chattering.

Her dry, knuckly, pink-nailed fingers push the hooked thread in and out. Push . . . hook. Push . . . hook. Her mouth looks gray and her false teeth are the same ivory-yellow as the hooking needle.

Gram says it's a sin to hate or to call another person a fool. Click-chatter, click-chatter, click-chatter. Push . . . hook . . . click . . . slish. Push . . . hook . . . slish. Fool. Damned fool, bottomless pit of the Devil. Bitch. Hateful jabbering gray-mouthed bitch. I hear my father's words and his voice in my head. The unthinkable has happened to us and I cannot think it. I want to see my father and know he is safe. I want my mother back.

The house smells like roses and fried chicken. The dining-room table is piled with food: honeyed ham with cloves stuck in the fat; fried chicken; pale, gummy mounds of potato salad; pickles; sliced tomatoes; cakes and pies. The greasy smell of fried chicken, the ache of a too full belly and death are linked forever in my mind. "Child, your mother is sick. Your mother is dead."

Click-chatter. Click-chatter. We wait and wait and wait. Dread piles on dread. Time stops. I seem to be turning to stone.

Finally, Daddy is there, standing with the light behind him in the dark doorway between the kitchen and the sunroom. His suit hangs slack and crooked from his shoulders and his face looks twisted and dark in the shadows. Somebody says, "Duke is not himself."

I start toward him, expecting him to pick me up. Instead, he turns his head and pulls away as if repelled by the sight of me. Suddenly I sense that, for all my mother's apparent weakness, it had been some secret strength of hers that had held us together. It may have been simply the strength of her illness and her need for us. Or perhaps the pure and primordial power of motherhood itself. Or some invisible force protecting us from the soul-destroying rage/terror that periodically erupted in Duke. I couldn't say. What I know is that, whatever it was, it is gone.

I cower before him, a tiny being in front of a giant wrapped in darkness. A howl rises up, up, up in my body. *Momma. I want my mother.* Before it gets out, a pain as harsh and palpable as a blow from a fist strikes my throat and blocks the words . . . i want my mother . . . momma. momma.

Who knows how a child reasons in a moment that threatens all hope of psychological and (so it seems) physical survival. Maybe

247

I thought it safer to carry my terror in solitude and silence than to add to the burden and rage of the only parent I had left. Maybe I instinctively deflected the combined impact of my mother's death plus whatever I already knew of my father's inability to cope by taking on his suffering rather than feeling the identity-shattering pain of my own. Perhaps my decision to protect him was simply a projection of my own need to be protected. Better perhaps to see myself as strong and him as weak than to see and feel the extremity of my own vulnerability and need for comfort and protection.

What I am certain of is that in that moment my mind and soul wrap around my father like a vine clutching at a tree that is still standing though sick at the center. The double weight of his grief and mine comes down on my shoulders, placed there, so it seems, by a hand from above. My childhood is over. My job now is to worry about my father, please him, placate him, and make his life bearable. My life seems to depend on it. That the task is impossible is of no consequence to me. If we are to have any chance at all, I think I must bear both his grief and mine and never speak of it and never upset him and never displease him. He wants me to succeed at everything I try. I'll do it. He wants me not to grieve. I won't. Without him, I am utterly alone, sunk in solitude too absolute and loveless to be borne.

"We are going to the beach tomorrow anyway," Duke says. And before I can get to him (to try to stop him from doing what I know he is going to do), he turns back toward the kitchen and says what I have been waiting for two days to see if he would say: "I don't suppose anybody would think it remiss if I took a drink now, under the circumstances." Someone makes a joke, grants permission, and laughs.

Bastards. Sons of bitches. Fools. Hateful. Stupid fools. Where is my mother? Where in the name of God is Momma?

248

I hear the cabinet door sliding, ice clinking, glasses on the table, laughter.

Hateful. Stupid. Fools.

He says it with a smirk, stilted and self-conscious, making "the circumstances" sound like nothing, like a flat tire or a lost toy. Terror turns to rage in my body. I can't breathe and my heart thumps like thunder. KathuHD, kathuHD, kathuHD. Duke is my only parent.

Suddenly I am out the back door, moving in fading sunlight toward the arbor where the morning glories that shouted at daybreak now hide in tubes of gray. Grass cut yesterday smells green and wet in the sun. Yesterday. Red dress. Fort Walton. Momma.

I feel eyes on me from the house. I keep moving, slow, my head up to keep them from calling me back. Leave me alone. I want my mother back. I want her the way she was before bad things started happening. I want her the way she was on Wilmington Road. The way she was the last time I saw her.

Maaamaaa. Maaamaaa . . . I want my mother . . . starts up in my throat. Stop it. Shut up. I don't want them to see me or hear me or stop me from leaving the house. A house like a rotting grave where everything dies.

I grab a handful of scuppernongs and glide away from the house toward the end of the arbor nearest the barn. I don't like the red muscadines that grow at that end—too dusty and sharp-tasting— but I pick a few anyway to give them time to stop watching from the house. I put a few in my mouth, then start picking them by the handful and tossing them at the sky. The greener they are, the better they throw. The better they throw, the farther they go . . . fhhiiiiit . . . fhhiiiiit . . . little lobbing sounds into the sky and back to earth, fhhiiiiit, fhhiiiiit . . . into the sky and back to earth.

Nausea rises greasy inside me. I inch toward the pasture, where I have been forbidden to go alone, because, they say, "that horse Dimples is *mean*, just as soon trample you *to death* as look at you."

Who   cares   .   .   .   whoooo   caaares   .   .   .
wuuuuhuuuuuuuuuuuuuuuuuuuu rises with the nausea.

I see a child set free by the thought of her own death. Who cares. Who cares. Who cares about anything.

Baptized in grief, she drops to the ground, rolling over and over and over. Crazy with sadness, she runs and spins and yells out of the great cave in the place where her chest used to be.

A child sick with grief, running and running, her face wet and dirty in pine straw and grass, her heart pressed to the ground, pushing, pushing, pounding like thunder, like drums. Puh . . . Pu . . . Pu . . . Puh . . . Pu . . . Pu . . . pressing hard and flat in the twigs and the leaves. Momma. Momma.

Outrage and disbelief bite into my heart. My mother is *not* dead. I didn't do anything wrong. She *did* love me. *Not* dead. If I don't find some way to keep loving her, I will die myself. Momma. Emily. Baby.

I walk up the hill toward the house. All the cars are gone. The house is dark except for the light in the kitchen. Bessie and Mamie stand behind the stove. Bessie's face shines cold-creamed and smooth as an egg. Mamie glows amber in the heat. They look like children playing house. Bessie promises to stay the night and read a grownup story about love and trouble.

The sky purples. Bats swoop. Crickets hum. The night air already has a touch of autumn in it. My mother is gone.

Nobody says Emily. Nobody says Momma. Nobody says anything about her for years.

Life After Death

Mamie, Gram, and Duke stand in the kitchen talking. Daddy says, "I'm not sending any of them anywhere, not to your house, Mother, not to Sonny's."

His voice has tears and whiskey in it. Even Gram has stopped pretending not to know how much he drinks. She thinks if she can "straighten things out for him at home," he will go back to the way he was before, which was, heaven knows, bad enough, but not like this.

Mamie says, "You know I'll help out any way I can, Mr. Duke, but there's LeRoy and all . . ."

She doesn't say, "I can't work here with you drinking the way you are and gone all the time and Miss Ila and Miss Bessie arguing over everything I do."

Gram doesn't say, "I can't—won't—live in this house with you drinking like this."

She says, "You don't want me out here all the time, and I don't want that either. I've already raised my children. I'll get you somebody."

The person she gets to come live with us is a middle-aged widow from her church I'm going to call Mrs. O'Connor rather than her real name, since what I have to say about her comes out of the heart of a child too distraught to know where her own grief stopped and the truth began. The truth notwithstanding, my first sight of this awkward, wide-hipped woman getting out of an old car and walking across the lawn (where Emily played croquet with us and Duke shot trap) and up to the front door makes my flesh crawl and raises the hairs on my arms. The cheaply cut pink dress she wears stretches too tight across her wide wide hips. Her round, fiftyish face is blotchy with age spots and her black hair is graying to steel.

She smiles a pious smile and carries herself in a way that manages somehow to be ingratiating and aggressive at the same time. She makes a maternal gesture toward me and I am filled with disgust. I think she is the most unappealing woman I have ever seen.

My aversion to Mrs. O'Connor is mitigated only by the fact that her twelve-year-old daughter, whom I call Ellen, comes with her. Ellen is a good sport who introduces me to her friends and helps me catch and saddle Dimples even though she herself is scared to death of horses. She seems as straight and comfortable to me as her mother seems twisted and perverse.

According to my nine-year-old view of such things, our mother-substitute is both attracted to Duke and terrified of him. As for him, he is so ill at ease in her presence that I can hardly stand to be in the room with the two of them at the same time. Whenever he can, he ignores her. When he has to talk to her, he squirms. When he is home (which isn't often), he drinks in his room and avoids us all.

And that is what life is like at home when Gram takes me to school for the first day of Mrs. Colquitt's fourth grade. Before I get there, the teacher tells the others to be nice to me because my mother has died. Whatever they have heard from their parents is neither to be talked about among themselves nor mentioned to me.

Some of Emily's friends had started the rumor—in resentful jest, I suppose—that my father had drowned my mother in the swimming pool in order to inherit her money. Some people said she killed herself on purpose with pills. If she did, my father was the only person who knew it for sure (besides maybe Mamie) and he would only have known if Emily told him—so maybe she told him that morning and I only remember part of it ("I don't want to die" and "Good God A'mighty"); maybe she told him one way or another in the ambulance on the way to town; maybe she said nothing or just kept saying "I love you" and "I don't want to die"; maybe she said, "Stop drinking and look after my children." She need not have said either, since it was not in him to do the one and not in him not to do the other.

What do I think? I think she loved us too much to take her own life deliberately, but that she may have overdone the barbiturates that put her to sleep when nothing else would and may have known what she had done and told my father, who carried it with him forty years to his own grave, telling no one, stiffening at the sound of her name. And perhaps they had argued that night, and perhaps—despite all the resolutions and all the new sweetness between them—one of them had taken a drink.

I think her body and spirit were worn out from the struggle she had waged with herself and my father and their marriage for too long—and too long a diet of too much alcohol and not enough food. I think she may have wished for death in the face of the insanity of going to Fort Walton with friends who drank.

I didn't know about the lecture Mrs. Colquitt gave the fourth-graders for a long time, and I certainly don't recall my classmates being any nicer to me than usual. What I remember is standing in the doorway with Gram, watching the others do arithmetic and remembering Emily teaching me Goldilocks in the kitchen on Wilmington Road and knowing that, because she thought I was smart and wanted me to do well in school, I was going to have to try harder.

Before that, I had been a casual and self-satisfied pupil, intrigued by everything that had to do with the written or spoken word and unfazed by my lack of artistic talent and my slowness in math. Before the year is out, my determination to excel will have turned school into a combination footrace and search for the Grail. The change comes, I think, partly out of an impulse to keep something of my mother alive inside me and partly as a strategy to blot out my grief over her death and my worries about my father's drinking and the tensions at home.

Jane and I lie in bed at night and listen to the sliding door opening and closing on the cabinet where Duke keeps his whiskey. We lie with our eyes open in our separate beds a few feet apart and count the drinks and say nothing to one another. One . . . maybe he'll stay home and not go out . . . two . . . maybe he'll stop now and go to sleep . . . three . . . maybe now . . . four . . . and the door slides, metal on metal . . . *krrrkshhh* . . . *krrrkshhh* . . . in both our minds for the rest of our lives.

Sometimes he gets drunk and leaves the house; sometimes he stays home and talks for hours on the phone to "Seabee buddies" all over America. Sometimes I hear him throwing up, a horrible, horrifying sound. And still, by the time we get up for school, he has already left for work.

Mrs. O'Connor wants Duke to stay home more at night, and thinks it is her job to keep him there. One night he stays home at her insistence and tries to get her (pious teetotaler that she is) to drink with him. She refuses, which doesn't stop him from getting very drunk himself and prancing around the house wearing only his shorts and an undershirt. In memory he is a ghostly, potbellied clown taunting us all: Nobody is going to tell *him* what to drink or say or do or *wear* in his own house.

Horrified, finally, at the combination of booze, underwear, and the futility of her sermonizing, Mrs. O'Connor gets hysterical, herds us upstairs, and calls Gram, implying that she is about to be raped and to see us molested. Duke yells up the steps, "Prissy bitch, a drink [and something else suggested] is just exactly what you *need*."

Ellen and Jane start joking to distract us all from what is happening. Duke prancing around with his chest puffed out like a frog in a puppet show and his bowed, skinny legs sticking out from under his baggy white shorts like a baby in diapers. They think this is funny.

Nothing about it seems funny to me. All I see are the new depths of chaos to which Emily's death and Duke's drinking have brought us—and added to it the creeping shame about sex and sexuality that infuses every interaction my father has with Mrs. O'Connor and somehow, by extension, with us. The yell I want to yell swells and sticks in my chest like a balloon filling with air. I don't want anybody to know how bad I feel. Not Daddy. Not Mrs. O'Connor. Not Ellen. Not Jane. Not anybody at school.

"It's a wonder she didn't call the police," Gram says after the prissy-bitch incident. "I told her about the drinking. She came with her eyes wide open."

She tells Daddy not to walk around in his underwear in front of Mrs. O'Connor. Gram doesn't mention his drinking. Nobody does. Yet everybody knows that things are hopelessly wrong at our house. Certainly Mrs. O'Connor. Certainly Gram. Certainly Mamie.

In their different ways, Gram and Bessie both condescend to the housekeeper they had somehow agreed upon (she spends too much money; doesn't get along with Mary Willie; doesn't dress us right; forgets to polish our shoes; is a terrible cook, a poor driver, too emotional) and whisper their concern over whether she is quite old enough to be out there in that house all alone in the country with Duke (so handsome, so young, and half out of his wits with grief). Gram's reservations reach new heights when she realizes the good Baptist she hired is flirting with Christian Scientism.

In truth, though Mrs. O'Connor does, indeed, read Christian Science literature in our presence and talk about it sotto voce on the phone to her friends, she does nothing to indoctrinate us—which is what Gram most fears. Nevertheless, Gram is soon campaigning for Duke to meet (and marry) a war-widowed Wilcox County cousin-in-law named Dorothy Moore McNeil. A lovely person, everyone says, a few years older than Duke and unable to have children of her own. Duke needs a wife. He should go meet Dot. Emily is, after all, "as dead as she'll ever be," Gram says, and Mrs. O'Connor just won't do for long.

Mamie doesn't stay at night much, because there is no place for her to sleep. One night Mrs. O'Connor and Ellen are gone and Mamie is there to sleep in Joan and Jim's room like she used to. I lie awake in black loneliness and call to her, "Come love me. Come love me," meaning give me another hug so I can go to sleep.

She comes one last time and says, "I *do* love you," meaning "That's enough." She has on blue cotton pajamas. Her skin looks dark brown in the dim light from the bathroom. She looks wearier and older and heavier than I think of her being.

Sometimes she sits in the kitchen and acts just like she used to, joking about Mrs. O'Connor's designs on Duke (and it may be from her that I got that idea) . . . Old Lady Sally want to jump-ty jump . . . Old Lady Sally want to bow . . .

No. Mamie, please stop it. It's not funny. Stop joking. Something goes dead inside me. My father is going to get married again. Not Mrs. O'Connor. I know better than that—but to somebody. I don't want anybody new. I want my father like he used to be. I want my mother back. I want somebody to help me remember she loved me.

Duke no longer comes home every night, and I am bolted upright every morning with the premonition that the night before will have been one of those nights when his bed wasn't slept in. "What is it that I must remember?" I ask my morning ghost as soon as consciousness strikes. "Your mother is dead," it says. "Your father is gone and will never come back." My losses stand all around me. New York. The war. Momma.

I creep down the front steps and look to see if his bed is rumpled. If the bed has been slept in, the anxiety lifts and I am free of worry for another whole day, until he comes home drinking or doesn't come home and it starts again. His smooth bed fills me with dread. I think, "He is drunk; he is dead; he has left and is not coming back." The next morning I look again. I look in secret. Nobody sees me looking. I look morning after morning after morning until my life and body seem constructed of looking and fearing.

He is gone, I worry. He comes home, I stop worrying and am free to do what I please for a while. I worry compulsively and begin to think my worrying is what makes him come home. Sometimes he goes off for the weekend and I don't worry until I know it is time for him to come back. I don't worry at Gram's and Bessie's or when he is home sober or when I know he is at the Greenhouse.

I call the Greenhouse to see if he is there and pray he won't catch on to what I am doing and be angry. I am almost as afraid of his anger as of his absence—but not quite. If he isn't there, anxiety explodes inside me and nothing can stop the pounding of my heart until I find him and elation-relief replaces the terror— until my life has become a vicious cycle of losing and finding my father. Terror . . . elation . . . relief . . . terror . . . elation . . . like two ends of a seesaw, up . . . down, up . . . down.

If I call the Greenhouse too often, he gets annoyed. Don't call, don't let them know what you are doing. Terror. Terror and trying to control it and failing and more terror. I want to know where he is, not because I want to be with him (which I don't, not like he is now), but because I want to stop worrying.

On December 7, 1946, four months after Momma died, the worst fire in the nation's history swept through the Winecoff Hotel in Atlanta, injuring a hundred people and killing 127, including a friend of Ellen's. A plump, blond, good-natured girl who sometimes spent the night with us is dead. How can that be? Swallowed up in an inferno we see pictured in the newspaper.

Ellen cries for a week. I have never seen anybody cry like that before. I want her to stop. Gram and Bessie say Ellen can't be that grieved and is just showing off and shouldn't act like that in front of us. I walk around the house with her and watch her cry.

Death doesn't seem real to me. How can a thirteen-year-old girl who used to spend the night with us be gone forever? People die and it is just the same as if they had gone on a trip. And, though they don't come back, it feels as if they are coming back. And that is what I can't believe, that my mother has gone and is not coming back.

By Christmas, Momma has been dead only four months, but our lives are so changed it seems like years. By the time Bessie arrives at our house on Christmas morning in a cab, Duke is already drunk. Mrs. O'Connor has managed to keep him home long enough to open presents with us. We sit on the floor in front of the tree. He slumps beside us, his face gone flaccid and gray. He hands Ellen the expensive blue-and-yellow watch plaid car coat he has bought and wrapped for her to make up for the many presents put under the tree for us. The magnitude of the gift flusters Mrs. O'Connor. Jane and I stand like wooden dolls in the light of a fire too hot for the day. Grief howls "Momma, Momma" all around us, but nobody says it.

I remember Christmas in New York when I learned to read IKE and on Wilmington Road when I got the tetanus shot and fainted and Jane and I wrapped presents by ourselves. I remember last year (so long ago) when Uncle Dan brought Dimples in the truck and Emily watched me ride.

"Let's go ride Dimples," Ellen says in a self-sacrificing effort to distract me from whatever it is that she sees on my face.

"No," I say, feeling my face shut down. I hate Christmas.

Bessie gives me Mary Webb's *Precious Bane* and W. H. Hudson's *Green Mansions* for Christmas and reads them aloud to me, skipping the erotic descriptions and the part about a girl standing in silhouetted nakedness before the man she loves. I take the books to school and read them to my friends at recess, until my teacher looks at the books and makes me stop.

"No reading at recess," she says. "Judy, leave those books at home." There is no hiding the sensuality (no matter how sublimated and spiritualized) of such books from the eagle-eyed Mrs. Colquitt, who has already offended me by suggesting that my reading aloud will have to improve if I am going to stay in the top reading group. I hate the way she tells me, squatting down at my desk and whispering in a condescending, poor-little-thing-her-mother-died tone of voice that makes me feel like screaming. I hate waiting my turn in the circle, listening to one child after another read a tedious story in a sequence of slow, halting paragraphs. By the time it gets to me, I am angry, resentful, and so bored I can hardly sit in my chair. Waiting scares me, makes me mad and cracks the door I have slammed on my sorrow. Waiting for Momma, who went off in an ambulance and never came back. Waiting for Daddy, who is in some ways as dead to me now as she is.

Besides, my friends like the way I read under the trees at recess, and I can read faster to myself than anybody else in the fourth grade. Nevertheless, I make a vow to pay attention and sit still and do better in the reading group, since things that imply failure are no longer allowed in my life.

Some time during the winter, Duke brings a woman to the house. She is athletic-looking, with dyed-blond hair and the pale, mottled skin of a drinker. She works at the airport and flies airplanes. Jane and I stand before them in the living room. Sun spangles the reds and blues of the Oriental carpet we got from Knoxie.

"This is X [if I hear her name, it doesn't register]," he says. "How would you like for X to be your new mother?" My heart goes watery with outrage and fear. I wait for Jane to speak. She doesn't. I cross my arms in front of me like Gram and say, "We wouldn't." Duke looks hurt, and I wish I hadn't said it. Dyed hair. Weathered skin. I don't like her.

They go out the seldom-used side door toward the pool. I remember Emily going out that door when she was pregnant with Joan and laughing about fattening herself up on buttermilk and biscuits. Duke dated the woman for a while, but I don't think we ever saw her again.

After Christmas I start taking riding lessons from Ty at the Narrow Lane Stables again. Duke takes me after school and goes to the airport and comes back to get me when my lesson is done. Ty is letting me ride a big, confident horse she calls Big Red, the best horse in the stable. I am getting better and better at riding and love the feel of the huge horse under my legs. My teacher stands in the center of the ring and shouts orders. I circle the ring with my back straight and my thighs tight and feel as if my mother were still here, leaning on the fence, standing in sun that reddens her hair.

One day Duke comes to pick me up. I get off Big Red and take him to his stall in the barn. When I come out, I see my father and Ty leaning close to each other, talking and flirting. He is lighting her cigarette and looking into her face, which, I suddenly realize, is prettier than I thought.

I go back to Red's stall and stand beside it, feeling more anger, jealousy, and grief than my body can bear. The sinking sun lights the inside of the barn as bright as if all the hay in the stalls was going up in flames. My head aches, and the light hurts my eyes. I look out across the field and see a woman my mother knew riding with her two children in front of the sinking sun. They look like the Three Wise Men crossing the desert to find Jesus in the manger.

I throw up on the floor of the barn and cover the vomit with hay. The barn is red. The sky is red. My mother is dead. I wish I were dead with her.

Even though Emily is dead and he and Gram are Baptists, Duke still takes Jane and me and sometimes Joan to the Episcopal church every Sunday. For Easter, I wear a pink dotted swiss dress Gram bought for me at a department store. It is not soft and smocked like the dresses Emily got for us, but I like the color and the little nubs of cotton sticking out of the cloth.

Joan is with us. Though she is still smaller than she should be, she is winsome and beginning to be pretty in a delicate, wide-eyed sort of way. Jane, Jim, and I are stockily built, light-haired and blue-eyed like the Patersons. Joan is frail, golden-skinned, and dark-eyed like Emily and Knoxie.

Sunday School is over. Duke stands on the sidewalk waiting for us to come out. The Greek Orthodox congregation, which holds services in the chapel at St. John's, is getting out, too. Everybody is dressed up because it is Easter. The Katechis family and the people they know crowd around my father and talk about his parents and grandparents and the "old store," the way they do at Thanksgiving.

"I remember," one of them says, "how, after your father died, you used to ride your bicycle to town every day and sit on the curb in front of the store. We'd look out the window and see that cap you wore and try to get you to come in and eat something."

I see him sitting there in one of those little round caps Gram made for him to keep him from catching the colds he was prone to, looking into the distance with his eyes squinted and his jaw set, grief sawing into his chest the way it saws into mine. "I remember," he says. "It was near Easter. I always smell the lilies when I think of it."

Emily's friend Mel, who used to come to the country and drink beer and cry and complain about her honeymoon, comes out of the church just behind us, immaculately groomed, wearing high-heeled shoes and a big hat. Ignoring the glum look on my father's face and the fact that he hardly speaks to her, she rushes up to him and pushes her face close to his. I am already stiff with knowing he is not going to like whatever it is she is determined to say.

With her face close enough to his to whisper and a look of maudlin sentiment on her carefully made-up face, she practically shouts, "Joan looks *just* like Emily and so *pretty*. She just loved them soooooo much, those poooor little *baaab*ies." Now she is crying. "And you, Duke? How are you? We . . . I . . . ."

He jerks away from her, puts us in the car, and slams the doors as if he (and we) had been insulted in some unspeakable way. Momma's name hangs hollow in the air, a cluster of sounds we are trying to forget.

We pass the Dexter Avenue Baptist Church, which had helped Will and Maggie start the Alabama State College for Negroes in Montgomery in 1887. We pass it every Sunday and every Sunday Duke reminds us of its significance to our family. Other black churches were important, too, the Old Ship AME Zion Church and the Beulah Baptist Church, which—along with Dexter Avenue Baptist—had rescued the school, the faculty, and the Patersons after they moved to Montgomery and the legislature abandoned them and shattered their dreams.

Duke always says the same thing, "The best colored people go there and run the college my grandparents started." And then he tells how Thomas Seay had known Will in Greensboro and then become governor and befriended the school; and how Governor-to-be Thomas Goode Jones had been among the first people in Montgomery to support his grandparents in their work; and how when they joined Montgomery's First Presbyterian Church, only one member, Mrs. Lucy Judkins Durr, ever called on them at home. The names of such people are not to be forgotten.

Though today Duke is not in the mood for a history lesson and says nothing, we look in the direction of the church (already activist and about to put first the Reverend Vernon Johns and then the Reverend Martin Luther King, Jr., in its pulpit), out of habit, and see a little girl wearing a pink dotted swiss dress like mine.

"Look," I shout without thinking. "That girl has on a dress just like mine."

Now Duke is really upset, not so much because I have gone to St. John's on Easter in a dress no better than what a colored child would wear (though that is part of it) as because he had feared all along that the dresses Gram and Mrs. O'Connor bought us would not be right. Grief and shame flood the car. Gram doesn't know the kind of children we are supposed to be. He misses Emily. His children need a mother.

Coda

One Saturday in the spring, Jane, Joan, and I get dressed up and go with Duke in his airplane to pick up Dorothy Moore McNeil at a little landing strip in what used to be a cotton field in Camden, Alabama. I am wearing the only one of the handmade dresses Emily bought that still fits—royal-blue velveteen with a white lace collar, gorgeous to look at, soft as a cloud on my skin. Jane's is just like it, only maroon.

From the air, I see a tall, strong-featured woman standing in a field with two of Duke's cousins. Though she is straight-backed and handsome, with lush auburn hair rolled in thick buns behind her ears, she is not pretty in the girlish way I am used to in women. Duke is thirty-four years old. Dot is a few years older, the childless widow of a Wilcox County kinsman killed in World War II. "He is going to marry her" drops like a bomb in the part of my heart where in some secret way I still think my mother may come back.

Dot flies back with us in the airplane. Duke points out the black-soiled counties beneath us: Wilcox, Lowndes, Montgomery. Rivers. Woods. Cotton. Corn. Kudzu. Peanuts. We sit silent and shamefaced. Nobody says Emily. Nobody says Momma.

One day not long after that, Mrs. O'Connor comes to school to get Jane and me and tells us that Duke and Dot have married and gone to New York on a honeymoon. She says it in a pious, pitying way that makes my stomach hurt. She expects us to be upset. Jane gets in the front seat with her and cries. I sit in the back with a face of stone. Somebody else should have told us. Gram. Daddy. Mary Willie. I don't want anybody to know how I feel about anything.

A friend at school explains honeymoons to me but says she thinks Dot and Daddy are too old for sex. Jane and I spend the weekend with Bessie, who takes us to Oak Park to feed Knoxie's parrot and tells everybody she sees how she brought us to the park because our father has remarried and gone on a honeymoon. I hold Bessie's hand and am comforted by the walking, the talking, and the reiterated themes of her life . . . She never loved anybody like she loved my mother . . . Jane and I are the most wonderful children in the world . . . The old ways, the old movies and songs are best.

We stand in front of the birds and monkeys and try to get Polly to talk. "This is Emily," Bessie says, pointing at me and squawking like Polly. "*Eeem* uhh *liii* . . . *Eeem* uhh *liii* . . ."

Polly stares past us and finally croaks, "Yawwwwk, awwwwk polliwannakrakkkaa . . . eemuh*li*."

A few days later, friends and relatives gather at Gram's to meet Dot. I am only half paying attention until they start talking about our Scottish ancestor, William Burns Paterson, and my new step-mother says, "You know, they tell me his wife, Maggie, was the one with the education, that she graduated from Oberlin College, the first college for women in America."

Silence falls, and then someone corrects her. "Not the first college for women; the first coeducational college." Then, sotto voce and to the side: "And the first to take Negroes. With whites, you know, before the war." Too new in the family (and originally from North Carolina) to understand the nuances that govern us, Dot glows with admiration for the seldom-mentioned Maggie.

Duke looks stonily at her, meaning "Don't go into that." I start asking questions even though I know the look includes me. Where is Oberlin? How did Maggie get here from Ohio? How did she meet her husband? Did Gram and Daddy know her? Duke says, "She was my grandmother. She died before I was born. No more questions." The Patersons prefer Will's story to Maggie's, and they want it told only in the foreshortened and stylized way they always tell it.

My Great-uncle Will—nearly seventy years old, half deaf, and bearing a sweet-faced resemblance to his father the Scotsman— stands in the doorway. "Let her ask questions," he roars. "That's how children learn."

Uncle Will leaves. Nobody says anything. My face goes hot with the realization that he is not so much telling them to answer me as apologizing for my persistence. For a long time, that is all I know of Maggie Flack Paterson, who came to Alabama to redeem the death of the father who died marching through Georgia to free the slaves.

What I already know is that we are a family of secrets and concealments and that I want to know all the things nobody wants to tell me. I also know that Dot, whom I am beginning to like, is not going to have an easy time of it in a network of families that includes Emily's relatives as well as Duke's.

As soon as she marries him, my stepmother starts trying to curb my father's drinking. She doesn't want him to drink every night. She doesn't want him to get drunk when they go out. She doesn't think he should drink around us. Soon there is so much tension between them over that (and who knows what else) that I can hardly stand to be in the same room with them.

Most days, I go to Gram's after school and stay until Duke leaves the Greenhouse for home. On the best of such days, we go straight to the country; on the worst, he stops at a neighborhood restaurant called the Sahara (the first turn he makes tells me whether it is a good day or a bad one) and sits at the bar and drinks.

"You wait here," he says, motioning to the front seat of the car, where I sit (already angry and afraid to say so) with my books in my lap. "I'll only be a minute."

I wait thirty minutes. An hour. Sometimes more. I read. I do homework. I stare at the red neon s-a-h-a-r-a blinking above me, and the three camels crossing the yellow-green façade in front of me. I look across the street to the drugstore we used to walk to from Wilmington Road and think of a time so distant that it seems hardly to have existed at all.

The night gets darker, the sign gets redder, and the camels fade. Sometimes, after I have waited a long time, I go in and ask Duke when we are going. He and the men he drinks with get up from their stools and look down on me with guilt on their faces. Duke says, "Get back in the car. I'm coming."

By the time he comes to the car, his face wears a sneer of contempt for everybody in the world, including me—including most of all, I suppose, himself. He doesn't say anything. He doesn't look at me. I am lonely for my true father and also furious, sullen, not speaking to this drunk man any more than he is speaking to me, holding my breath till I can get home and take my books to my room to get out of the way of the battle that is sure to ensue between him and Dot, who for reasons I don't understand seems as angry with me on these occasions as she is with her new husband.

One day, after I have waited and fidgeted in the car in front of the Sahara for what seems like forever and been unable either to stand it any longer or to muster the courage to face my father's displeasure and the shamefaced grins of the other men, I get out of the car and start walking to Gram's. I don't decide to do it. I just open the car door and start walking.

I move fast at first, my heart pounding as if someone were

chasing me. I slow down. It's almost dark. The air is cool and
still. A few stars shine in the sky, and suddenly I am striding
through the night as loose-limbed as an animal that has gnawed
its way out of a trap and is on its way home. The air holds me
in its hands. I am safe. I am free.

By the time I get there and find Gram in her lighted kitchen,
it is long past dark. I tell her how long I have waited and how
afraid I am of my father and how much I hate being stared at
and pitied by the men at the bar. She calls Duke at the Sahara.
He thinks I have been kidnapped and has called the police. He
comes to get me. He and Gram talk in another room with the
door closed. He takes me home in the car. We sit a foot apart like
prisoners in separate cells. We don't talk about it that night—or
ever. I don't tell anybody, not even Jane, and in the end I am so
ashamed of having made my father ashamed before his mother
that I never do anything like that again. It didn't stop him anyway.
Nothing did.

Sometimes Uncle Sonny comes to Gram's in the afternoon and
gives me sentences to diagram that are harder and more complicated than anything Mrs. Colquitt puts on the blackboard. Sometimes he does them with me and tells me about the famous writers
who wrote them. I like the pure logic of the dark words on white
paper. I understand this. I can do it.

Gram wants to buy me a typewriter to stop the teachers from
complaining about my handwriting and because she thinks all girls
should know how to type. "She should be a teacher," Sonny says.
"It runs in the family."

They talk for months about how much typewriters cost and
which is the best one for me to have. They read the papers; they
call people on the phone. One day we get in the car and go to an
office-supply store downtown and pick out the little Smith-Corona
that will serve me twenty years and slip obsoletely out of my life
before I understand that it had been given me as a birthright. The

Patersons are workers, scholars, serious people. People with talents are supposed to use them.

I am standing in Gram's kitchen one afternoon after school, wearing a favorite blue-checked cotton dress. We face each other over the white metal table that stands between the refrigerator and the stove.

"Judy," she says in a tone that sounds accusatory, "Dot doesn't think you love her as much as the others do. I know you wouldn't want her to think that."

My face shuts down and my body goes still. A stream of stymied words burns in my throat. I look past her and mumble, "I guess I love her."

What I mean is that I like her all right. She gets me to school on time and tries to stop Daddy from drinking so much and lets my friends (except for the ones from Wilmington Road and the ones whose mothers she doesn't like) spend the night. But she is not my mother, whom I still ache for and imagine (though I know better) may still be coming back. Most of all, I don't like being coerced into acting some way I don't feel—by Gram especially, who has always let me say and do whatever I pleased.

She turns away, embarrassed, I believe, at having used a tone of voice to make me say something I don't want to say, so she can tell my stepmother she has done it. Something turns cold and stubborn inside me. I'll love whom I please, the way I please. Or I won't love anybody at all.

Mamie stands in the upstairs bathroom in the country, staring into the mirror and sucking her bottom lip. I stand beside her, wearing the same blue-checked dress, trying to draw her attention toward me and away from her own reflection. "This dress is getting too little for me," I say, feeling the tightness in the shoulders and the belt hitting high above my waist. Mamie looks mad and says nothing. She doesn't like Dot; she is going to leave.

Dot and Gram are standing downstairs in the hallway by the kitchen. Mamie has just come back from being gone with LeRoy. "Mamie's back. Mamieeeee," all four of us squeal, clamoring down the steps at the sound of her voice, hugging her and kissing her and hanging all over her.

"You know," Dot says to Gram, "when Mary Willie is here, those children just run *wild* . . . and they kiss her on the lips . . . I just don't like to see white children kissing a colored woman *on the lips* like that."

Lights go wobbly in front of my eyes. Words fly around me like bullets. Gram nods, purses her lips, and says, "Well . . . she always ran things. Emily . . . you know . . . just couldn't manage without her."

Though Dot can't get rid of the house (which was built with Emily's money and now—according to the courts—belongs to her children, and which I believe my father loved more than any living person), everything she can get rid of that has anything to do with my mother, she wants to get rid of. I don't know whether she wants the past forgotten mainly out of jealousy (wanting my father to love her like a wife and always fearing he had married her mostly to give his children a mother) or whether she wants it forgotten mainly because she thinks that is the only chance she has of saving Duke (and by extension herself and us) from his memories.

Some of our Paterson cousins come to the country on a Sunday afternoon that summer and set up a movie projector in the sunroom and start showing home movies made when the house in the country was new. There I am, and the playhouse, and the sliding board, and Shag, and the teenage Mary Willie beaming at the camera with Jane in her arms. Someone yells, "*EE*m'ly. There's Em'ly."

And there she is, big on the screen in a plain cotton dress, moving fast in the slew-footed way I remembered, waving, clowning, mugging the camera, a cigarette held down at her side. My heart stops. I can't believe I am seeing her. I can't believe someone is yelling her name in our house.

Her resurrection is as fleeting as it is sudden. The reel speeds up . . . fluuuuuupf, fluuuuuupf, fluuuuuupf . . . and stops. Duke is angry (or is it grief?). Dot doesn't know what to do. Our cousin turns off the projector, puts the film back in his car, and walks down to the pool with Daddy. Someone says, "You know how Duke is sometimes."

Mamie leaves again, and years pass before I admit to myself that she is not coming back. Many more before I let myself think, "Never see her again." More after that before I realize how angry (and how despairing) I was at what little recourse I had over the things that happened to me that year and how unmindful everyone was of the feelings of four children battling the death of their mother and the emotional collapse of their father.

Mamie went once after that to talk to Bessie, so I've been told, and to ask if she could see us. "No," Bessie said, sitting, as I imagine it, in the Victorian parlor at the Sophronia. "Don't go out there. The children are fine. You would only cause trouble."

The last I heard of Mary Willie, she had gone to Detroit with LeRoy, who had written my father asking to borrow a hundred dollars, which Duke had sent. Though I never saw her again, she lives in my memory as young and beautiful as she was then and as I imagine her now, an old woman standing in a kitchen or a yard somewhere, singing about an old lady who goes jumpty-jump or a man with a heart like a rock cast in the sea.

Some time during the summer after Duke married Dot, Bessie sold the boarded-up house at 410 South Court Street and bought a huge antebellum-style place on the edge of town nearest the Ware plantation. It wasn't right, she said, for all the "family things" to be stored away where no one could see them. With all her siblings dead and most of her cousins moved away, she wanted, I think, to house her sense of who the Ware–Walkers had been and memorialize Knoxie and Emily, the most recently dead members of her disappearing family, and the ones she had loved the most.

Bessie was in her sixties by then. Moving "made no sense" (as Duke never stopped telling her, though in the end he helped her do it) and took all the energy for life she had left. Though she would live another thirty years, Emily's death and the sale of 410 drained her of the physical and mental stamina that had made her such a force in my life when I was small.

I don't remember much about the move except helping her pack. I see myself standing on a chair taking a round hatbox out of a tall, dark wardrobe. The box is full of dust, scraps of newspaper, and a bill of sale for a slave named Ellen whom Bessie's grandfather, James Anthony Ware, had given to his wife as a personal servant a few weeks before the birth of their first child, a boy who as a student at the University of Alabama would fight the Yankees in the last days of the war and die two years later of a congestive chill.

Bessie remembered Ellen, who had been known as a nurse with great healing powers at the Confederate hospital Grandmother Jane had helped create during the war (and where the suffering she saw on both sides brought her to her knees and—I can't say how or why—turned her from a Baptist back into an Episcopalian). After the war, the tall, capable Ellen had stayed with the family, "as if nothing had changed," and run the household until she was old and feeble and Bessie was almost grown.

Bessie tells again some of her favorite stories about Ellen, who was very stern and proper and didn't like for children to veer from the straight and narrow. Though my sister and I had always liked these stories because they often ended with the children outwitting the adults, I had not known before that Ellen had been a slave; and still, at that time, had too slender an understanding of the place where I lived to grasp the implications of Bessie's characterization of Ellen as a former slave who stayed with the family "as if nothing had changed."

We pack and Bessie talks all day about Ellen, her grandmother, her father, her brothers, and the undeserving Knoxie, to whom she had devoted so much of her life. She was grieving, I now know, for all that had gone before and all that was lost. She was grieving most of all for Emily, I think, whose name she mentioned only when her tongue slipped and she called me by my mother's name instead of my own.

Ty and Dot want me to ride in the big horse show that is held at the end of every summer in Wilcox County, where Gram was born and where Dot lived before she married Duke. I practice and practice and get better and better.

When the day comes, Ty takes the horse in a van, and I ride in the car with Dot and my father, past Selma, where Maggie Flack went in 1875 to teach the freedmen. We drive deeper and deeper into the cotton-blighted hinterlands where most of the people are black and many of the white people are kin to me.

We arrive at the fairground and start getting ready for the show. We wait and wait for my time to come and Daddy goes off drinking with his cousins. I want him to come back before I ride. I get scared. It is August, around the time my mother died. I don't want to do it without her. I don't want to do it alone.

"I'm scared," I say to Dot and Ty. "I don't want to do it. Where's Daddy?"

"He'll be here soon," they say.

"You have to do it. We came all this way and told everybody you were riding. What will they think if you don't ride?" my stepmother says in a tone of voice that makes me feel ashamed and angry at the same time. I keep asking for Duke, who isn't there, and missing my mother, whom, in a year, everybody but me seems to have forgotten—a year of so little consolation that my need for it seems to be contained only by the strength of the bones in my body to keep it inside me.

It gets dark. I go into the ring under the lights. Big Red acts crazy and doesn't do what he is supposed to do, and instead of trying to stop him, I start kicking him and making him act worse. I am furious. I know the sky is dark beyond the lights, but it looks red as far as I can see. My mother is dead, really dead; my father has turned me over to a woman whom I hardly know and who seems not to know me at all; and unless I do things I don't want to do (like ride in a ring under lights, being stared at by people I don't know), there will be no one to look after me at all.

Suddenly and as palpably as a seizure of physical pain, my heart drops to my belly and goes as stubborn and private as a rock dropping to the floor of the sea. I make up my mind. I won't love Dot and I won't forgive Duke, and I won't trust either one of them ever again. I'll make them think I have forgotten my mother, but I won't forget. I'll go on loving her in secret and I'll remember what she wanted me to be and one day I will be it.

And so it happened that in that time after my mother died, a piece of my heart froze inside me as cold and lonely as the heart of little Kay whisked off to the realms of the Snow Queen. Until pretending to forget had turned to real forgetting and the person who came and went in my body hardly remembered the child who had spun in pink light on a hill and sunk her shoes in wet snow and hummed to the *slurpurp . . . slurpop* of the waters on the shore and been loved by her mother and father.

And there my childhood remained in an eerie black-and-white still life of forgetting until a winter's day in 1964 when I walked into the unexpected warmth of a sunset and found my daughter standing with her shoes in her hands, welcoming a spring we hadn't known was coming. And this is the story of what came

275

back to me of a childhood and a time in which the joys and the sorrows were so mixed that it was not possible for one to come back without the other. And this book is the "help" note finally written, not only for the suffering that was mine, but for all who suffer in childhood and think, as I did, that the pain of forgetting is less than the pain of remembering. For without the remembering, no matter how painful, we have no life to call our own.

Acknowledgments

Sweet Mystery is based on my own memories, combined with the recollections of many other people and much research into family and local history. It is as true as I could make it. I have changed the names of a few people to protect their descendants from whatever errors may remain in the remembered perceptions of a bereaved child.

As I wrote, I was influenced by the ideas and research of a number of writers interested in the way loss, stress, and trauma affect both children and adults. I found the work of the psychoanalyst and author Alice Miller extraordinarily pertinent to what I was doing, both in her early books on how abuse and neglect affect children, especially bright children, and in her later writing on the importance of remembering the damage done in childhood and challenging the patterns it sets in place. The work of psychiatrist Robert Jay Lifton and his associates on how trauma re-creates itself in memory and in subsequent life experiences also influenced me, as did some of the things Elie Wiesel has said about the importance of remembering and trying to communicate events too painful to be fully represented in words. I was intrigued both by the importance Dr. Murray Bowen and his followers assign to family history research in psychotherapy and by French psychoanalyst and theorist Jacques Lacan's ideas about the relationship between early consciousness, memory, and language. I found what Michael Dorris says in *The Broken Cord* about the effects that a mother's drinking during pregnancy can have on the emotional and intellectual development of her children to be both informative and deeply troubling. Gerald G. May's assessment of addiction as a spiritual problem helped me understand my parents.

I was also helped along the way by counselors and mental-health experts and greatly encouraged and supported by friends who shared their experiences in addictive families with me and listened to my endless early attempts to turn my own long-hidden memories into a story that made sense. I am grateful still to all who labor in a field of knowledge and treatment that did not exist when my siblings and I were young.

I owe a boundless debt of gratitude to the local and family historians, librarians, archivists, and courthouse clerks who helped me from the beginning. Grants from the University of Maryland, the John P. McGovern Foundation, and the Virginia Center for the Creative Arts encouraged me early on and gave me time to travel, do research, and interview people. The enthusiasm and interest of my students lightened my spirits and kept me going through long periods of seemingly endless toil.

Though many people helped me fill in the gaps in my memories, I am especially indebted to my mother's friends Gene Daniel Bentley and Mary Helen Scott Foster, who offered me not only their uncensored recollections and help with dates and places but also photographs of my mother that I had never seen and letters she had written to them when she was young. My Aunt Mary Lou Hillman offered a wealth of useful information and opinion in the last years of her life. And although I cannot say that I learned the true nature of her relationship with my mother, I am grateful that the nurse whom I call Connie Turner was willing to talk to me.

My quest for my childhood and my heritage made an enormous number of friends along the way. I think of all of them often, though I have only mentioned a few. Without the skill of my agent, David Black, and the sagacity of my editor, John Glusman, the pilgrimage would never have become the book it did. The book it did become would, I think, have been almost impossible to finish without the hospitality and goodwill of the nuns at the Convent of the Holy Child Jesus in Rosemont, Pennsylvania, where the most difficult parts of it were finally written.

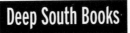

The University of Alabama Press

HOWELL RAINES
Whiskey Man

JUDITH HILLMAN PATERSON
Sweet Mystery: A Book of Remembering

MARY WARD BROWN
Tongues of Flame